GERTRUDE
LAWRENCE

GERTRUDE LAWRENCE

A BIOGRAPHY BY
SHERIDAN MORLEY

PAVILION
MICHAEL JOSEPH

This edition published in Great Britain in 1986 by
Pavilion Books Limited
196 Shaftesbury Avenue, London WC2H 8JL
in association with Michael Joseph Limited
27 Wrights Lane, Kensington, London W8 5DZ

British Library Cataloguing in Publication Data
Morley, Sheridan
    A bright particular star: a biography of Gertrude Lawrence.
    1. Lawrence, Gertrude
    2. Actors – Great Britain – Biography
    1. Title
    792'.028'0924   PN2598. L28
    ISBN 1-85145-063-7

Picture research by Linda Poley

Printed and bound in Great Britain by
Biddles Ltd, Guildford & Kings Lynn

For Juliet,
another starry lady

═══ CONTENTS ═══

≡ ILLUSTRATIONS ≡

(between pages 116 and 117)

With Leslie Howard in *Candlelight* in 1929 *(Mander & Mitchenson)*
With Noël Coward in *Private Lives* in 1930 *(London Theatre Museum)*
In *Lord Camber's Ladies* with Gerald du Maurier *(National Film Archive)*
With Laurence Olivier in *No Funny Business* *(National Film Archive)*
Gertie and Noël Coward in 'Family Album' *(Mander & Mitchenson)*
Noël Coward and Gertie in 'Shadow Play' *(Mander & Mitchenson)*
As Liza, the *Lady in the Dark*, Broadway, 1931 *(Vandamm)*
Gertie as a driver for the American Red Cross *(Pamela Clatworthy)*
On a naval tour of the Pacific *(Pamela Clatworthy)*
Gertie and Richard Aldrich at the time of their marriage *(Dorothy Wilding)*
The Aldriches at the Cape Playhouse *(Pamela Clatworthy)*
Gertie and Raymond Massey in 1946 *(Pamela Clatworthy)*
In Daphne du Maurier's *September Tide* (*Angus McBean, courtesy Harvard Theatre Collection)*
In *The Glass Menagerie*, 1950 *(Pamela Clatworthy)*
With Yul Brynner in *The King and I* *(Vandamm)*

QUOTATIONS

Sometimes, in *Private Lives*, I would look at her across the stage and she would simply take my breath away; I can think of nobody living or dead who ever gave to my work as much as she did. *Noël Coward*

Poor Richard Aldrich: he thinks he is marrying Miss Lawrence, but he will very soon find out that it's Myth Lawrence. *Constance Collier*

She didn't have a shy bone in her body. *June, Lady Inverclyde*

She was generous to the point of recklessness. *Cecil Beaton*

She spent money like an entire fleet of drunken sailors. *Fanny Holtzmann*

She could see a Maurice Chevalier film in the afternoon and play her entire performance that night as Maurice Chevalier; she was infinitely suggestible. *Douglas Fairbanks*

In the cerebral sense, she was scarcely an actress at all. *Ronald Bryden*

Her moral victory was that she learned how to act when she, above all women, could have been a successful actress without taking the trouble. *Rebecca West*

When she enters, the stage becomes visibly brighter. *Cedric Hardwicke*

It wasn't that my mother ever really intended to be unkind or difficult; it was just that she could never discover precisely what a mother was supposed to do. Our relationship was a disaster. *Pamela Clatworthy*

xi

Vitamins should take Gertrude Lawrence.

Harold Cohen

She can't sing, but who cares?

Agnes de Mille

There was one element of a working relationship with Gertie that I have never experienced in working with any other actress, and that element was sheer unalloyed fun.

Moss Hart

She was a light that danced and swayed, that burned not with a dull lamp's steady glow but with all the divine uncertainty of flickering candles on a Christmas tree.

Daphne du Maurier

When Gertrude Lawrence has a good time, everybody has a good time. Or else.

John Chapman

She regarded her own divorce and bankruptcy proceedings as accidents unrelated to her, like falling off a horse. It could have happened to anybody.

Cole Lesley

She loved life, she loved people, she loved the theatre and she loved applause.

Yul Brynner

Her features were irregular, with a strange blob of a nose, but she had beautiful eyes and hands, wore clothes like a dream, and danced with exquisite grace; although her voice was never very good (she wobbled if she had to sustain a high note and was frequently out of tune), she had learned to use it with beguiling charm.

John Gielgud

She was a blazing great star, and we shall never see another quite like her.

Laurence Olivier

Once you had worked with Gertie, you could work with anyone.

Anne Leon

I am not what you'd call wonderfully talented, but I am light on my feet and I do make the best of things. All I really lack is a private life.

Gertrude Lawrence

PREFACE

She may not always have been the best, but she was certainly the brightest. Others of her generation were better singers, better dancers, better actresses; Gertrude Lawrence was a better star. For her, the Gershwins wrote *Oh, Kay*; for her Noël Coward wrote *Private Lives* and *Tonight at 8.30*; for her Richard Rodgers and Oscar Hammerstein wrote *The King and I*. It was Gertrude Lawrence who first sang Coward's 'Someday I'll Find You', she who made hits out of the Gershwins' 'Someone To Watch Over Me' and 'Do, Do, Do', she who first sang Weill's 'Jenny' in *Lady in the Dark* and much of Cole Porter's score for *Nymph Errant*. For a brief but memorable time she was First Lady of the musical comedy stage on Broadway and in the West End.

She was a bright, particular star who rose above the limitations and variations of her talent to personify the brittle glamour of a post-First World War generation which was hiding its disillusion under an often cynical smile.

When she died, suddenly and unexpectedly of undetected cancer in September 1952 at the age of only fifty-four, they dimmed all the theatre lights not only along Broadway, where until only a few weeks before she had been playing Mrs Anna in *The King and I*, but also in the West End, which, apart from one postwar appearance in a play by Daphne du Maurier, she had forsaken after the run of *Tonight at 8.30* in 1936. It was a unique tribute to an actress who had started out in 1911 at Olympia as one of a hundred and fifty child choristers in *The Miracle* and who was inclined to view her entire career from then onwards as something of a miracle in itself.

But by the time those lights were shining again, most traces of Gertrude Lawrence had disappeared; she died before television had begun to immortalize its artists on tape, before radio shows were regularly recorded, and though she made half a dozen films, her appearances in them are mostly undistinguished and give no clear impression of a radiance which could hold theatre audiences spellbound. True, there are a few recordings of her best-known numbers, but again they are inclined to emphasize her technical failings without giving any real idea to the present-day listener of what kept her close to the top of her profession for the best part of thirty years.

What follows, then, is an attempt to chronicle that career through her own words and the memories of those who knew and worked with her on both sides of the Atlantic and the war. Gertrude Lawrence left behind her just one brief and less than wholly trustworthy autobiography, published in 1945 as *A Star Danced*; a decade later, soon after her death, her second husband (the American theatrical manager-turned-diplomat Richard Aldrich) published an account of the time in which he knew her, a period from 1939 to 1952 interrupted by the four years he spent at war. But both these books have now been out of print for the best part of twenty years, and to them needs to be added the hitherto unheard evidence of her only child Pamela, who has been kind enough to give me much of her time and many of her recollections of a not always easy relationship.

The rags-to-riches life of Gertrude Lawrence often sounds like the script for a singularly appalling Hollywood musical (and once indeed it did become just that—a film called *Star!* for which she was impersonated by Julie Andrews, a lady bearing about as much resemblance to her as to Mickey Rooney); an active sex life led Gertie through two marriages and a series of affairs with the likes of Douglas Fairbanks Jr and Captain Philip Astley, and her lifelong inability to refrain from spending instantaneously any money that came to hand, and often a great deal that did not, led her at the height of her fame into a prolonged and, for its time, scandalous bankruptcy hearing.

Not always the most brilliant selector of scripts ('Nothing that can't be fixed' was her reaction to the first offer of *Private Lives*, to which Coward replied, 'The only thing to be fixed will be your performance') Gertrude Lawrence yet managed to attract the most distinguished composers, lyricists, lovers, playwrights, directors and managers of her day. 'Her quality was to me unique', wrote Coward when she died, 'and her magic imperishable'; it is as a critical record and a pictorial celebration of her magic and her quality that this book is intended.

For all their help in putting it together, my sincere thanks must go not only to Mrs Pamela Clatworthy but also to the following: Mrs Philip Astley, Felix Barker, Peter Bull, Dr William Cahan, Constance Carpenter, Rosalind Chatto, Dorothy Dickson, Daphne du Maurier, Marlene Eilers, Charles Evans, Douglas Fairbanks Jnr, Milton Goldman, Morton Gottlieb, Michael Gough, Cathy Haill, Radie Harris, Kitty Carlisle Hart, Alice Heggen, Raymond Mander, Joe Mitchenson, Timothy Morgan-Owen, Graham Payn, Jason Pollock, Pamela Webb, Arnold Weissberger and Evie Williams.

I would also like to thank my editor at *Punch*, Alan Coren, for his customary generosity in giving me time away from the office to finish the book, and my publishers Weidenfeld & Nicolson in London, Colin Webb and John Curtis, as well as Beverly-Jane Loo at McGraw Hill in New York for their unflagging enthusiasm.

In further research I have as always been much helped by the staffs of the Theatre Museum at the Victoria and Albert Museum, the British Film Institute, and of the Billy Rose Theatre Collection at the New York Public Library, Performing Arts Research Centre.

BABE IN THE WOOD

Gertrude Lawrence was born, appropriately enough, on Independence Day: 4 July. The year was 1898, though later she was to put 1901 in the reference books, a practice not unknown in the theatrical profession. Her parents were then living in a less-than-desirable residence at 6 Bath Terrace, Newington, London. They christened her Gertrud Alexandra Dagmar and her father's surname was Klasen, though by the time of his only daughter's birth he was already working as Arthur Lawrence.

Gertie's father was a Dane whose family had moved from Schleswig-Holstein to London when he was two; there, in later years, he had begun to carve out a career for himself in the theatre, as Frederick Willis recalls:

Marie Lloyd was always principal boy at the Crown Theatre, Peckham, but at Drury Lane she was always principal girl. At the Crown she'd have a first-class company to support her, and among the lesser lights there was Arthur Lawrence. He was Demon King for years at this theatre, and being a bass singer was usually billed as 'A bold bad demon with a bass voice in everything'. He delighted us with 'Asleep in the Deep' and other old favourites, and held us spellbound as he descended lower and lower down the musical scale. When he reached rock bottom he breathed a sigh of relief . . . He loved a drink, was very thin, very active, very social and always had a new story to tell. None of us had much hope that he would ever reach the top rank . . . and the last time I saw him was in the Strand [in 1905], when he told me that he was among the resident choir at the new London Coliseum, a novel and short-lived feature of that variety theatre in its early days.

Gertie's mother (born Alice Louise Banks) came from a faintly more 'genteel' family background: her father had been a master builder and there was considerable ill-feeling among the relatives when she ran off to marry a none-too-profound *basso profundo*. Moreover their worst fears about him were rapidly realized; though Arthur behaved well enough during his courtship ('We were never ever out together after ten o'clock' Mrs Klasen proudly told her daughter, much of whose life and career was to be based on being out after ten o'clock), once married he took rapidly to the bottle. 'His gaiety,' remembered his daughter later, 'his charm, his blond good looks disappeared. He became ugly in disposition and demeanour. Mother left him soon after I was born, and I grew up with no memories and no real knowledge of him.'

When, in the late 1940s, Gertrude Lawrence came to write a graphic and romantic but perhaps rather less than wholly factual account of her early life (which she called *A Star Danced*) she gave lengthy descriptions of a waif-like cockney London childhood. Few street corners in the Clapham district of the early 1900s appear to have been complete without a barefoot Gertie, dancing to the music of the barrel organs and singing, at the age of six, her first big number:

> Oh, it ain't all honey, and it ain't all jam,
> Walking round the 'ouses with a three-wheel pram,
> All on me lonesome, not a bit to eat,
> Walking about on me poor old feet.
> My old man, if I could find 'im,
> A lesson I would give.
> Poor old me, I 'aven't got a key,
> And I don't know where to live.

It was left to Noël Coward, Gertie's lifelong friend, critic and partner, to remark of his own similar South London childhood: 'I was born in Teddington, Middlesex, an ordinary middle-class boy. I was not gutter. I didn't gnaw kippers' heads in the gutter as Gertrude Lawrence quite untruthfully always insisted that she did. But nor was our first memory the crunch of carriage wheels in the drive. Because neither of our families had drives.'

After the departure of Arthur Lawrence, his wife remarried and entertained occasional gentleman callers. Family life for little Gertie was therefore not strictly uneventful, but nor was it a matter of abject and utter poverty. This legend grew in later years, notably in American press interviews where Gertie, realizing that journalists expected some kind of a story and never having been reticent with the press, was inclined to exaggerate a childhood of genteel lower-middle-class deprivation into one of near-starvation.

1898, the year of Gertrude Lawrence's birth, was also the year the United States took possession of Hawaii, the year Kitchener defeated the Dervishes at Omdurman, and the year Pierre and Marie Curie discovered radium. More relevant to Gertrude Lawrence's subsequent career, it was the year of the first-ever flashlight photograph. Bernard Shaw wrote *Caesar and Cleopatra* that year, Oscar Wilde wrote the *Ballad of Reading Gaol* and another notable star born in 1898 was Paul Robeson.

The British theatre at this time was led by Sir Henry Irving, and it was still the high summer of the actor-managers; melodramas were beginning a long, slow decline, and, in general, revivals were preferred to new plays by actors and audiences alike. W. S. Gilbert called the British dramatists of this time 'steady and stolid', while the critic J. T. Grein noted that 'so long as Shakespeare still draws the crowds . . . we need not bewail the poverty of our contemporary drama', though in fact both Bernard Shaw and, in Ireland, W. B. Yeats were writing prolifically by 1900, while Pinero and Jones were still at their height.

Quite what drew Gertrud Klasen into the theatre is unclear; she can have had only the vaguest notion of what her father did for a living, and though there may well have been 'something in the blood', by her own account she simply started with a concert party at the seaside at the age of six. The fact that she was beside the sea (in fact at Bognor) at all suggests that there was a little more money in the family than she later cared to admit, for in 1904 a Bognor holiday would not have been exactly routine for a family living in the depths of South London poverty. For Gertie's only daughter Pamela, there is still a certain mystery about how and with whom her grandmother was living in the earliest years of Gertie's childhood:

I've an intriguing family group showing my grandmother with a whole lot of people in the back-yard of the house in Clapham, and by the time I went to live there years later Granny was sometimes known as Mrs Dewing and sometimes as Mrs Bentley. I know that she got her divorce from Arthur Klasen, who took to calling himself Lawrence off-stage as well as on, once the anti-German feeling started, but

I've never been quite sure whether she then married both Dewing and subsequently Bentley or whether only one of them. I do remember Mr Dewing, a lovely man he was, with a yellowing moustache and a roll-top desk, and he used to take me on his knee and tell me that if my grandmother hadn't met him she'd have been a great lady.

Given that somewhat shadowy domestic arrangement, Gertie was herself less than forthcoming about the precise details of her early childhood; she did, however, once give a vivid account of her first professional engagement:

The summer of my sixth birthday, my stepfather [presumably either Dewing or Bentley] must have had a streak of unusual good luck with the horses, because he took Mother and me to Bognor for the bank holiday. It was boiling hot, I remember, and the sands were crowded. I had never been to the sea before; the bathers, the picnic parties on the sand, the strollers along the front fascinated me. A concert party was entertaining, and Dad paid for us to go in. At the close of the regular bill the 'funny man' came forward and invited anyone in the audience who cared to, to come up on the stage and entertain the crowd. A push from Mother, and the command, 'Go on, now, Gertie, and sing your song', was all the urging I needed. 'It ain't all honey and it ain't all jam', I carolled lightly, twirling on my toes with my skimpy pink frock held out as far as it would stretch. The applause and the cheers were gratifying, even without the large golden sovereign with which the manager rewarded me after a little speech.

One day some student of twentieth-century British theatre will research the influence of seaside concert parties in the first decade of this century; their habit of inviting talented (or simply shameless) children from the audience to leap up onto the stage provided not only a cheap and easy finale but was also the fore-runner of innumerable television talent shows of equally horrendous fascination.

In 1907, just three summers after Gertrude Lawrence's starring debut there, Uncle George's Concert Party, a pierrot troupe also working the sands, offered a large box of chocolates in a spontaneously-organized competition to see which of the children in the audience was willing to sing the whole of 'Come Along With Me To The Zoo, Dear'. The winner was a seven-and-a-half year old Noël Coward.

Back in London in the autumn of 1904, Gertrude Lawrence and her stepfather and mother, a lady who was not only Irish, Jewish and cockney but also ambitious for her daughter in an almost classic 'stage mother' fashion, took to a kind of involuntary tour of South London as Gertie later explained:

When times were good, we lived in rooms at Kennington Oval; but only as long as luck was with Dad on the horses. Then we'd move, as we frequently did. There was a regular ritual connected with these movings which varied only as we moved up or down in the economic scale. If the move was occasioned by good fortune, Mother added a piano to the furniture she ordered to be sent around to the new address. There was something undeniably genteel about a piano in the house, even if no one could actually play it.

If the move was in the other direction, a van drove up and men smelling of sawdust and beer carried away the piano and the rest of the furniture which we had on the hire-purchase plan . . . Mother was always on her dignity with them. She refused to be commiserated with, and the impersonal air with which she watched the men from the hire furniture company stagger down the front steps under the pseudo-Jacobean fumed oak dresser was a triumph of dramatic genius. As the rooms became emptier, you felt that Mother was merely clearing her decks for bolder action, and that when we had furniture again it would be on a nobler, more elegant scale.

Meanwhile Dad would have slipped round the corner and entered into negotiations with the neighbourhood greengrocer whose account had been paid up and whose friendship could therefore be relied upon. Not until after dark, when there would be no prying eyes, would Mother take down the window curtains and pack the few possessions rightfully our own . . . then, close to midnight, the grocer's boy would arrive with his cart. Dad would tiptoe down the stairs with the parcels and baskets and pile them on the cart while the boy leaned on the railings and kept a lookout for 'nosey Parkers'. In all this there was nothing original; we were merely following a tradition long recognised in Clapham and other less-favoured districts. This manoeuvre was known as a 'moonlight flit'. Obviously it was a move to cheaper lodgings in another district where we and our straitened circumstances were as yet unknown. Equally obviously, it was without the landlord's knowledge. There must have been families whose moonlight flits were sad and shamefaced. Not ours. There was something daring and whimsical about this sort of move which challenged all that was adventurous in our three natures.

None of the three men in Gertie's mother's life seems to have enjoyed what might be called a steady income or a regular job, and by the time her daughter was ten there had been one too many of the moonlight flits. Mother decided therefore that the only answer was to get a job herself and this she did, in the back of the chorus for the Christmas pantomime at the Brixton Theatre.

That year, in 1908, it was *Babes in the Wood* and though the title characters had already been cast, it so happened that: 'The theatre manager wanted a child who could sing and dance with nine others in a troupe, and one who could be trusted to be on time for the show and not get into mischief. Mother promised she would take care of all that, and I was taken on. We children were little robin redbreasts in the forest ballet when the ''Babes'' got lost in the wood. Dressed in brown tights, very wrinkled at the knees, our skinny bodies clad in musty feathers and with hats which had beaks in front, we covered the two unfortunate children with artificial leaves to keep them from the cold until they were rescued by Robin Hood and his Merry Men. Mother was one of the Merry Men.'

So, little Gertie Klasen was already on the stage; not, at this time, due to any burning ambition or recognizable talent, but partly because it was worth the princely sum of six shillings a week and mainly because, encouraged by both her mother and her grandmother, she recognized in the theatre a kind of escape from a suburban South London world of genteel poverty and moonlight flits, one which had already claimed rather too many of her neighbours. The theatre was not at this time an especially 'respectable' profession except in its highest reaches: Irving had been granted his knighthood (the first ever given to any member of his profession) in 1895, but from *Hamlet* at the Lyceum to *Babes in the Wood* at Brixton was a considerable distance; if not geographically then certainly socially and professionally. Yet precisely because very few self-respecting families of the middle and upper classes would willingly allow offspring of theirs in through a stage door, the theatre was considerably more open to children a little lower down the scale or of professional families. There was a constant demand for stage children in the early 1900s, since they were widely considered to be audience-pullers, and this demand could as often as not be met by those (both parents and children) in need of an escape from the reality of an unprofitable and unsuccessful existence. The stage was, after all, a place where anything could happen and sometimes did.

One pantomime does not make or even adequately launch a career, and it rapidly became clear to little Gertie and her mother that if she was to have any hope at all of a life on the stage, even for a decade or so until she was old enough to catch herself a financially suitable husband, she would first need some sort of training. Backstage at Brixton, there had been rumours concerning a lady called Italia Conti:

Miss Italia Conti held a unique place in the world of the British theatre. She had a basement studio just off Great Portland Street where the boys and girls she accepted as pupils practised dance steps, did acrobatic exercises on the horizontal bar, and were taught elocution and the rudiments of the drama. The studio was a big room lined with mirrors in which you could see yourself from every angle, and at one end was a small stage with a piano. Mother had no money to pay for dancing and singing lessons for me. Dad had suffered a run of bad luck for months, and we had moved to cheaper and still cheaper lodgings. My education did not benefit by these flittings about Clapham and Brixton; whenever we moved into a new district it usually meant my entering a new schoool. It also meant finding myself one of a new group of children, who stood off and eyed me suspiciously. The boys and girls at Miss Conti's eyed each other too, but their glances were different. They looked at me critically, not at my clothes or where I lived, but for what I was able to do. Many of them had been born into theatrical families. All of them aspired to stardom. I sang and danced for Miss Conti, and she thought me sufficiently talented to offer to give me free lessons. On these terms I was enrolled one afternoon a week for a six weeks' trial period. If I showed promise, I had the opportunity of staying on as a pupil-teacher, thereby repaying my tuition.

She showed promise. Not a lot, at first, but enough to get into another Christmas show, and Reinhardt's Olympia epic *The Miracle* (as one of 150 child choristers), and then a fairy play called *Fifinella* which starred those two subsequent stalwarts of Hollywood character acting, Eric Blore and Estelle Winwood. Though rehearsals were held in London, *Fifinella* was to open at the Liverpool Repertory Theatre in December 1912, then under the direction of Basil Dean. Dean was (and remained for the next fifty years or more) a distinguished director but something of a martinet, and there was a widely held theory in the British theatre for most of the twentieth century that if as a child actor or actress you had started your career with Basil Dean, then there wasn't much else they could do to you in later life that didn't come as some form of a rest cure. A demanding and hard taskmaster, Dean was later to recall his first meeting with Gertrude Lawrence as uneventful: 'Among the lively pack of stage children supplied by Italia Conti was one, Gertrude Lawrence, a rather plain child with pigtails who seemed to feel the thrill even more than the rest of us, jumping in and out of stage trap-doors intended not for her but for the Demon King.'

The success of *Fifinella* led Basil Dean and the Liverpool Repertory on to another show requiring a large number of children, Hauptmann's dream play *Hannele* with which Stanislavsky had enjoyed a considerable success in

Moscow a few years earlier. By now it was the beginning of 1913, and one of the children cast for *Hannele* was Noël Coward, not in fact a Conti child (despite that lady's later inclination to claim him as one of hers) but already achieving a considerable reputation for himself as a boy actor after seasons in *The Goldfish* and *Where The Rainbow Ends*. The job in *Hannele* was, however, the first for which he would be required to leave London and the tender clutches of his adoring if ambitious mother. Noël wrote twenty-five years later:

I was engaged at a salary of two pounds a week. In due course I was seen off by Mother at Euston, and in company of about ten other children and Miss Conti, travelled to Liverpool. It was a pleasant journey. We ate sandwiches and chocolate and played card games on a travelling rug stretched across our knees. Some of the children I already knew. Gracie Seppings and two sisters, Ivy and Dorothy Moody, had been in the *Rainbow* with me, and a very perky little boy in a yachting cap called Roy Royston I had met at one or two parties. The others were strangers, and still are, with the exception of Harold French and a vivacious little girl with ringlets to whom I took an instant fancy. She wore a black satin coat and a black velvet military hat with a peak, her face was far from pretty, but tremendously alive. She was very *mondaine*, carried a handbag with a powder-puff and frequently dabbed her generously turned-up nose. She confided to me that her name was Gertrude Lawrence, but that I was to call her Gert because everybody did . . . She then gave me an orange and told me a few mildly dirty stories, and I loved her from then onwards.

She was then fourteen; he had just turned thirteen. Privately, it was the start of a beautiful if sometimes stormy friendship. Professionally, it was the most important meeting of both their lives.

2

CHILD ACTRESS
AND DANSEUSE

At some point in her Italia Conti schooldays, after 1910 and before the meeting on the train with Noël, Gertrud Alexandra Dagmar Klasen had become, for reasons not unconnected with posters and programmes and the then remote but just conceivable possibility of a name in lights, plain Gertrude Lawrence. Though she still never saw her father, his stage name had been the obvious one for her to adopt, and the Gertrud had acquired a final 'e' in the interests of sounding English (which she anyway was, at least by birth if not by parentage) at a time when to sound even faintly German was not the best of ideas.

As for the meeting with Noël, it is hard if not impossible to over-estimate its importance; until Gertie's death just forty years later, they were to remain privately and publicly a double-act of unique and imperishable talent and charm known simply as Noël and Gertie. Their interest in each other was everything save sexual; sometimes brother and sister, sometimes father and daughter, sometimes just tetchily good friends they travelled together and apart through four decades of British and American theatrical history. But for Gertie there would have been no *Private Lives*, no *Tonight at 8.30*; but for Noël she might have stayed forever in the mindless revues of the early 1920s.

In fact, Noël and Gertie were after this first production only to share the same stage in less than half a dozen other shows; but their partnership was not simply a matter of shared curtain calls. It informed and conditioned both their careers more deeply than (in her lifetime) either of them cared to admit. Already, at the time of *Hannele*, they had in common a similarly unglamorous South London childhood (true, Noël's family were slightly better off, running as they then did, a boarding house) and an early realization that the theatre could provide them simultaneously with an escape and a career. Noël's family had certainly never indulged in the moonlight flits which Gertie was to recall so vividly, and technically he may have been a notch or two above her in the social order; but there was, as she had already noted, a great levelling among stage children, whose hierarchy depended not on background or dress but on the size of the role then being played and the nearness to the footlights that was allowed them by the director.

The director in this case was again Basil Dean, who wrote later: 'It was in my production of *Hannele* that Gertrude Lawrence and Noël Coward first acted together, appearing as members of the Angelic Chorus in the dream sequences, although from their subsequent careers it does not seem that either of them was markedly influenced by the experience. Gertie was just over fourteen . . . and suffered her first professional heartbreak when she discovered that her surname had been spelt with a U instead of a W in the programme. Noël was a pimply, knobbly-kneed youngster with an assured manner'.

Unlike Gertie who was already more independent, Noël's 'assured manner' masked a deep and desperate homesickness; things did, however, brighten up a bit when, after Liverpool, they played Manchester and Gertie hit Miss Conti's sister over the head with a rounders bat. In Gertie's view Noël seemed at that time to be 'a thin, unusually shy boy with a slight lisp'. There was the memorable night when the two of them were given a large box of peppermints on condition they shared it with the rest of the cast: 'Noël and I managed to forget this admonition and to eat most of the sweets ourselves in the taxi on the way to the theatre. Soon I began to feel queer, and when we went on in the heaven scene the other celestial beings seemed to float and bob dizzily around me. I stole a glance at Noël. He was positively green. Presently the audience was permitted an unexpected vision of heaven in which two small angels were being violently sick.'

After the show each night Miss Conti's little band of stage children would return to a drab lodging house in Manchester's Acker Street, where Noël shared a room with Roy Royston and Harold French, who later remembered: 'One night after we three boys had undressed – last to bed turns out the gas – there came a subdued tapping from outside. Noël threw on a dressing-gown and gently opened the door. Standing there was Gertie and two friends. "How about a little game of Nap?" they wanted to know. My pack of cards was produced and we settled down. The girls had brought their purses so it was money, not matches, we played for. After a while Noël, never an avid Nap player, opted for bed. Gertie too got bored and while Roy, the other two girls and I went on trying to win each other's ha'pennies, Noël and Gertie chatted—she sitting on the side of his truckle bed—till far into the night. It was in that rather sordid little room in Manchester that Noël and Gertie started a friendship, deep and true, that was to last until she died.'

Fourteen years later, the British theatre being a small world, it was the author of that memoir and Gertie who were together to sing George and Ira Gershwin's 'Do, Do, Do' in the first London production of *Oh, Kay!*

But with *Hannele* closing at the end of its Manchester week, Gertie returned to London more than ever determined that it was to be an actor's life for her; she even spent some of her salary having a hundred cards printed:

LITTLE GERTIE LAWRENCE
Child Actress and Danseuse

If they did not immediately bring her in any more work they did at least confirm in print her new-found career.

At home things were not going too well; because there was no money and Miss Conti's generosity, though considerable, was something less than infinite, Gertie had to withdraw from further lessons. With no work forthcoming for herself, her mother or her stepfather, family life became a series of more or less bitter quarrels about the future; these were interrupted by the occasional joy such as a trip to the seaside at Brighton during which, if Miss Lawrence is to be believed, she invested in a penny-in-the-slot fortune telling machine which duly delivered her a card reading 'A star danced, and you were born', a message Gertie chose to interpret as meaning that she was already a dancer and would one day be a star.

To be a star, however, meant first getting herself back into the theatre, and although Harold French, Noël Coward and her other card-playing friends from *Hannele* were having little difficulty in carving out careers for themselves as boy actors because it was a career chosen by precious few male teenagers, for a girl it was considerably more difficult — there was no shortage of *them* whatsoever. For Gertie to get back into the theatre meant knowing somebody already there, and in a position to advise or introduce:

Mother and I were out shopping one day when suddenly she stopped to read a poster stuck up on a wall. . . . Heading the cast as the star appeared the name Arthur Lawrence. 'That's your father,' said Mother, pointing. I stared at the name, trying to accustom myself to the idea of a relationship between this man and me. No one had ever told me much about my father. I could not remember having seen him or heard of his taking the slightest interest in my existence. . . . We walked on, and no more was said about my father. I would have liked to have gone to the theatre to see him and hear him sing, but Mother did not suggest it. I only had to look at her to realise the subject was closed. But the sudden discovery that I had a father who was a success in the theatre set me thinking . . . a plan began to develop in my mind. . . . One evening several months later, when Mother was out, I decided to carry out my plan, and I packed a few belongings in a small straw portmanteau. I then collected all the empty bottles and jars in the house, returned them to the grocer's, and got the money I needed for the journey. Wearing my best coat and a large mushroom-shaped hat, and carrying the portmanteau, I took the tram to the theatre where I knew my father was appearing. A note left on the kitchen table told Mother of my decision to join my father, and that she was not to worry.

And Mother didn't; backstage at the theatre Gertie sent in her printed card and 'presently a man stood there – a very tall man who leaned forward to peer at me in the dim, flickering light. He was in his shirt-sleeves and collarless. One half of his face was smeared with grease and burnt cork. Out of the black face a pair of very blue eyes stared at me in utter incredulity. He spoke in a deep, quiet voice: "Who are you? What are you doing here?" "I'm Gertie," I said. "And I've come to stay".'

Viewed from the present distance, three-quarters of a century later, it is not easy to establish whether the early life of Gertrude Lawrence really did resemble one of the weepier penny-dreadful novels of the period, or whether those were merely the terms in which she later chose to recall it. Certainly she did at this time leave her mother for her father, certainly he was then singing in travelling variety shows. Whether she really said 'I'm Gertie and I've come to stay' only he and she would ever have known, but later evidence indicates that she was a character of remarkably limited imagination, immensely susceptible to anything she had recently read or seen or heard. Her life was to be lived out in a series of clichés, and her talent lay in either turning those clichés inside out or simply in rising above them. If anyone could have played that stage-door reunion with a father in those terms and got away with it, then Gertie would have been the one.

Life with father was, however, not a lot easier than life with mother had been; for six years now he'd been living with a chorus girl called Rose, who initially was understandably reluctant to take on the responsibilities of watching over a teenage girl as well as a drunken lover. Eventually, though, it was agreed that little Gertie would tour with them in her role as 'child *danseuse*', handing over any money she could make to her father and Rose in return for her keep. Father, meanwhile, had agreed to write a weekly letter to his ex-wife reporting on their daughter's progress and whereabouts, although as the drink slowly but surely got the better of him, these letters were more and more often written by Rose.

After a while, the endless routine of casting offices and stage-door tips about who was looking for whom in what sort of show led Gertie to another chorus-and-understudy job, this one in a touring revue (the first to attempt a kind of up-market vaudeville) called *Miss Plaster of Paris*. For fifteen shillings a week, most of which still went to her father, she was required to sing and dance a bit, sit atop a column in one tasteful tableau (a role she got by having the smallest bottom in the company) and above all understudy the leading lady, who happened to be married to the show's producer-star. On a Saturday night, after a few drinks, it was his custom to beat her up a bit, which usually meant that Gertie played the Monday night show while she recovered.

Miss Plaster of Paris bred a sequel, *Miss Lamb of Canterbury*, and by the time that tour came to its close a number of things had happened, not least the start of the First World War. This, like most wars, did nothing but good at the box office; there had never been a greater need for entertainment, and within a year of Sarajevo the London acting community's unemployment problems had been cut by something like a half.

The war, however, impinged on Gertie's life a good deal less than a major family decision which she had recently reached in conversation with Arthur's hitherto faithful Rose. The two girls decided that so long as either of them were there to dry him out and bring home any kind of a salary, his drinking would only continue. The answer, they decided, for his sake as well as theirs, was to leave him to his own devices.

As it happened, they needn't have bothered; before they were able to announce their decision to him, Arthur told them both that he'd been offered a year-long tour of South Africa in a variety show which was also to feature a young Victor McLaglen, and that he would therefore be leaving in the morning.

Gertie was never again to live with either her father or her mother as a dependent, though she kept in touch with them both and, when times were good, sent money. She was now just sixteen, and alone.

For a while she lived at the Theatrical Girls' Club in Greek Street, leaving London to tour in any show that would have her in its chorus. Her experience was by now not inconsiderable; since *Fifinella* and *Hannele*, she had done the two revues, a musical called *All Aboard*, which rapidly sank, plus a show with her father called *The Little Michus* about a French pastry-cook and his troubles with twin daughters, one of whom was conveniently played by Gertie. Then, in 1916 came a disastrous engagement as a dancer in a touring company which ended in Shrewsbury, a country town not generally regarded as the centre of British theatrical activity. The company manager, affectionately known to the girls as 'old four-eyes' on account of his thick spectacles, was a shy man; so shy that when the money ran out before the end of the week, leaving him a bit short for the wages, he decided to return to London rather than get himself involved in any nasty verbal altercations with the cast. Thus he was able to keep most of the box-office takings.

Stranded quite literally penniless in Shrewsbury, Gertie got a job serving behind the bar in the hotel where she was already staying; luckily it was Shrewsbury's busy season, with the flower festival in full swing, and after a month behind the bar she had made enough not only to pay off her hotel bill but also to continue living there in reasonable comfort.

What she was waiting for was, of course, the arrival in the town of another touring company, and sure enough eventually one did come through, in need as always of a little local talent to take care of the roles for which they had not thought it worthwhile paying any actresses' train fares from London. Thus it was that each evening around 7 p.m. Gertie would leave the bar of the Red Lion, cross the road to the theatre and, dressed as a nun, sing 'My Rosary' as the prelude to a religious drama. By the time that run came to an end, she had saved enough to head back to London.

Now, with her father's departure for South Africa and the break-up of what had become her second family, Gertie received some parting words of advice from Rose: 'Go on your own. You've got something and I think you're going to get on. You're not exactly pretty, and you're too thin for everybody's taste, but you've got *class*. You need to be seen by the West End toffs.'

Not that there were too many West End toffs to be found in Swindon, which was where Gertie went next with a show called *Money For Nothing*. As usual she was in the chorus, dancing a little and singing a little and understudying stars who were never ill, and hoping against hope that this would be the show which finally got her off the road and the outer-London circuit and into the West End. It wasn't; but it did get her noticed by people who were able, in the end, to do her a bit of good. To London in 1913 had come a celebrated American revue couple called Lee White and Clay Smith; during 1916 they decided to visit Swindon. Staying overnight, they also visited the local music hall and there, in *Money For Nothing*, they found Gertie.

Quite what they saw in her is not known; but something about her work that night, something about the moment or two in the show when she had a fraction of a song or dance to herself, impressed them enough to offer her dinner at their hotel. They wanted, they said, to help her and they believed that her talent would justify their interest; they made it clear that there was nothing on offer at the moment, but they would always like to know where she was in case anything came up.

Gertie, a prolific and constant postcard-writer then as later in life, took to sending Lee White and Clay Smith lists of her touring dates; later, when she was playing Yarmouth, there came a telegram: WE HAVE RECOMMENDED YOU FOR A JOB IN NEW CHARLOT REVUE STOP COME AT ONCE.

Gertie was half way to the station before a fellow chorus girl, chasing after her, pointed out that although there was nothing specific in writing to tie her to the present tour, if she left in midweek and headed for London only to find that Charlot couldn't use her, she would doubtless be replaced at Yarmouth and then find herself once again out of work. Caution prevailed, and she replied with another telegram: DOES YOUR WIRE CONSTITUTE A CONTRACT?

YES, IF YOU CAN COME AT ONCE, came the answer. She did. Collecting the fare from some friendly soldiers who happened to be in training at Yarmouth and to have seen her show, she headed for London and *Some* in June 1916, one of a long line of revues presented by André Charlot. Though largely forgotten today (he was to die a sad and impecunious death in Hollywood after the Second World War) Charlot was the architect and founding father of the twentieth-century British 'intimate' revue and was once described by J. M. Barrie as 'the whole British theatrical profession in a nutshell'. While Flo Ziegfeld on Broadway was more concerned with the spectacle of large numbers of lovely ladies descending staircases very slowly, it was André

Charlot who pioneered the concept of the 'intimate' revue in which elements of comedy, dance and song would be merged to provide an altogether more thoughtful and coherent spectacle. Where Cochran and Ziegfeld worked almost exclusively for the eye, Charlot worked also for the ear, giving in his shows as much importance to the words as to the music.

Some (an eccentric title partially explained by the fact that the words 'More Samples' were printed on posters and programmes directly below it, referring audiences back to an earlier show by the same authors, Grattan & Tate, which had been called simply *Samples*) opened at the Vaudeville Theatre in London on 29 June 1916. It was a company show with a cast of twelve, and the top billing was given to Clay Smith and Lee White together with an eighteen-year-old Toronto-born comedienne called Beatrice Lillie. It was specifically to understudy Beatrice Lillie that Gertie had been brought from Yarmouth, and *Some* was to prove the start of a professional partnership between the two women which continued well into the 1920s.

In the opinion of the then drama critic of *The Times*, *Some* was 'an evening of excellent fooling', which had an intriguingly original opening number in which the entire cast were seen outside their own stage door, desperately trying to get taxis home. After this, the revue was a mixture of songs, dance numbers and sketches, the latter including a satirical attack on the hopelessness of London's new telephone system ('always a fitting butt for good-natured banter' wrote one critic prophetically).

For Beatrice Lillie, just six weeks older than Gertrude Lawrence but already considerably further advanced in her stage career, having reached the West End within three months of her stage debut at the Chatham Empire in 1914, the arrival of Gertie at rehearsals for *Some* meant not only the grandeur of having her own understudy but also the discovery of a kindred spirit with whom to lark around backstage and sometimes even on stage:

I was young and callow enough to be elated over the acquisition of my first understudy, and a quick glance at her showed enormous blue eyes in a vivid, elfish face . . . after we had been running for several months at the Vaudeville, news came that America had entered the war. That April [1917] evening, a number of mine was cut so that our American star Lee White could sing a song which her husband Clay appeared to have composed in a matter of minutes. He stepped out from behind the curtains to announce his brand-new rouser, *America Answers The Call*; the front tabs were drawn and there stood Lee, tall and majestic, giving out in her strong contralto:

America answers the call, America answers the call—
Tramp, tramp, tramp, tramp, tramp,
The boys are marching . . .

There was no resisting the impulse. Standing behind the drop-curtain to hear what Clay had wrought, my feet began to feel a twitch. In a moment, I was marking time, then I started marching out myself to the beat of the drummer, to and fro behind Lee. Feeling the same impulse, Gertie fell into step behind me until the curtains were swaying as if in a high breeze.

Within seconds, an irate Clay Smith was backstage, accompanied by an equally irate 'Uncle' André Charlot. Both Bea and Gertie were immediately given ten days' notice to quit the show.

It was not an auspicious start to Gertie's first West End engagement.

3

A STAR DANCED

The following morning, Charlot sent for the two girls and told them that they would not be dismissed after all: Bea, he said, was irreplaceable (a home truth in the comfortable knowledge of which Miss Lillie was to revel for the rest of her eccentric career) and Gertie had been reprieved at the special request of Clay Smith, who was not (at least at that time) a man to bear a grudge.

The reprieve did not, however, make either Gertie or Bea any better behaved backstage; they were like a couple of naughty schoolgirls and their relationship from this time forward was akin to that of two incurable pranksters let loose in a world which, already unreal enough, could easily be sabotaged with highly enjoyable results. A week or two after the saga of the 'Tramp, Tramp, Tramp' song, Bea noticed that Lee White (who like her husband Clay Smith had money in the show and therefore a considerable share of the solo numbers) was doing a song in the second half called 'Have You Seen The Ducks Go By?', which required a number of the chorus girls, including Gertie, to cross the stage behind a wall, revealing only their hats which were, suitably enough, in the shape of ducks. This was altogether too much of a temptation for Gertie: 'I couldn't help making my duck frisk about and behave as no properly drilled duck would ever do. Nor could I resist popping my head up over the wall in the wrong place, winking at the audience, and laughing when they laughed at me. Naturally Lee did not like this in the least. But Bea Lillie adored it, and would join us in the chorus and pop her head up over the wall, minus the duck head-dress but wearing a man's straw hat and a false moustache . . . finally both Lee and Clay stopped speaking to us at all.'

Quite apart from the ingratitude shown by Gertie to the couple who, whatever their inability to share a joke, had actually taken the trouble to get her out of a second-rate touring revue and into the West End, to anyone used to the more formal atmosphere of present-day theatre, Bea and Gertie's lively behaviour on-stage must be rather surprising. The reason that they got away with it seems to have been that Bea was considered by Charlot as too important to dismiss, and Gertie too insignificant. To the question of motive, Gertrude Lawrence herself once came up with an eminently satisfactory answer:

I suppose a psychologist could find a reason for the irrepressible impulse to play pranks which obsessed me for several seasons after I got started on the London stage. They were the kind of pranks that usually only schoolchildren think are funny – fake telegrams, keyholes stuffed with soap, coat sleeves sewn up at the cuffs so that the victim found it impossible to make a quick change of costume. If it seems strange that I should have taken such liberties after I had been at such pains to get an opportunity in a London production, I can only explain these idiosyncrasies of mine on the ground that I must have been making up for those years when I had been working at a time when most children my age were playing games. Perhaps, it was just something I had to get out of my system. Perhaps, too, it was the not abnormal reaction of a girl who suddenly found herself made much of for the first time in her life. On looking back it seems to me extraordinary the patience which André Charlot had with me during those seasons. I must have been an unmitigated nuisance – to him and to all the other members of the company. What I needed was to have someone tick me off.

But that time was still to come. Meanwhile, her one-show engagement at the Vaudeville was turning into a permanent Charlot season; as *Some* came to the end of its run there, the decision was made to replace it with another Charlot revue. This one, which opened early in 1917, was called *Cheep!* and again it starred Clay Smith and Lee White. Harry Grattan was billed as sole author (though a footnote added 'Songs by Clay Smith, Bert Lee and R. P. Weston') and it was further announced in the programme that 'This show is staged by the Author because we could not afford a real producer.' The rest of the cast stayed much the same, with Bea Lillie getting billed now in thicker type than anyone save Lee White, and the critic of the *Observer* thought that this was 'without exception the wittiest, most amusing and prettiest revue to be seen in town'.

Gertie was still being used in the chorus and to understudy Bea, who had thus far not missed a single performance of either show; her freedom of manoeuvre on stage was (probably because of her behaviour during *Some*) severely curtailed, and Charlot made very sure that she would never again get the chance of the kind of disruption she had earlier managed to create with the ducks. As a result, she was getting thoroughly bored and looking for a way out of *Cheep!* when one unexpectedly presented itself. On 11 July 1917, from her shared dressing-room at the Vaudeville, she wrote to André Charlot:

I have heard today that *Some* is to go on tour in a few weeks' time, and I want to ask you if I might be allowed to join that company? You see, Mr Charlot, I feel an awful outsider in the show here at present, especially after all my little parts in *Some*, and as I have done a good deal of male impersonation I am daring to ask you – if you haven't settled on somebody else already – might I take Miss Lillie's roles on the tour? Or failing that Billie Carleton's? The latter is a very easy task, and after having played Blanche Marie on tour in *The Little Michus* for eight months I think I am quite capable. Anyway, will you try me? I do so want to make good, and seem to be making very little headway here at present. Do answer this, or let me see you myself. Awaiting your reply, Yours very sincerely, Gertrude Lawrence.

Grasping the chance to separate Gertie and Bea at last, and perhaps also recognizing that there was indeed in Gertie something special which was not exactly being brought to the fore by a job in the back row of a chorus at the Vaudeville, Charlot agreed to send her out on tour doing the Bea Lillie material from *Some*.

By the time that tour ended and she was back in the chorus of *Cheep!*, certain things had become abundantly clear to Gertie. First, though she had enjoyed at last having a go at Bea's numbers, she had also discovered that there wasn't much point in starring in towns so obscure that nobody in the audience would ever be likely to do you any professional good. Second and more important, however, she had discovered that she could handle a star number. It had been nearly a decade since Italia Conti and the ballet mistress Madame Espinosa had first taken her into their classes, nearly a decade since some singing teacher had put a piece of paper under the strings of a piano and told her that was what her tinnily vibrating cockney voice sounded like, and that she would have to work on it if it was ever to sound even faintly musical.

Now it did, but who was to hear it? Back at the Vaudeville, Gertie put the problem to Beatrice Lillie, who quickly came up with her own brand of solution: 'My understudy may have been a latent star, but she needed assistance to help her shine. She had to have a chance to prove herself to Charlot and the rest of the cast by playing for me. After a certain amount of soul-searching (was it the right thing to do, to put friendship ahead of my public, etc.?) I telephoned the theatre one morning. ''I'm in bed'', I lied in a croaky whisper, ''with a temperature of a hundred and three. If it goes any higher, I'm going to sell.'' So that night, with the same delicious feeling you get playing hooky from school, I took a busman's holiday and went to see Oscar Asche in *Chu-Chin-Chow*.'

So for that one night in late 1917, Gertrude Lawrence made her starring debut in the West End 'due to the indisposition of Miss Beatrice Lillie'. By all accounts she did well enough, but Bea did not intend to stay phonily 'indisposed' for more than a single night, so the next day it was back to the chorus, which was where Gertie stayed for the rest of the run of that revue.

Away from the theatre, her life was becoming romantically active enough to take her mind at least temporarily off her boredom at the Vaudeville. Though she was still too far down the cast list to attract the attention of any of the wealthy admirers who would later be found at so many of her stage doors, she had briefly become engaged 'to a boy then serving in the balloon barrage which protected London'. That romantic wartime liaison finished however almost as rapidly as it had started, and Gertie had then met one of Charlot's dance directors, a Blackpool man by the name of Francis Gordon-Howley: 'Frank was twenty years my senior, and I was immensely flattered by his attention. Moreover he belonged to my world—the world of the theatre. He spoke my language—that of the theatre. He was a director, and he talked to me of his future plans in which I figured as his star. Other boyfriends had expected me to marry them and leave the theatre; Frank expected me to marry him and stay in the theatre.' And she did. By the beginning of 1918, without missing a single night at the Vaudeville, Gertrude Lawrence had managed to get herself married—and pregnant, though whether by Frank Howley or the 'barrage balloon boy' was never entirely clear. Howley was a modest and by all accounts charming character, no Svengali, and Gertie was by now certainly not some wilting Trilby; yet there's no doubt that their relationship both before and during their short-lived marriage was more one of father and daughter than of husband and wife. Quite apart from the twenty-year difference in their ages, Howley was – though never too successfully – a talent scout and a moulder of singers and dancers, and just as he recognized in Gertie 'someone to do something with', so she recognized in him a father she had never had and a manager who might do something to get her still uneventful career off the ground. The trouble, although it didn't become apparent until several months later, was that Howley (unlike Charlot) was not a man who would ever manage to become an all-powerful impresario.

For the time being, life proceeded reasonably calmly; Charlot had raised Gertie's salary from £3.00 to £4.00 a week at the Vaudeville, and she and Howley took a small flat in Carlton Mansions, Maida Vale, where they were soon joined by Frank's two brothers. Howley wasn't actually working at this time, or indeed at almost any time during their brief marriage, but the idea was that he would raise the money to form his own production company, which would then present shows in which Gertie would naturally be the leading lady. Quite where this money was to come from never became altogether clear, but before she had too much time to worry about that there was better news for Miss Lawrence (as she was still known). *Cheep!* was to be replaced at the Vaudeville in May 1918 by a third Charlot revue entitled *Tabs*. By now Clay Smith and Lee White had returned to America and the stars of *Tabs* were therefore to be Bea Lillie and a young singer-dancer with whom Gertie was to work frequently in the near future, Walter Williams. But the best news about *Tabs* was that there in the poster billing (admittedly in thirteenth place out of a cast of fourteen) was at last the name Gertrude Lawrence and, more important still, two of the twenty-two numbers in the show were to be hers.

Overall credit for the words and music of *Tabs* was taken by Ronald Jeans and an up-and-coming Welsh composer by the name of Ivor Novello, though Gertie didn't sing any of Novello's music; her two numbers were 'I Love You For Loving Me' (lyrics Ronald Jeans, music Bob Adams) and 'Dinkey Diddle-Ums' (Mills-Scott-Long), both of which appear to have sunk more or less without trace – certainly they were not exactly on the lips of every whistling messenger boy who passed the Vaudeville on his way up the Strand in that last summer of the First World War.

Tabs opened to the glowing reviews that Charlot had by now come to expect, but Gertie had begun to get more than a little careless about understudy rehearsals, with the result that Charlot had taken that job away from her and re-assigned it to a young girl named Jessie Matthews. As Bea

Lillie was renowned for never being 'off', the whole question of who should understudy her seemed to Gertie more than a little academic. Luckily, however, her husband began to miss the extra pound or so a week which the understudying paid, and after a month or two convinced Gertie that she should go back to it which, with Charlot's benevolence, she did. And only in the nick of time.

One morning in July Bea Lillie, as was her wont, went out riding in Hyde Park as part of what one gossip column described as 'a merry group including Eileen Molyneux, Princess Clementine and Prince Napoleon'. Only that morning it wasn't quite so merry; Bea's horse threw her to the ground, resulting in medium concussion, a bent collarbone which had to be in plaster for the next month, and Bea's celebrated comment, 'The next horse I ride on, I'm going to be tied on.'

Gertie's big chance had come and not, in her view, a moment too soon. There was just one snag. She was by now seven months pregnant:

My chance – the chance I'd longed for for years. The chance every understudy dreams about – the star suddenly ill, or meeting with an accident, and the little understudy having to step in and take her place. Now this had happened to me. As I stood there in Bea's dressing-room and her dresser helped me with swift, experienced fingers I thought 'The irony of it. It has happened to me just now when I'm feeling so ill' . . . In a couple of numbers Bea was doing male impersonations. For these she wore a white tie and tails. The black broadcloth suit was cut perfectly and fitted her slim, straight body like a glove. I held my breath while the dresser laced me up tightly; then I got into the trousers and white waistcoat . . . When my call came, I went on and for the first time in my life on the stage I knew anxiety. Bea was a tremendous favourite. Most of the audience had come on purpose to see her. Could I satisfy them? If I could hold that audience, if I could make them laugh and applaud and like Gertrude Lawrence, then the rest of my career was assured. If I failed. . . .

But she didn't; when she finally came offstage two and a half hours later Charlot was standing in the wings grinning broadly. It was all Gertie needed to know and for the next two months, getting ever more pregnant, she played show after show until finally a message came from Bea: 'I don't know about the horse, but I'm fit for work again.'

It was agreed Bea would return to *Tabs* the following Monday; that Saturday, Frank went up to Liverpool where he had heard of a possible directing job. His two brothers were in the Maida Vale flat with Gertie, both in bed with influenza. Feeling distinctly queasy, she left alone for the theatre and played both houses; as the final curtain fell, she knew she was going to have the baby. Not in a matter of days or weeks, but in a matter of hours. Leaving the stage door, she decided the best idea would be to go home to mother, with whom there had been a sort of uneasy *rapprochement* since her marriage. Cabs were not in those days inclined to travel all the way to Clapham, especially since raging over London that night was one of the worst air raids of the war. Eventually she stopped a policeman who in turn bullied a cab driver; once arrived in Clapham she was bundled by mother straight into a nearby nursing home and by the Monday night, as Bea Lillie returned to her starring role in *Tabs*, her understudy was the proud possessor of a little girl called Pamela.

When, for the first and last time in her life, she became a mother (she eventually had an operation to prevent a recurrence of the event) Gertrude Lawrence was just twenty and had been married less than a year; the baby, she announced firmly in her autobiography, was in any case 'several months premature'. Though the drama of Pamela's birth nearly fitted the 'born in a trunk' cliché and neatly belonged to the scenario of the cut-price romantic novel within which so much of Gertie's life was already being lived, the arrival of a child broke the traditional requirements of romantic fiction by totally destroying rather than saving the already tattered Howley marriage.

Frank returned from Liverpool still jobless, pawned one of Gertie's rings to cover his expenses, and left her to settle the nursing home account. There being virtually no money at all now, the lease of the Maida Vale flat was given up and Gertie took the new baby home to Mother, leaving Frank to his own resources. After a spirited but all too characteristically unsuccessful attempt to kidnap his own child, Frank decided that enough was enough. He asked for one last meeting with Gertie, at the Lyons' Corner House where they had first planned to marry, and agreed that if she would give him all the money then in her purse, which came to about £5, he would go to live in Manchester and run a casting agency for pantomime dancers; which, until he took to running a boarding house there, was precisely what he did.

The failure of the marriage had not of course been his fault alone, as his daughter Pamela discovered some years later when, as an adult, she finally got to know him:

When my own eldest child, his grandson, was about three my father came down from Manchester to stay with us, and he brought his second wife, an ex-Tiller Girl, who had, unlike my mother, been able to make him very happy. It was only about the third time we'd ever met; once he'd come to visit me at Roedean and once when I was on tour in Manchester with a play he came backstage and bought me a hideous blue tulle evening dress, which, to be fair to Daddy, I chose myself because of the diamanté scattered over it like something out of *Come Dancing*. But when he came to stay with us he told me, and I believe it, that he had decided on purpose not to see me because he didn't want me to feel torn between two parents. He was very modest, very unassuming and I think that what went wrong with their marriage was quite simply that Mummy had begun to be a success and he hadn't. In those days if that sort of thing happened at all it usually happened the other way around, with the man getting bored of the wife he had married when times were hard, and then going off in search of something more glamorous when times got better. In this case it was the wife who outgrew the husband; my mother just left my father behind. It was as simple as that: he'd married an understudy and by the time I was born a few months later she'd taken over a starring role. She wasn't about to go back to the chorus, and she knew that he didn't have anything to offer that she hadn't already outgrown. I wasn't enough to keep them together, but what month-old baby ever could have been?

4

FORCED TO TOUR

So, as the First World War dragged to its November close, Gertrude Lawrence found herself at the head of a one-parent family; so far as she, none too regretfully, was concerned, there was to be no further contact with Howley and divorce proceedings were soon under way. She and her baby were now safely installed with mother in Clapham, and though the terraced house at 14 Lydon Road was less than glamorous, it did represent a kind of security.

Charlot, in recognition of Gertie's new-found status as a mother, increased her salary at the Vaudeville to £6 a week, but with Bea now fully recovered from her fall, Gertie found it difficult and depressing to return to her old chorus-and-supporting status. In December of that year, however, *Tabs* was replaced by a fourth Charlot revue entitled *Buzz, Buzz*, in which she was given not only such solos as 'Winnie The Window Cleaner' but also some straight romantic numbers with Walter Williams. Bea Lillie had by this time left the Vaudeville team, but Gertie was not her clear heiress apparent; certainly she had at last escaped the line of girl dancers, yet without managing to establish herself as the company's leading lady either.

The relationship with Charlot continued to deteriorate as, soon after the first night, Gertie returned to her old on-stage tricks in an attempt to alleviate what looked like the boredom of a long run and her depression at not having been allowed to step straight into Bea's shoes. Off-stage, however, her life took an altogether more cheerful turn: the little money she was earning was at least regular, and she soon realized that her mother would be happy to keep Pamela with her in Clapham even if she, Gertie, were not actually to return there every night. Early in 1919, she therefore took a share in a small Mayfair flat and proceeded, carefully and insistently, to work her way into high society.

One of her Charlot understudies, June (later Lady Inverclyde) recalled:

She was a wraith of a girl, not at all pretty but extraordinarily magnetic, who appeared to live on an inexhaustible fund of nervous vitality. Her sole mainstays were guts and gallantry and a driving determination to succeed. The men pouring back from the war were eager for carefree enjoyment and Gertie handed it to them in hunks. They filled the stalls and boxes of the Vaudeville and every night her chintzy little dressing-room housed bevvies of young officers. I used to see them lolling against the walls, lounging on the couch, and hear their laughing responses to Gertie's saucy wit. There did not seem to be a shy bone in her body. She didn't care what she said or did in public, so long as it drew attention to her . . . I think she would have dyed her hair pink if she had felt the occasion warranted it. She adored playing to the public both on and off the stage. For her, the unwritten law that actresses should only be seen across the footlights did not exist. Gertie was seen everywhere: wearing a flying helmet or ludicrously swinging a tennis racquet at the newly-founded Hendon Flying Club; lunching in the best restaurants; dancing at the best nightclubs; peering into Cartier's windows. Her moods were mercurial and she began to cultivate a variety of accents; rowdy, county, blasé, – all to be used at the right time in the right place.

These were just beginning to be the years of the bright young things, the Café Society and Coward's poor little rich girls; the years when any reasonably attractive chorus girl who was half-way good in bed could be fairly certain of marrying, if not actually into the aristocracy (though that too often happened), at least into an altogether better social and financial circle than the one she had been born into. Theatre at this time was a social rather than an intellectual event, and it brought together as never before or since two totally separate worlds: most theatre people of the era came from backgrounds they were fast trying to forget, and were in any case the first generation not to be made to feel ashamed of their trade. Most of the young male aristocracy, already jolted by war, were having a hard time settling back into country life with girls who reminded them all too clearly of their mothers or sisters. For both teams of escapers, the stage door provided a meeting place, a kind of neutral territory where, safe from their own and each others' families, discreet liaisons could be formed and pursued through innumerable late-night suppers and Mayfair flats.

Moreover, at a time when progress in the theatre tended to be accidental and arbitrary, rather than the result of careful career-planning, a girl with the right friends, who turned up in the right nightclubs and therefore next morning in the right gossip-columns, was more likely to catch the eye of a producer than a girl who spent her spare evenings at ballet classes. To become a star in the theatre, unless an exclusively Shakespearian career was envisaged, you had also to become a star outside the theatre and it was, however sub-consciously, to that project Gertrude Lawrence now turned her attentions.

It led her at first into a good deal of trouble. In organizing for herself some sort of private life away from mother, the baby and Clapham, she turned first to her old child-actor friends; Noël was already hard at work in *Scandal* at the Strand Theatre, but he and Ivor Novello (whom she had first met as the composer of Charlot's *Tabs*) separately introduced her around and about to a whole new world of late-night suppers and discreet attachments, which added to the strain of still doing eight shows a week at the Vaudeville rapidly led her into a state of exhaustion. Pleading a combination of lumbago and tonsillitis, she persuaded the long-suffering Charlot to release her from *Buzz, Buzz* for a fortnight while she recuperated. All might have been well had she not agreed, towards the end of the fortnight (when she was already feeling distinctly better) to join a party Novello was making up to go to a new Ethel Baird opening night. As luck would have it, in the theatre seat next to hers sat André Charlot. And that was it. He'd put up with nearly three years of Gertie fooling about on stage and off, and his patience was now exhausted. She had been away from his show for more than six performances, which allowed him to cancel her contract, and the next morning she received a note from him in which he did just that. 'If you are well enough to go to other people's plays' his note ended, not unreasonably, 'you are well enough to come to your own'.

She was out of a job and, what was worse, in London's small and tight-knit theatrical community, every other management soon knew why. Codes of behaviour were at the time curious but distinct: no producer much minded what a young actress got up to in her spare time, but she was still expected to be on stage eight times a week. Already Gertie had broken that rule and was being considered 'unreliable'. Moreover her West End career had been solely in Charlot revues at the Vaudeville, which were a law, and a language, unto themselves. There was no reason to believe she could do anything else but Charlot revues, and it was from a Charlot revue that she had just been sacked.

Gertie was not one to take that sort of thing lying down; having rapidly discovered that stage doors were now barred to her, she looked around for another job and rapidly found one. One of the newer London landmarks of this time was a nightclub called Murray's; far-sightedly joining in the new cabaret craze, it began providing its upper-crust customers with the best floorshow in town, a carefully choreographed all-singing, all-dancing extravaganza, a miniaturised version of one of the Cochran or Charlot revues. Its over-riding attraction was that you could eat and drink, maybe even talk, during the entertainment and that its stars were expected (if not actually forced) to join your table for a little champagne afterwards.

Early in 1919 Gertrude Lawrence applied for a job there, and Murray's was to become her professional home for almost the whole of the next two years. It is difficult now to assess whether she or the club got the better deal. From the club's point of view, it acquired for the first time a 'legit' singer and dancer, somebody who had actually worked with Charlot and Bea Lillie at the Vaudeville instead of on the usual showgirl-club circuit. From Gertie's point of view, she was able to star (only, admittedly, in a forty-minute show) in the West End still, but was now able to get into direct contact with her admirers without having to run the risk that the most promising or desirable of them might not bother to make the journey round to the stage door.

It was at Murray's that Gertie caught the eye of the Duke of Kent and the future Edward VIII; it was there too that she began to be noticed, not only by the 'beautiful people' of her day but by journalists and by stars and directors from the legitimate theatre (still her first love) who, by dropping in to the club's midnight show on the way home from their dressing-rooms, were able to see and applaud Gertie as they never would had she been playing a show with the same curtain-times as theirs. In a social if not in a professional sense, her nightclub work at Murray's was the making of Gertrude Lawrence, for it was there that she was first seen by Captain Philip Astley.

The son of a wealthy country clergyman, Astley had been born at Chequers, the country house later given to the nation as a weekend residence for the Prime Minister of the day. Not only that, noted Gertie eagerly, but, 'He was christened in the robes of Oliver Cromwell, and educated at Eton and the Royal Military College, added to which he was desperately good-looking and had unparalleled charm. We had to fall in love with each other: it was as natural and instinctive to us as to breathe.'

Though later each was seriously to consider marriage to the other (usually at different times), for the present there could be no thought of it; Gertie was still officially Mrs Gordon-Howley, and for Astley to have been involved in divorce proceedings would have ruined a promising career in the Household Cavalry. Astley fast became almost everything to Gertie: lover, escort, friend, adviser and above all tutor in the social ways of the world to which Gertie still most wanted to belong.

'Philip', recalls his last wife, 'was at that time the perfect young man about town: he was handsome, he was rich, he was experienced, he owned a positively enormous car complete with chauffeur, and his family had by now grown accustomed to him going out with actresses. There had been one before Gertie, and when Philip went to see his mother to tell her there was a problem she simply reached under her pillow and brought out an envelope full of pound notes and said, "I think you'll find that will solve it." '

This time it was rather different; Philip was rapidly falling deeply in love with Gertie, and they were to stay together for the best part of the 1920s until, much to Gertie's regret and rage, he eventually married Madeleine Carroll. But Astley's influence on Gertie, and his importance to her, was as crucial in the social sphere as was Coward's in the theatre and it was Noël's friend and biographer Cole Lesley who once explained the significance of the Astley-Lawrence partnership: 'Gertie was taught everything by Philip, who guided her taste in clothes and everything else and she, monkey-quick, picked up from him every trick of behaviour and social jargon until the girl from Brixton emerged during their long relationship as a perfectly polished product of Mayfair.'

Gertie did not come of a generation who took pride in humble origins; she was genuinely ashamed of her social background, eager to forget both mother and daughter in Clapham and to rebuild herself in the image of the early 1920s lady about town, a fitting partner for Captain Astley and a guest who would not disgrace herself with the wrong fork at dinner with the Prince of Wales, for that was now the exalted circle in which the girl from Murray's was starting to move:

I'll never forget dashing into my dressing-room one night to find the Duke of Kent

34

seated before my mirror, trying on a wig of long, false curls . . . I was often invited (because of Philip) to the parties which the Prince of Wales gave in his apartment at St James's Palace, at which everyone sang and danced and did stunts. These parties were always informal and entertaining. You met people of all sorts and from every walk of life and profession, but never anyone who was dull or stuffy. He invited international tennis champions, the newest blues singer, a guitarist who was all the rage in Paris, as well as his own intimate set. It was amusing that all this fun went on late at night inside the solemn old pile, with the sentries keeping up their march along the pavement just outside . . . the Prince once took me on a tour of the state apartments in the palace. We paused at the window from which, according to the centuries-old tradition, every new sovereign is acclaimed on his accession to the throne. Each of us was thinking silently that someday the King's herald would proclaim from the balcony outside that very window: 'The King is dead – long live King Edward VIII' . . . at that time, during the early 1920s, no one in London had even heard of Mrs Wallis Warfield Simpson.

They were, however, beginning to hear about Gertrude Lawrence; her fame at Murray's was spreading to such an extent that even André Charlot came to see her there. She was good, he admitted, so good that it was high time she got herself back into the legitimate theatre rather than run the risk of becoming London's leading nightclub girl. Gertie saw that danger, as did Philip; but Charlot wasn't going to take her back even now, and no other West End manager who came into Murray's came clutching a contract for her.

To her credit (and perhaps also because of the increasingly sensible advice about her career she was getting from Astley) Gertie gave up a lucrative engagement at Murray's towards the end of 1920 and began to work her passage back into the straight theatre. At first all she could get was a touring revue called *The Midnight Frolics*, followed at Christmas 1920 by a job understudying Phyllis Dare as the Princess in *Aladdin*, that year's pantomime at the London Hippodrome. But part of the deal was that she would be allowed to play some matinées, which she did, and when that closed she spent the best part of 1921 touring music-halls in London and around the country as part of a double-act she'd formed with Walter Williams.

Williams was by now enjoying a considerable success as the singer of 'K-K-Katie' and together, billing themselves as 'Straight from London' and using some of Charlot's old revue material without worrying too much about copyright fees, he and Gertie managed to get themselves some good top-of-the-bill bookings on the old Moss Empire circuit, vaudeville experience that was to stand her in good stead when fifteen years later she came to play in Coward's *Red Peppers*.

But the touring life of a music-hall act did not suit Gertie's highly social domestic arrangements, and what she wanted was a show in London. When one did not materialize, she decided to take a few months off and (with a little financial help from Astley) rented a summer cottage by the Thames near Windsor. There, for the first time (and again at Astley's prompting) she began to get to know her now two-and-a-half-year-old daughter, whom she had invited along with her mother to stay with her. Gertie later recalled: 'Among our gay [an accurate description in its current usage] companions at that time was Lord Lathom, and several times he and Philip and the others would stop at Buck's Club, pick up a hamper of chicken, fruit, champagne et cetera and we would all roar down to the cottage and get mother out of bed to act as hostess . . . one night, we gave her a real surprise. We all arrived without warning, as usual, and routed her out of bed. Down she came, and we had supper. Suddenly she realised that there was a stranger in our midst and that we were calling him 'Sir'. Her gaze shot down the table, past his face, and fixed itself on my delighted grin; I nodded. I knew she had recognised the Prince of Wales.'

Somehow it all seemed a long way from Clapham and the moonlight flits, but it was not advancing Gertie's theatrical career. Indeed she might have stayed by the river at Windsor giving gracious surprise supper parties for the rest of the 1920s (many ex-showgirls did) had it not been, in that late summer of 1921, for a magical and almost eery repetition of events from her recent past.

André Charlot was again preparing a new revue to be entitled *A to Z* and, since it was destined for the Prince of Wales Theatre, it would have to be on an infinitely larger scale than anything he had ever done at the Vaudeville. A starry cast was to be headed by the famous American close-harmony Trix Sisters and Jack Buchanan; the other leading female role Charlot had given to his stalwart comedienne from the Vaudeville, Beatrice Lillie. In September they began rehearsing and by the end of that month Bea was in hospital with a recurrence of back trouble. *A to Z* had an opening date fixed for October, sets were built, musicians hired, and there was no way they could wait for Miss Lillie to return. Charlot thought back to the last time this had happened, and decided that if history was repeating itself then so would he; messages were sent to the riverside cottage and by the following morning Gertie was rehearsing Bea's numbers.

Though the best of the songs were supposed to go to the Trix Sisters, there was one, 'Limehouse Blues', which had somehow got away and was set up as a duet for Gertie and Jack Buchanan, who had not worked together before; later the song became one of her most constant and profitable hits on record. Written by Philip Braham and Douglas Furber, it began:

> 'In Limehouse, where yellow ladies dance and play,
> In Limehouse, you can hear those blues all day . . .'

'Limehouse Blues' led *The Times* critic to describe *A to Z* as 'all Charlot, Charm and Chinatown'. The score also featured Novello's 'And Her Mother Came Too' as a solo for Buchanan. All in all, *A to Z* had so much going for it that they survived at the Prince of Wales for 428 performances, a run of fourteen months, which allowed Bea Lillie eventually to step back into the numbers that had originally been meant for her. The success of *A to Z* did both Buchanan and Gertrude Lawrence a power of good; while the programme was advertising *diners dansant* and nightclub suppers for eight shillings a head, Gertie could relax in the knowledge that she was back in the real theatre at last.

Her friendships now divided into two distinct categories; there were her theatre friends — Noël, Bea, Buchanan — and then there were her 'grand' friends; and the two groups sometimes led her into considerable social uncertainty. Bea Lillie once recalled how she and Buchanan were being shown by Gertie around an especially palatial new flat she had rented:

After she had taken us on a conducted tour of its splendours, Jack asked, 'why do you need a place as big as this?'

'Oh, but wait,' she said. 'You see, I now have a chauffeur and three mehds.'

'Three whats?' I said.

'Mehds.'

I still didn't get it. 'How do you spell it?'

'Mehd. M-A-I-D. And then I have a butler, and . . .'

I don't remember whether it was Jack or I who threw the first cushion at her. I know we knocked her down, literally. It did her good now and then. She was a darling, but she sometimes behaved like an Empress of China.

As she settled in to the Prince of Wales Theatre, where she was to spend almost the whole of 1922 happily engaged in *A to Z*, Gertie at last had the chance to get herself into some sort of order; with Philip Astley in almost constant attendance she was able to lead the kind of social and theatrical life that until now had been at best an ambition. In the West End she, Buchanan and Charlot were already part of a team, one that would go on soon to conquer Broadway as well; more important, they were working in a comparatively new theatrical form of 'intimate' revue, which perfectly caught the somewhat frenzied spirit of the times. 'Revue', wrote Herbert Farjeon, one of its greatest practitioners, 'is a form of entertainment so designed that it matters neither how late you reach it nor how early you have to leave it.' The sequence of songs, short comedy sketches and dance numbers, each more or less self-contained and unlikely to last more than a matter of minutes, was ideally suited to audiences who were apt to find their attention wandering. The 1920s were not a time of deep dedication to a single topic for a long period of time, which was why on balance revues usually did better business than straight plays. This was the era of revue, and of revue Gertrude Lawrence was now the newest and brightest star.

Privately, too, things were going very well: several years later stars as diverse as Madeleine Carroll and David Niven were to acknowledge the importance of Astley's friendship and advice, but Gertie was the first, best and most important of his 'creations'. It was because of him that her dressing-room was filled night after night not only with flowers but also with princes of the blood royal and, so linked at that time were stage and society, that the more fashionable she was off stage, the greater her box-office value was too. For all that, the mockery of Bea Lillie was a low price to pay. Gertrude Lawrence was now the flavour of the month and the problem became not how to make it, but how to make it last.

A to Z, apart from being among the very best of all Charlot's many revues, proved a splendid showcase for Gertie's now considerable talent. Whether doing the

> Poor broken blossom
> And nobody's child,
> Haunted and taunted
> You're just kind of wild

despair of 'Limehouse Blues' or the infinitely more upbeat and jolly double with Buchanan:

> A cup of coffee, a sandwich, and you,
> A cosy corner—a table for two . . . .

she was proving night after night and twice on Saturdays that, unlike many better actresses, she had the gift for instant changes of mood, lightning switches from comedy to song to dance and back again. Moreover she was a quick study, able to accept new material suddenly thrown at her an hour or two before the show in an attempt to keep it topical through changing newspaper headlines. In an age before radio or television, when most London theatres were hermetically sealed with unchanging productions, revues were able to alter themselves from week to week according to changing public moods. They were of the moment for the moment, and so was Gertrude Lawrence.

After the show, the dinner parties were usually at Rule's in Maiden Lane, where Gertie later recalled 'walls lined with signed photographs of actors and acresses, boxing champions, cabinet ministers and marble busts of Shakespeare and Beerbohm Tree . . . the place was just the same as when Edward VII, then Prince of Wales, had given supper parties to Lillie Langtry in the private room upstairs. This was the room in which we had our parties and our young Prince of Wales sat where his grandfather had sat, enjoying our gay chatter.'

Towards the end of the year Charlot took Gertie out of *A to Z*, giving Bea the chance she should have had a year earlier, and put her instead into an unenthralling but respectably successful Joseph Coyne musical comedy called *Dédé*, which ran through the winter at the Garrick; in Christmas week Charlot again moved her, with several other stars from shows of his all over London, to play in cabaret at the Hotel Metropole in *The Midnight Follies*, a task Gertie found considerably more sociable and therefore more enjoyable than working with Coyne at the Garrick. Then, early in 1923, it was time for another Charlot revue.

This one was to be on Charlot's home territory at the Vaudeville and was bizarrely entitled *Rats*, presumably in the hope that someone would then pronounce it a Rattling Good Show which several critics dutifully did. Its stars were Gertrude Lawrence and two male comedians, Alfred Lester and Herbert Mundin, and one of its more eccentric showstoppers was Gertie in full Ku-Klux-Klan costume singing a hymm to lynchings. Critics found the proceedings generally enchanting; 'Miss Lawrence', noted *The Times*, 'is dashing, full of assurance, extraordinary in facial expressions and with humour radiating from every limb and feature. It is high time she appeared in a stage comedy.'

5

PARISIAN PIERROT

On a skiing holiday in Davos early in 1923 Noël Coward, Charlot and Lord Lathom worked out the basis for a revue which, in honour of the newly-established British radio network, was to be known as *London Calling!* It was understood that the revue was to star Gertrude Lawrence, Maisie Gay and Noël himself together with one other comedian, but in view of Coward's total inexperience where revue was concerned, and because Charlot was less than enthusiastic about some of the material that he had already written, Ronald Jeans was brought in to help with the book and Philip Braham with the music—both men already tried and tested through countless earlier Charlot revues. Tubby Edlin was cast as the principal comedian, and there then developed some doubt as to whether or not Coward himself would actually appear in the show. Charlot was only offering him a weekly £15—less than half what the others were now getting—and the salary did not therefore much appeal to Noël who held out for rather more on the grounds that, unlike the others, he was risking his prestige as a straight actor by appearing in revue.

Charlot, unmoved, refused to go over £15 and decided to find someone else for the job. He had, however, overlooked a clause neatly inserted in his contract by Noël, guaranteeing himself as part-author the right to approve or veto all major casting. For the next few weeks Noël regularly, politely and firmly objected to the casting suggestion of every juvenile lead in the business. Finally, with *London Calling!* on the very brink of rehearsal, Charlot was reluctantly forced to make him an offer of £40 a week, an offer that Noël was graciously pleased to accept with the demand only that he be given the right to escape after six months.

This granted, Noël began work on his singing and dancing, talents which had been left unpractised since his days as a child actor. Enlisting the help of Fred Astaire, who at that time was conveniently enough appearing with his sister Adèle in the London production of *Stop Flirting*, Noël learnt enough to get through such numbers as 'Other Girls' and 'You Were Meant For Me' which he sang and danced with Gertie to choreography by Astaire himself.

After two postponements for alterations and more rehearsal, *London Calling!* (with costumes by Edward Molyneux) opened with no pre-London tour at a matinée on 4 September 1923 at the Duke of York's Theatre; the matinée was Charlot's idea, his theory being that as the entire company of artists and technicians were already exhausted by four long, hard and difficult weeks of rehearsal, the matinée (to which no critics were invited) would tire them even further, thus ensuring that the first evening performance, played entirely on raw nerves, would be remarkable for its nightmarish vivacity. The gamble worked; the first night went superbly and the reviews were ecstatic.

This first version of *London Calling!* included twenty-six numbers of which half were composed by Noël, although only 'Parisian Pierrot', which he wrote for Gertie and which, according to Cecil Beaton, she made into 'the signature tune of the late 1920s' managed to outlive its original setting. This was the first hit song Noël ever achieved, and he had written it during a brief holiday in Germany: 'The idea of it came to me in a nightclub in Berlin in 1922. A frowsy blonde, wearing a sequin chest-protector and a divided skirt, appeared in the course of the cabaret with a rag pierrot doll dressed in black velvet. She placed it on a cushion where it sprawled in pathetic abandon while she pranced round it emitting guttural noises. Her performance was unimpressive but the doll fascinated me. The title ''Parisian Pierrot'' slipped into my mind, and in the taxi on the way back to the hotel the song began.'

Of the show itself, Noël later recalled: 'I appeared constantly, singing and dancing and acting with unbridled vivacity and enjoying myself very much indeed.' But the critics at the first night of *London Calling!*, though still in love with Gertie, tended to be unimpressed by Mr Coward's musical gifts:

'He cannot compose', said the *Sunday Express*, 'and should sing only for his friends' amazement'. One number, 'Sentiment', staged by Fred Astaire, was particularly tricky for Noël: 'I would bound on stage immaculately dressed in tails, with a silk hat and cane and singing every couplet with perfect diction and a wealth of implication which sent the words winging out into the dark auditorium, where they fell wetly like pennies into mud.'

Months later, in New York, Noël was to watch Jack Buchanan bringing the house down nightly with that same number, and had to admit ruefully to himself that Jack's seemingly effortless revue technique was then, as always, vastly superior to his own. But the reviews for *London Calling!* were not by any means all bad, though most critics found it a little long and Noël better at the writing than the performing. Two papers offered him, amidst all the praise for Gertie, dubious personal tributes. One called him 'the most promising amateur in the West End' and the other noted that he was 'unmistakeably talented, though not yet another Jack Hulbert'.

London Calling! settled into the Duke of York's for a lengthy run, despite Noël's rather grudging press and a celebrated feud with the Sitwell family who thought they recognized in one of the numbers, 'The Swiss Family Whittlebot', an all too accurate parody of themselves and their verse; just after the first night Osbert remarked acidly that as he was leaving town for the weekend he would have to miss the show, since it would doubtless have closed before he got back, to which Noël retorted that on the contrary they were in for a long run and he would be happy to place a stage box at the Sitwells' disposal from which they could see the show with *all* their supporters.

This was all good publicity, as were the full-length pictures that started to appear in the glossy weeklies of Gertie in her 'Parisian Pierrot' costume. She also had one or two numbers that required a certain amount of acting, not least 'Early Mourning', in which she played a society hostess hearing the awful news that her husband has just jumped off Waterloo Bridge, and then being told the even more awful news that he has not. But Gertie was still being thought of as a singer rather than an actress, and it was as a singer that Charlot was to take her to New York within a few weeks of the London opening of Coward's first revue.

No sooner was *London Calling!* safely away and running than Charlot had an even more ambitious idea. For the past year or two he had been casting vague glances over the Atlantic, made aware by the occasional offers that were reaching both him and his revue stars that Broadway had nothing quite like the kind of shows he had pioneered in London, and that it would pay well for them. In the autumn of 1923 he therefore decided to form a company of his own leading players, lift the best songs and sketches from his last half-dozen London revues, and take them all to New York.

This meant recasting *London Calling!* within three months of its opening (which did not much please Coward, who was left to play it on in London with a distinctly second-rate company) as Charlot took from the West End not only Gertie (who gave over her material in *London Calling!* to Joyce Barbour) but also Jack Buchanan and Beatrice Lillie to form the nucleus of his American company. Under the management of the American Archie Selwyn and Charlot together, they were to open on Broadway as *André Charlot's London Revue of 1924.*

Charlot himself had already been over to prepare the way and try to alert Broadway audiences to what they were to be asked to buy seats for: 'When the American public is given a chance to see my London revue,' he told the press, 'they will understand the difference between this type of show and vaudeville in America . . . over the years we have developed an intimate understanding between players and audience such as you do not know in this country. The mixture is hard to define since it depends not only on a company in which everyone – not just the principals – can sing and dance and act, but also on lighting and scenic effects which are simple but artistic. I intend to offer outstanding melody, humour, good taste and distinctive charm.'

In short, Charlot was offering Broadway not just three unknowns, but three unknowns in an unknown kind of entertainment. Aware that he would therefore need all the help he could get, the first person he hired in New York was a press agent Walter Wanger, later to be better known as the Hollywood producer of the epic Taylor-Burton *Cleopatra* and countless other films.

Wanger arrived in London, took a look at *London Calling!* and announced that though quiet good taste was all very well in its way, what Charlot would need for a Broadway hit could best be described as 'Oomph'. This he proposed to inject into the proceedings by arranging a talent contest to find 'The Most Beautiful Blonde In Britain', who would duly be given her chance to appear on Broadway in the chorus of the revue. Leaving nothing to chance, Wanger also selected the winner, a lady called Bobbie Storey who was then working as a barmaid at Rule's.

André Charlot's London Revue of 1924 did a week's English try-out (in what was still actually 1923) at the Golders' Green Hippodrome where, noted the press, 'the Prince of Wales laughed as loudly as anyone else in the audience'. Carrying therefore an unofficial royal seal of approval, the company then set sail on the *Aquitania* for New York.

Both Gertie and Bea Lillie were leaving their small children with their grandmothers, but Bea seems to have felt rather more maternally deprived than Gertie, who was in any case now well accustomed to living apart from Pamela. The crossing was, by Bea's own account, a jolly one: 'Gertie and I made a shipboard friend of one of the season's glamour boys, Alastair McIntosh, who later married Constance Talmadge. When Gertie, Jack and I all told him that we had no idea where to stay in New York he ordered another drink all round and told us that he had a friend who owned the Ambassador Hotel on Park Avenue and that we'd be very happy there.'

Lord Beaverbrook (then still Max Aitken) was also on board the *Aquitania*, where he christened Lawrence, Lillie and Buchanan 'the Big Three', a useful description which was to stay with them throughout their joint Broadway lives. The welcoming press conference held while they were still docking, was, however, less than successful for them; carefully briefed by Wanger, the gentlemen of the New York press and their photographers hurtled straight past the Big Three to get the story on Bobbie Storey, Britain's Most Beautiful Blonde Barmaid, who would now be appearing in the show as a result of the talent contest.

The others took it badly. Buchanan went down to the desk to ascertain what time the next ship was leaving for London, Bea felt 'that somebody had shot a hole in my middle' and it was left to Gertie to guide them both to the suites that had been reserved in their names at the Ambassador. It being still early morning, and Christmas Eve at that, Gertie ordered up the first editions of the evening papers: 'With cheeks that the mist and fog of London had tinted the colour of English roses' one report read, 'and with appearances as neat as the hedgerows in springtime, with eyes that glowed as brightly as the lights that illuminate Big Ben at night, and lips that laugh merrily, twenty-five beauties from the tight little isle across the sea who are due to appear in the André Charlot revue tripped lightly down the gangplank of the *Aquitania*.'

One of those beauties was a totally unknown sixteen-year-old Jessie

Matthews for whom the reality of New York was a little less than wonderful: 'I sat on my trunk in the customs shed and wondered what had hit me . . . it was nine o'clock on Christmas Eve and no one wanted me . . . a burly customs guard said ''You can always spend the night on Ellis Island, kiddo.'' '

Back at the Ambassador, things were going slightly better until Gertie ordered them a sizeable breakfast: 'sausages, eggs, slices of ham and bacon by the dozen; a bakeshop's fill of toast and muffins, firkins of coffee and glistening sections of a fruit none of us had set breakfast eyes on before called grapefruit.' The only thing wrong with that was the bill, which came to twenty-five dollars without the tip.

Guided by Buchanan's ever alert grasp of financial affairs, the three of them rapidly worked out that if twenty-five dollars was what the Ambassador was charging for breakfast, then none of them could afford to stay for lunch, let alone several weeks. The only solution was to leave, and leave fast.

'We shall need a cab, of course,' said Gertie.

'Can we afford it?' asked Jack.

'No', replied Bea, 'but you know Gertie.'

This dialogue summari es almost too perfectly the characters and their relationships to each other. In the cab they headed straight for the Algonquin, which they had heard offered sanctuary to impoverished artists, writers and actors and had even in those early days a special affection for the British.

There was, after all, no indication yet that *Charlot's Revue of 1924* was actually going to succeed on Broadway, and in the meantime its stars could see little purpose in throwing money around even if there had been any to throw. Buchanan was at this time still walking down to the docks most evenings to enquire what times the boats left for London; Gertie and Bea, though faintly more optimistic about their theatrical chances, were less than reassured by their week's try-out in Atlantic City, where Bea overheard Selwyn himself muttering, 'Jeez—it stinks.'

By the time they got back to New York the entire cast was so enveloped in gloom that Bea didn't bother to unpack her suitcase, thinking she'd leave that task until she caught the boat home to England in what would doubtless only be a day or two. Nor were any of them much more reassured by their first glimpses of Broadway. 'Before our New York opening,' wrote Gertie later, 'Jack, Bea and I were taken to see all the shows on Broadway. We were very much impressed and rather frightened by the obvious lavishness of the productions in comparison with our intimate revue. As Jack said, ''It seemed to us that what New York wanted was hundreds of girls dressed in feathers, with tons of scenery studded with diamonds and ten-dollar bills.'' We saw Grace Moore sing ''Orange Grove in California'' for which song the entire theatre was perfumed by orange blossom. We wondered if we could compete, with our tiny show and our British humour.'

That remained to be seen.

6

LILLIE AND LAWRENCE, LAWRENCE AND LILLIE

In most, if not all, of her subsequent interviews for American papers, Gertrude Lawrence was to claim that she 'fell in love with New York on first sight'. The reality was something rather different; neither she nor Buchanan nor Bea Lillie had much cause to love their American impresario after Selwyn's celebrated remark about their show, nor had they much reason to believe – judging from the neighbouring shows they had already seen along Broadway – that what they had to offer would be of much interest or excitement to New York theatregoers who then seemed to prefer the trappings of shows to the contents.

They therefore went into the Broadway opening of *André Charlot's London Revue of 1924* with a kind of resigned tolerance, genuinely anticipating rapid closure and already quite looking forward to a speedy return home. Only the young Jessie Matthews, understudying Gertie, was able to find much magic backstage:

I used to stand out there in the darkened wings watching Gertie Lawrence rehearse a number. She was as lovely as a dream in her satin Pierrot costume, and I'd never seen such a beautiful stage picture as the set for 'Parisian Pierrot'. There were black velvet hangings and on the stage were masses of huge coloured velvet cushions . . . in my room at the Martha Washington Hotel, I'd scrape my hair under a tight handkerchief and pretend it was the little black skull cap that Gertie wore. I'd pull the pillows from the bed and lie on the floor like she did and sing 'Parisian Pierrot'. Every gesture that Gertie made I had practised, every movement I copied. By the time opening night arrived I was a little, undersized, immature carbon copy of Gertrude Lawrence. I knew every song, every dance, every nuance with which she held her audience in thrall.

Opening night was 9 January 1924; Selwyn had pleaded with Charlot and his company to 'Americanize' their material but they had all staunchly refused, preferring to keep to their original agreement, which had been to show Broadway the best of their London songs and sketches unchanged. And they were right. The sheer, unexpected originality of the *Charlot Revue* took the six Broadway critics (Heywood Broun, George Jean Nathan, Percy Hammond, Burns Mantle, Ring Lardner and Aleck Woollcott) by storm; they had quite simply seen nothing like it in their entire theatregoing lives: 'When André Charlot's company stepped out on the stage last night with their opening "How do you do?" number, there was an immediate response between actors and audience. That cordial relationship continued throughout the evening and when the curtain fell, the fact was established that in *Charlot's Revue*, Broadway has something altogether new in the way of musical comedy.'

What Woollcott and the others were experiencing was something which in London had been taken for granted, since there it had always been the rule for revues rather than the exception: the idea that an audience was composed of individual customers, guests in fact, who should be treated the way they would be treated by the best maître d'hôtel in the best restaurant in town. Buchanan above all, and to a lesser degree both Gertie and Bea, had stage presences which allowed them to play a number as if only to a single spectator at a time. The audience thus became a part of the show, just as diners become a part of a restaurant, and it was something no vaudeville house had ever achieved. It was, in a word, intimacy.

Admittedly there was a certain anglophile snobbery in all this; Woollcott was then just making his name as a drama critic, and like all critics on the make he needed something to hang his hat on; fortunately for those involved with the *Charlot Revue*, he chose the English theatre and was to remain for the next two decades the best publicist any London actor or actress in New York could have desired. Besides, as became clear from Woollcott's very first column on the show, there was always a good story in the triumph of the underdog: 'It is fair to suspect that Mr Ziegfeld and Mr George White [of *Follies* fame] must have fairly laughed themselves into a coma at the innocence of this London manager for thinking that any revue so airy and so unpretentious would not be trampled underfoot in New York. Why, the chorus was not half so populous as that of the *Follies*, and there wasn't so much as a yard of gold cloth in the whole thing.'

Others were less amused; Walter Pidgeon, then an up-and-coming musical comedy star, told Michael Marshall that as the first-night curtain fell to tumultuous applause Irving Berlin was to be seen sitting motionless and ostentatiously refusing to clap. 'Sour grapes?' asked Elsie Janis; 'No', replied Berlin, 'I was just thinking that this entire production has cost less than the finale of one of my Music Box revues!'

Heywood Broun commented, 'Beatrice Lillie, Gertrude Lawrence and Jack Buchanan are worth a good deal more than their weight in gold cloth and velvet hangings' (another dig at Ziegfeld and White). By the time those notices hit the streets the Charlot team were the hottest performers in New York. It was from this moment that Gertrude Lawrence began to love the city which has always cherished its successes and cruelly rejected its failures.

Soon a little rhyme was to be on everyone's lips:

> Lillie and Lawrence,
> Lawrence and Lillie,
> If you haven't seen them,
> You're perfectly silly,

and as the queues formed morning after morning outside the Selwyn Theatre, the cast settled down to a prolonged celebration. By staying at the Algonquin (which reminded Gertie, she said, of a really good cheap hotel in the Midlands) the Charlot stars found themselves in the midst of precisely the people who were most enjoying and most able to publicize their show. The present and future members of the Round Table there were all fervently pro-British, and were keen to promote something which seemed to rock the current Broadway establishment. Bea and Gertie (and to some extent Buchanan, though he was always more inclined to keep himself to himself, especially when abroad) became the Algonquin's favourite rebels, and it was there that they in turn met some of its greatest stars. The press were constantly requesting interviews; one morning the phone rang in the suite Gertie was still sharing with Bea and it was the latter who got to it first.

'Is this Miss Lillie from England?' asked a professional journalistic voice.

'This is the *New York Sun*. We'd like to be able to tell our readers, Miss Lillie, your feelings about the death of President Harding.'

'Who?'

'Our President, Miss Lillie, Warren Gamaliel Harding. He's dead. How do you feel about it?'

Even Bea was momentarily at a loss for words and Gertie, across the other side of the room, was no help either.

'Well,' Bea finally flustered, 'Well, I mean, it's a great loss, isn't it? A man like that. What a terrible thing! How will you find another President now?'

There was a pause at the other end of the line. Then the reporter spoke again. 'As a matter of fact,' he said, 'President Harding died last August. I hope you will do better next time.' It was the American playwright Marc Connelly.

Despite the fact that due to an electrical fault on the neon sign outside the Selwyn their show was very often billed as HARLOT'S REVUE OF 1924, or maybe precisely because of it, tickets were by now virtually impossible to come by. No foreign artists, at any rate since Jenny Lind, had been welcomed quite like this and Woollcott took to claiming most of the credit – except that when he got too insufferably patronizing either Gertie or Bea would sidle up to him and enquire, 'Tell us, Uncle Aleck, what is the Statue of Liberty actually there for?'

By now the two girls had moved out of the Algonquin and into a duplex apartment on West 54th Street which was, wrote Percy Hammond, 'first among the famous places every visitor to New York should head towards'. Most did, and a good many of the residents too: Gertie once listed Dorothy Parker, Jeanne Eagels, Bob Sherwood, Richard Barthelmess, Laurette Taylor, Jimmy Walker, Oscar Hammerstein, Arthur Schwartz, Jerome Kern, Rodgers and Hart, Jascha Heifitz, George and Ira Gershwin, Clifton Webb, Vincent Youmans and Irving Berlin – and that was just at a single party, though it's unclear who got to the piano first.

After the first three months Buchanan returned to London; he had only signed for that long on Broadway as he had a West End show to go back to, and Charlot brought out the celebrated English comic Nelson 'Bunch' Keys to replace him. It is some indication of the concern that Charlot was causing rival Broadway managements, however, that on Keys' arrival in New York Ziegfeld tried to prevent him going on stage by claiming that he had a prior contract with the comic. He didn't, and Keys duly opened for Charlot. Gertie meanwhile had started giving long, gracious dressing-room interviews to the press, mostly about the struggles she had endured on her way to the top: 'I have been through the hardships, the unending torture of financial insecurity and the untiring labours that the Theatre demands . . . now of course I am a Star, but my struggles have made me all the more aware of the pleasures of success.' One can hear very faintly in the background through most of these press interviews the hysterical giggles of Bea Lillie, never one to take herself or her work quite so solemnly.

The English on Broadway could still do no wrong: papers published little notes explaining that 'Toodleoo' and 'Cheerio' were synonyms for 'Goodbye', and one added that Miss Lawrence would be most grateful if aspiring American songwriters would cease sending her their material as she already had more than enough to read.

Originally the idea had been for *Charlot's Revue* to close on Broadway at the beginning of June, as was then the custom for most shows there; but business was so good that instead of closing at that time they simply moved from the Times Square next door to the larger Selwyn Theatre and played there right through to the end of August, thereby making Broadway history and setting a pattern which the other really big hit shows were, eventually, to follow. It was Robert Baral who finally summarized the importance of this first Broadway season: 'Gertrude Lawrence and her co-stars definitely dented the prestige of the *Ziegfeld Follies* and similar annual shows overnight, and set off a chain reaction throughout Broadway. The girlie-girlie revues were now definitely passé after this first Charlot import, and the accent was now on wit. Beatrice Lillie and Gertrude Lawrence lit up the sky with their sheer versatility—Miss Lawrence alone had over twenty-five changes of character, from glamour to drab.'

Jessie Matthews was still in that chorus, as was another young English girl called Constance Carpenter who, just twenty-eight years later, was to succeed after Gertie's sudden death to the Broadway role of Anna Leonowens in *The King and I*.

Through the summer of 1924 Gertie grew increasingly capricious; though her social life was still in the whirl she had grown both to love and to need, her sexual life was considerably less exciting. She was still deeply in love with Astley and he, three thousand miles across the Atlantic, with her; for this

BELOW LEFT Gertie at ten, (above) at twelve, and as
Leader of the Frolics at Murray's night-club in 1920.

ABOVE Family album: mother, father and the grandmother who brought her up.

BELOW As one of the Beauty Chorus in *Buzz, Buzz* at the Vaudeville, London: Gertie is fourth from the right.

OPPOSITE:
ABOVE LEFT 'Someone to watch over me . . .': Philip Astley in 1920.

ABOVE RIGHT Child stars no longer: Gertie and Noël Coward in his *London Calling!*, 1923.

BELOW Charlot and his three stars (*left to right*, Gertie, Bea Lillie and Jack Buchanan) arriving in New York on the *Aquitania* to conquer Broadway, Christmas Eve, 1923.

RIGHT
'Parisian Pierrot'.

BELOW 'Poor
Little Rich
Girl'.

BELOW RIGHT
'Fallen Babies': Gertie
(*left*) and Bea Lillie in
the Charlot parody of
Coward's *Fallen
Angels*.

ABOVE After the midnight first-night of *Charlot's Revue*, 1925: (*left to right, back row*), André Charlot, Joseph Coyne, Herbert Mundin, Peter Haddon, Jack Hulbert, Leslie Henson, George Grossmith, Noël Coward, Laddie Cliff, Henry Kendal, Jack Buchanan and Morris Harvey; (*third row*) Fay Compton, Phyllis Dare, Phyllis Monkman, Maisie Gay, Lillian Braithwaite, Violet Loraine and Zena Dare; (*second row*) Cicely Courtneidge, Gwen Farrar, Nora Blaney, Isabel Jeans, June, Heather Thatcher and Ivy St Helier; (*front row*) Rosaline Courtneidge, Irene Browne, Tallulah Bankhead, Beatrice Lillie, Gertrude Lawrence and Dorothy Dickson.

BELOW *The Battle of Paris*, Gertie's first film (1929), co-starred Arthur Treacher and Charlie Ruggles, and the songs were Cole Porter's first for the screen.

Gertie and Pamela in 1929.

BELOW Faces in a crowd; Gertie and 'Young Doug' (Fairbanks) applauding a Spanish bullfight.

Racing greyhounds at White City, London.

With P. G. Wodehouse during rehearsals for *Oh, Kay!*

With George Gershwin in rehearsal for his *Treasure Girl*.

BELOW Gertie with her Bentley on Broadway.

Gertie, who had a long career in advertising, seen dining at
Grosvenor House, London, with Doug and a well-known pale ale.

enforced separation they were to stay remarkably and almost entirely faithful to each other, but that didn't make Gertie any easier for the rest of the company to live with.

She would appear at the theatre every night (indeed she never missed a single New York performance) but began taking against certain numbers, notably 'Parisian Pierrot', which, though critically acclaimed, was curiously not a great applause-getter. In the heat of a Broadway July she began to get tired of it; sending the costume up to Jessie Matthews in the understudies' room, she would, once Jessie was dressed in it, decide that she would do the number herself after all. This happened two or three times until Jessie, who was just as headstrong an understudy as Gertie herself had once been, insisted that either she did the number or she didn't; Gertie, amused at such presumption, agreed that she would *not* be doing it, and for the rest of the New York run 'Parisian Pierrot' was duly sung by Jessie Matthews.

Early in September they finally closed at the Selwyn; business was still good, but Charlot had heard that there was even bigger money to be made on the road. Their last night on Broadway was, therefore, in the nature of a triumphal send-off; Bea played one entire number sitting in the lap of Aleck Woollcott in the auditorium, and Gertie wrote:

After the finale the entire house rose and cheered us. They pelted us with flowers. When the orchestra struck up 'Auld Lang Syne' the audience and the company joined in the singing. Everyone took hold of the hand of the person next to him. The chain of friendly hand-clasps stretched across the stage, across the footlights, and continued throughout the house. When the audience was finally pushed out of the theatre several hundred of them merely adjourned to the stage door, where they formed such an imposing mob scene that traffic was clogged in 42nd Street. When Bea and I came out, laden with flowers, to get into our waiting taxi we found the roof of the vehicle packed with the more ardent revellers, who escorted us through the streets of New York singing our own songs to us.

The tour opened in Boston, where Gertie caught a severe cold; by the time they reached Toronto it was showing signs of turning into something much worse, but she refused to give up the show or (Toronto being Bea's birthplace) the inevitable parties which carried on most nights between the ending of the applause and the rising of the sun. By the final week of the Toronto booking, a doctor had diagnosed double pneumonia and a mild form of pleurisy, and as the company travelled on to Detroit she was left behind in a local hospital to reflect on the folly of her ways.

Reports that Gertrude Lawrence was 'dying' spread rapidly through the world's press, unnerving not only Philip Astley back in England but also Jessie Matthews on the tour who, though she had prayed like all understudies for her principal to fall ill, did not want an actual death on her conscience.

Gertie spent Christmas and a total of fourteen weeks recovering in that Toronto hospital, and early in 1925 Philip, who was now by her bedside, got a doctor's report to convince Charlot that she should not return to the tour. Joyce Barbour had (much to the fury of Jessie Matthews) already been brought out to replace her, and Philip took Gertie straight back to New York. From there they sailed for France where Philip, typically, had friends who would lend them a villa on the Riviera in which Gertie could complete her recovery. This she duly did, much helped by a leisurely springtime drive down to Sicily.

There was just one problem. Charlot wanted the British public to be well aware of the Broadway success of his 1924 revue; when it finally closed in the spring of 1925 it had lasted fully fifteen months, or rather longer if the British staging is included. He planned therefore to stage a massive homecoming for his American company, starting with a triumphal disembarkation at Southampton and climaxing in a gala midnight matinee before the cast went straight into rehearsal for his new 1925 revue. But of the three Broadway principals, Buchanan had long since been at work back in London, Gertie was sunning herself on the Riviera, and only Bea had soldiered on to the end of the tour. Though an impressive lady, she could scarcely constitute a gala homecoming all on her own. It was Philip Astley, in conversation with Charlot, who came up with the solution: he and Gertie would motor up from their Riviera villa to Cherbourg, and there join the ss *Olympic* on which the rest of the company had already sailed from New York. Photographers at Southampton a few hours later were therefore able to photograph 'Lillie and Lawrence, Lawrence and Lillie' leading the Charlot players triumphantly down the gangplank onto home soil. If you hadn't seen them, you were (in the words of the song) perfectly silly.

To welcome them back to London, from the most triumphant mission so far in twentieth-century British theatre, casts of all the other shows in town gathered at the Prince of Wales Theatre, now Charlot's London headquarters, for a midnight matinée which bore the proud title 'Charlot's

Revue as seen in America'. One critic wrote that the matinée was 'the greatest single event in the whole history of British stage revue'. Bea Lillie was more specific:

The midnight show was the first of its kind in the modern London theatre. My dear, you should have been there. There were 31 – count them, 31 – stars of the stage and silver screen in the boxes and the stalls. Jack Buchanan, who later joined the show again, was typical, coming over from the Empire Theatre when his own musical was over. Like Jack, most of them just had time to change from theatre costumes into evening clothes. During the interval, they all trooped up on stage with us for a swallow of champagne. Noël, who'd written some of our new numbers, sat with Lilian Braithwaite who was playing his mother in *The Vortex*; John Barrymore was with Lady Diana Cooper (not to be confused with Gladys Cooper, *The Bohemian Girl*, also there) and Ivor Novello. George Grossmith, my leading man in a later Hollywood movie, appeared in a box sporting a monocle and so did his boxmate Heather Thatcher. Zena Dare wore black, and Tallulah Bankhead a mammoth bunch of orchids. There sat Fay Compton and Leon Quartermaine, Phyllis Monkman all in pale pink and gold tissue, and Fanny Brice in the flesh.

So good was all this home-coming publicity that Charlot decided not to risk closing his theatre while a new revue was prepared for the rest of 1925. Instead, the company would simply carry on playing the old material from Broadway, and then gradually feed in new numbers and artists as the time came for a change. Making a virtue of this financial opportunity, Charlot (now quite adept at publicity after a year in New York) then announced proudly that his revue would be the only one in town to 'change' every month, though he never specified exactly how much of it would change at any one time.

By the summer a good deal of new material had found its way into the revue; Gertie and Bea were now doing a 'Broadway Medley' and, inspired by what they had seen in New York of the Trix and Dolly Sisters, they were also doing a burlesque sister act as well as parodies of Fanny Brice and Sophie Tucker. Charlot was constantly at them to try something new: 'We have not', he told his two stars, 'come all the way back from America merely to rest on our laurels,' and it wasn't long before they had introduced their celebrated 'Fallen Babies' routine as two alcoholic one-year-olds falling about inside their prams, an oblique tribute to the West End success that Noël was now having with a grown-up comedy called *Fallen Angels*.

Late in the summer of 1925, by which time Buchanan had rejoined the revue and they had also taken on an unknown chorus girl by the name of Marjorie Robertson (later to achieve fame as Anna Neagle), Charlot announced that it was time for the leading members of the company to start thinking once again about packing their bags. They could easily be replaced by other stars at the Prince of Wales, but Broadway expected once again to see the Big Three.

This time Gertie, Bea and Buchanan set sail in October aboard the *Caronia*; also aboard for that star-studded crossing were Michael Arlen, who had recently published *The Green Hat*, the playwright Frederick Lonsdale, ex-Prime Minister Lloyd George and H. G. Wells; though Gertie had again left both Pamela and Philip behind, Bea was now accompanied by both her son and her husband, Sir Robert Peel, in whose honour a mass band of pipers was assembled on the quayside in New York. When it was tactfully pointed out to them that neither Sir Robert nor Lady Beatrice Peel had any discernible Scottish connections whatsoever, the pipers looked a little disconsolate, until the ever tactful Jack Buchanan mentioned that he came from Scotland and they could therefore pipe him ashore instead.

By the time they all arrived in New York with the Charlot company, Noël Coward and Lilian Braithwaite had already opened on Broadway in *The Vortex*, as had the stage version of *The Green Hat*; the start of the first full-scale English invasion of the Great White Way had already happened, but Broadway theatregoers didn't forget their first visitors and of the opening night of the new *Charlot's Revue of 1926* Aleck Woollcott was able to write: 'It was not a performance – it was a reunion.'

7

SOMEONE TO WATCH OVER ME

Charlot's Revue of 1926 opened on 11 November 1925 at the Selwyn Theatre on Broadway and by now, in New York even more than in London, the Buchanan-Lawrence-Lillie trio really were very big stars indeed; even before their new show opened, the box office had taken a $200,000 advance, and as a reflection of that the joint Charlot-Selwyn management was now paying each of them $2,500 per week. For Gertie, who less than five years earlier had still been getting £6.00 a week from Charlot back in London, it was at this point that money, fatally, began to lose much of its sense of reality. She began to spend, and she never really stopped.

Many of her contemporaries, not least Noël Coward, had come as she had from suburban London backgrounds, but the effect of sudden fame and wealth on Gertie was rather different. Noël, until the day he died, drew a kind of strength from his boarding-house childhood; he was infinitely proud of his mother for having managed to support him and his father and brother through some difficult times, and equally proud that he had managed to rise above those origins and through his own considerable talent move into a much higher level of society. He never forgot his past.

But Gertie saw nothing in her childhood that was really worth remembering, drew no real sense of achievement from an equally rapid climb out of the suburbs. The past was never a source of strength or support, and it gave her none of the innate caution or sense of economic survival which it had given Noël. The present was all that ever mattered to her, and in that present as fast as the money came in she spent it. It was, in one sense, fool's gold.

Moreover, although Bea Lillie now had the support and love of her husband to keep her in touch with some kind of off-stage reality, Gertie only had her stardom. Philip Astley's duties with his regiment were as usual keeping him in London, which is also where Pamela was still living with Gertie's mother. Gertie was on the town.

For the 1926 revue she was still doing highlights from earlier Charlot shows in London and New York (audiences of the time had apparently little objection to seeing favourite sketches and songs done time after time), though it was now, for the first time, that Broadway saw her in two of Noël's numbers from *London Calling!*, 'Russian Blues' and 'Carrie'. She had also taken over his 'Poor Little Rich Girl', which Alice Delysia had done in London the previous summer as a number in a Cochran revue called *On With The Dance*. But for Noël himself, still playing on Broadway in *The Vortex*, 'It was thrilling to see the three of them, Gertie and Bea and Jack, hailed as great stars by the whole of New York. It invested them, for me, with a new kind of glamour as though I was discovering them too and had never seen them before in my life. The appreciation of American audiences certainly gave an extra fillip to their performances. There was a shine on all of them, a happy gratification bursting through. I could swear that they had none of them ever been so good before.'

Woollcott, still the most vociferous of the Charlot trio's American admirers, now singled out Gertie for special praise: 'She dances with magical lightness and her voice is true and clear; the personification of style and sophistication, she can also convulse an audience with a bit of cockney horse-play or bring tears to its eyes with a sentimental ballad. She is the ideal star.'

Though she could hardly have known it at the time, this *1926 Revue* was to mark both the high-spot and the end of Gertie's partnership with the other Charlot stars; each was to be involved in later revues, for Charlot and for other managers, but the unique alliance of Bea, Gertie, Jack and André was now drawing to its close, having set a new financial and artistic standard for revues on both sides of the Atlantic. Not that Charlot himself was yet losing any of his old energy or acumen – no sooner had the revue opened at the Selwyn than he decided that there was a little extra money to be made if his company would also go into cabaret; after all, as the *New York Times* had already noted, 'the Charlot principals are now regarded by their audiences as good and personal friends.' How much better therefore to have them play not just across the footlights and orchestra pit but around dining tables as well. To this end, Charlot took a lease on the Rendezvous Club on West 45th Street and its opening was described in the *New York American* as 'one of the most brilliant gatherings of the nightclub season . . . at New York's newest "gin" [bootleg] club, where Jack Buchanan, Gertrude Lawrence and Bea Lillie made their cabaret debut, the scene was reminiscent of some New York millionaire's private party. Some of those present were Harpo Marx, Ethel Barrymore, Irving Berlin, Edmund Goulding, Elsie Janis, Marilyn Miller, Clifton Webb, Grace Moore and the William K. Vanderbilts.'

Gertie and Bea were already being described as 'first ladies of Broadway' and though Bea was always more nonchalant about these honours, to Gertie they meant a great deal. America in general and New York in particular were now 'hers'; there she was in this her twenty-eighth year, acquiring everything she had always longed for at home—money, fame and applause.

Though she remained reasonably faithful to Astley, she was seldom short of an 'escort', and somehow the longer she stayed out of England the more distant and unreal it had begun to seem to her. That, after all, was the past; America was the present and she was loving every single day of it. Nor had Charlot any intention of letting her return home, even had she wanted to: after the *1926 Revue* closed on Broadway in the early spring there was another coast-to-coast tour in the contract.

The new tour started in Detroit, made its way to Chicago and from there to Los Angeles where it opened in Hollywood's then new El Capitan Theatre in the middle of April. Though she was only destined to make one film there, and that a quarter of a century later, Gertrude Lawrence took to California on this first visit like a duck to water: 'I began to go about with bare legs, stockingless, which I found both comfortable and economical, and, as soon as it was announced in the press that Gertrude Lawrence was going around bare-legged, the papers began to interview fashion experts and other actresses to get their opinion of the fad I had started. Marilyn Miller, when interviewed, expressed ladylike disapproval of the innovation and announced that she had brought back from Paris two hundred pairs of silk stockings which she had every intention of wearing. Carmel Snow, fashion editor of *Harper's Bazaar*, was quoted exclaiming in horror "The idea is disgusting. It will never be done by nice people."'

The Hollywood run was a spectacular success until its closing night. As Gertie wrote later:

Then we gradually noticed that all the big Hollywood stars in the front seats were leaving before the finale. This worried us terribly; we couldn't understand such behaviour. Well, Jack went on in his full Highland costume and sang the opening of the last song; I followed, dressed as Flora MacDonald; and then on came Bea as Bonnie Prince Charlie. By this time there wasn't a single Hollywood male star out front. We all sang bravely and laughed gaily, trying to carry off our dismay, when suddenly one by one onto the stage came the missing males. They all had their trousers rolled up to the knees; Valentino had on a Scots head-dress borrowed from the chorus girls; Charlie Chaplin had his dinner jacket tied round his waist like a kilt; Richard Barthelmess had a tam o'shanter on; the Marx Brothers all wore red beards; and Jack Gilbert carried a ladder, for what reason no one knew. They took over our whole finale; they made speeches and Chaplin, who at that time was refusing to do 'talkies', made his speech in dumb show.

Then it was on with the rest of the tour, by the end of which Gertie had come to certain decisions about her future. The first and most important was that she had had enough of revue; it had given her a marvellous start in London, and a superb introduction to America, but now she sensed, before any of the others, that its days were numbered. Despite glowing reviews, *Charlot's 1926 Revue* had actually done rather worse business both on Broadway and on tour than its predecessor.

Secondly, though she had every intention of returning to England for a summer holiday and to be with Philip and Pamela, she was still very much more enthusiastic about working in New York. London had always had other stars in her field; Jessie Matthews was now coming up fast, having replaced her in the London versions of *Charlot's Revue*, and though she could always be sure of getting good work in the West End there was at this time less enthusiasm for her on home territory. There, after all, she was just another 'local girl made good' on the stage; in New York she was something special, foreign, different. There was nobody else on Broadway quite like Gertrude Lawrence.

She therefore let it be known that if anybody had a show for her she'd be available on Broadway for the autumn of 1926, and meanwhile she returned to London for the summer. Her days with the Charlot team were over.

One thing might perhaps have changed those Broadway plans of Gertie's: back with Philip at a flat in Mayfair it occurred to her that he might now propose marriage. It would not be difficult to get her divorce, since she and Frank had been living apart for fully seven years. No proposal came, though Philip did change one aspect of Gertie's family life now and for the foreseeable future. He made it clear to her that no self-respecting mother could continue to leave her only child with a grandmother; Pamela was her daughter, and as such should live with Gertie wherever Gertie happened to be. That autumn, when Gertie returned to Broadway, Pamela went with her.

Among those who had heard that Gertie was looking for a Broadway show were George and Ira Gershwin, both admirers of hers from the Charlot revues, and Gertie's fellow-Londoner P. G. Wodehouse, who was already working then with Guy Bolton although at that time their usual composer was Jerome Kern, hence the legendary Broadway rhyme:

> This is the trio of musical fame
> Bolton and Wodehouse and Kern,
> Better than anyone else you can name,
> Bolton and Wodehouse and Kern.
> Nobody knows what on earth they've been bitten by;
> All I can say is I mean to get lit an' buy
> Orchestra seats for the next one that's written by
> Bolton and Wodehouse and Kern.

For their new show Bolton and Wodehouse planned to work with the Gershwins, and Bolton already had his eye on Miss Lawrence:

I had seen her performing in the Charlot revues and had written her a note saying that I was willing to provide her with a straight comedy, a musical comedy or a revue, whichever she preferred. I slipped in a reference to my collaborator, Pelham Grenville Wodehouse. I thought that might fetch her. It did. She replied by telegram – twelve sheets of it, saying that as soon as she was free of Charlot she would put herself in my hands . . . but she had never played in a 'book' show and she wanted to be sure of her ground, of not making a mistake.

The play we wrote for her was a saga of those romantic days the Prohibition Era. It was laid at Montauk at the tip of Long Island with the Rum Fleet anchored twelve miles away, the hero's beach house boarded up for the winter, its cellars loaded with bootleg liquor, and Gertie, come ashore from her brother's liquor-laden yacht, bent on finding the man she had met for one magical evening and fallen in love with.

Apart from having to change his shirt three times every morning on account of the heat, Wodehouse recorded in his diary that he had a happy summer writing the new show with Bolton. They had already done *Have a Heart* and *Oh, Boy!* (or *Oh, Joy!* as it was known to non-American speaking audiences) and *The Riviera Girl* and *Sally* and *Leave It To Jane* among a dozen other shows so they were not exactly unaccustomed to the Broadway musical form, although, wrote Wodehouse, 'This time I shall have it easy. George Gershwin being the composer means that Ira Gershwin will write the lyrics, so that I shall simply be helping Guy with book as much as I can.'

While Bolton and Wodehouse were concocting their Prohibition plot, the Gershwins were at work on a vintage score; one which was to include 'Clap Yo' Hands' and 'Do-Do-Do' and 'Maybe' and above all, 'Someone To Watch Over Me.' When they went into New York rehearsals early in September 1926, all they lacked was a title. The show was variously known as *Mayfair*, *Miss Mayfair* and *Cheerio!* until, just before the Philadelphia opening, the authors decided to settle for the fact that it was developing into another of their *Oh!* shows. This one then became known as *Oh, Kay!* and of its first night at the Imperial Theatre on Broadway in November 1926 the *Herald Tribune* critic wrote: 'All of us simply floated away on the canoodling notes of "Maybe" and were brought back to Broadway by such flesh and bony anthems as "Fidgety Feet" and "Clap Yo' Hands".'

But the show-stopping moment was when Gertie, alone on stage, sang a wistful number to a strange rag doll that George Gershwin had bought her, shortly before opening night, in a Philadelphia toy shop:

> Won't you tell him, please, to put on some speed
> Follow my lead?
> Oh, how I need
> Someone to watch over me . . .

As a summary of Gertie's own off-stage needs at the time this was pretty accurate.

Oh, Kay! was enough of a triumph to carry Gertie all through 1927 on Broadway and almost all through 1928 in London. Her first big starring musical could not have been better, either for her or for its audiences, and it established her away from Buchanan and Bea as a star all on her own, capable of carrying a Broadway show virtually single-handed, though she was of course in the best of all possible hands: 'The book of *Oh Kay!*', noted Burns Mantle simply, 'was written by Guy Bolton and P. G. Wodehouse, than whom there are no better librettists writing for our stage.' And the Gershwins weren't too bad either.

With Astley still in London, Gertie's need for someone to watch over her led her that winter with reasonable speed into the arms of an American lover, Bert Taylor. The scion of a wealthy American family (his sister was the legendary socialite Countess di Frasso) Taylor was a Wall Street banker, already living apart from a wife and two small children. It was, for Gertie, love at first sight all over again:

Immediately my life changed . . . this tall, dark-haired, stunning-looking American was like someone one only reads about. With a snap of his fingers, a glance, a quiet word, he had the power to bring about miracles. Bert had been born with a golden spoon in his mouth. His father was President of the New York Stock Exchange and Bert had rolled up an enormous fortune of his own during those years when Wall Street was still holding carnival . . . he knocked me off my feet. From the moment of his entry into my life I began to live in a storybook world. While New York streets were glazed with ice and the sky sent down showers of sleet, my apartment was abloom with Spring and the fragrance of American Beauty roses. A banker in Bert's position could, and not infrequently did, make a profit of a hundred thousand dollars in a day's trading on the Stock Exchange and, exhilarated by this achievement, on his way up town to his club he would drop in at Cartier's and spend a part of the day's bag on a gorgeous bauble to please the lady of his heart.

Bert Taylor had little difficulty in sweeping off her feet a lady who, by her own admission, was there just waiting to be swept: 'From the start of my friendship with Philip Astley we had both known that we had no real future together. Circumstances to which we both had to submit [presumably Gertie's love for the stage and America, Philip's for the Guards and England] kept us apart, and although for several years I had been happy with half a loaf, I was inevitably now getting both lonely and restless.'

Gertie was, however, still very fond of Philip and well aware of all that he had done for her back in London; she therefore wrote to him with news of the Taylor affair. Philip took the next boat to New York and asked her to marry him. She refused.

Had he asked in London a year or two earlier, Gertie later wrote, she would have been very happy to become Mrs Astley. But by now things had changed. Her love affair with New York (and America in the person of Bert Taylor) was at its height, and deep down she knew very well that what Philip was offering was not just marriage but a life away from the stage, a life in the country bringing up children; the life that so many of her London chorus-girl contemporaries had happily chosen as an escape from their own families or the grind of yet another Charlot revue. But Gertie was now no longer doing that; she was doing a Broadway musical by the Gershwins, and she loved it. What is more, she had begun to doubt if she was ever going to be able to be happy away from the theatre; from the age of ten, the theatre was all she had really known. Life outside the theatre usually meant trouble; trouble with husbands, mothers, fathers, children. It was unglamorous, uneasy and usually, in her case, unsatisfactory. In the greatest and oldest of the many backstage clichés in which Gertrude Lawrence lived out her life, she was only really happy once she got through a stage door. The endless fuss about the decoration of dressing-rooms (which was to become a feature of her later career) was not just the usual starry insecurity or temperament on display. She cared passionately about the decoration and state of her dressing-room because that was the only home she ever really wanted or understood or recognized. Her life had been and always would be the theatre, and, when Philip Astley finally offered her a different one, Bert Taylor became a wonderfully convenient excuse for not facing up to the fact that she could never successfully be Mrs anybody. It will doubtless be argued that she did eventually manage to become Mrs Aldrich, to which the only answer is that in a marriage which lasted twelve years he was at war for five and she was on the stage for seven.

Philip Astley, whose manners were as impeccable in defeat as in success, took Gertie's rejection of his proposal like the officer and gentleman he always was and caught the next boat back to England while Gertie stayed in New York to finish the Broadway run of *Oh, Kay!* With his departure, she lost not only a lover and a friend but also the only man who might have been able to see her safely through the 1930s:

> Tell me, where is the shepherd for this lost lamb?
> There's a somebody I'm longing to see
> I hope that he
> Turns out to be
> Someone to watch over me.

8

OK WITH OH, KAY!

Although Philip had never managed to instil into Gertie any sense of the value of money, he had managed to persuade her to put a thousand pounds into a twenty-year trust fund for her daughter, one of the very few intelligent investments she was ever to make. But with Philip now back in England, mother and daughter weren't getting on very well together in New York as Pamela later recalled:

I was suddenly taken out of this working-class Clapham environment where I'd grown up with my grandmother and there were constant soapsuds around the front door because Granny still boiled the laundry in the copper, and thrown into this frightfully sophisticated New York world where my only relationship with Mummy was being lined up next to her for photographs. She got me into a boarding school fairly rapidly, but there were still the holidays and I remember waking up every morning and asking Mummy's maid Dorothy what sort of mood she was likely to be in that day, and if it was bad then I'd just get out of the house as soon as possible. It wasn't that she ever really meant to be unkind or difficult, it was just that she had absolutely no idea of what being a mother really meant. How could she? Her own family had broken up when she was barely ten, and she had just never seen or known any kind of domestic life. She had no idea what mothers were supposed to do. She was terribly irritable with the staff she hired, kept firing people and then begging them to stay because she couldn't manage without them, but she never really knew where a daughter fitted in to the household or what she was supposed to say to me. I made her very uneasy; not because I was a good-looking child, or any kind of a threat to her, but simply because she had never really met a child before and had no idea what she was supposed to be doing with me. Later we got on better, because she could visualize herself as a kind of older sister offering advice, but in the early days she was constantly protected from me by servants and agents and she was never really there when you needed her, or if she was then her maid would say 'Don't bother your mother now, dear – she's tired.' Going to day school in New York meant being up early for breakfast in the dining-room, just me because Mummy was still asleep or having breakfast in bed, and then when I got back in the afternoons she'd be getting ready to go off to the theatre. I don't think she was consciously trying to avoid me, but our lives just never seemed to overlap except if there were holidays when she wasn't doing a play and I was home. But then we used to find that, because we'd been apart so much, we had nothing to say to each other.

As if aware of the gap that Philip's departure had left in her life, Gertie soon began to surround herself with other people; not just Bert Taylor but secretaries and maids; there was also Helen Downes, a wealthy New York lady who was to stay with Gertie for several years as a kind of unpaid aide. The only difference was that where it had been Gertie who had once listened to Philip, it was now all of the others who listened to Gertie; none of them really had the courage or the authority to check her spending, which was now reaching epidemic proportions, or her greater excesses of temperament; there were only two men who could ever do that, Philip and Noël, and they were both back in London.

For a while, none of that much mattered; the Wall Street crash was still nearly two years off, Bert was still around to pay some of the more expensive bills, and money was still a joy rather than a problem. Gertie's attitude was, then as always, one of easy come—easy go; she took considerable pride in the fact that she was not, unlike many of her friends and contemporaries, ever totally 'kept' by anyone. Though she had never objected to Philip, or now Bert, accounting for a certain amount of her living expenses, her own considerable theatre salary was never banked against a rainy day. It too went towards the ever-increasing cost of just being Gertrude Lawrence.

Oh, Kay! which had made Gertie the first British actress to star in an American musical on Broadway, ran on through to the midsummer of 1927, and the management then decided to move it and Gertie straight to London for the following autumn; after some slight anglicizing (notably the casting of Claude Hulbert as 'The Duke of Datchet') they opened at His Majesty's in late September to good business but some rather grudging reviews. Playing opposite Gertie now was her old child-actor friend from *Hannele*, Harold French.

'At the first reading we assured each other again and again how wonderful it was to be working together again. That lasted all of two weeks. Our scenes worked wonderfully, dance routines presented no problem, my body, legs, arms and feet found no difficulty in obeying the demands of the choreographer. But before we went into the dance, duets had to be sung. Great numbers, all of them – 'Maybe', 'Do-Do-Do', 'Someone To Watch Over Me'; Mr Gershwin was no slouch. We were into the third week when I first noticed it, ''it'' being a slightly puzzled look on Gertie's face as we were singing our first duet together . . . I thought nothing of it until we had finished the dance and made our exit. Then, casually, she enquired ''Who's your singing teacher, Harold?''.'

It rapidly became clear that Harold French was going to have more than a little trouble with the numbers, and this was reflected in such first-night notices as 'he knows how to move about the stage but is no canary' from St John Ervine in the *Observer*. Indeed the whole experience of *Oh, Kay!* not only cooled the French-Lawrence friendship but also cured him of any further desire to work in musicals; from then on he was to have a distinguished straight-theatre career as a director, most notably of the plays of Terence Rattigan.

That apart, *Oh, Kay!* worked well enough in London: the full score still included a ravishing number called 'Dear Little Girl' which was then to disappear without trace for forty years, only to resurface as a piano duet for Julie Andrews and Daniel Massey in the otherwise appalling Gertrude Lawrence film biography *Star!* If the reviews found *Oh, Kay!* rather thin, they were at least marvellous for Gertie herself who, in the view of *The Times*, was 'a brilliant and happy girl combining in the most remarkable manner a variety of talents. She has looks, grace, humour, voice, dignity, acting ability and immense charm. She can play the gamine and the lady; she can range in voice and gesture from the good-natured cockney slut to the well-bred woman; and she has an unfailing fund of invention that enables her to fill an empty phrase with fun. Her mere mumbles are comic, and she has that indefinable radiance which compels an audience to concentrate its attentions on her. In Miss Lawrence we possess an actress of genius.' As homecomings go, that one can't have been considered bad: Gertie was, as the song said, OK with *Oh, Kay!*

Philip Astley, though no longer quite the devoted escort he had been, continued to drop into her dressing-room, and Gertie decided the time had come to get at least the rest of her private life into some sort of order; to this end she leased a large and costly flat in Portland Place from the Marquis de Casa Maury, installed Pamela along with André Charlot's similarly-aged daughter at a Catholic girls' boarding school near Margate, hired the ever-fashionable Sybil Colefax to do some interior decoration at the flat, and set about getting her divorce in case Bert Taylor's thoughts might be turning towards a proposal.

The divorce itself wasn't too difficult to arrange; Frank had, after all, left her (admittedly with some encouragement) holding a month-old baby and that was now almost ten years ago. He was not, therefore, in the strongest position to contest Gertie's suit, and some tribute to the stunning performance she must have given in the witness box can be gleaned from press reports of the judge's summing up:

'This,' said Lord Merivale, noting evidence of Howley's adultery at a Hull hotel, 'is one of the worst cases of which I have ever heard – in which a girl of nineteen was seduced by a man at a time when he was in a position of authority in the theatrical profession to which she belonged. They were married and a child was born, but the husband never maintained his wife and child. Apparently the view of the husband was that from that time onward he might live on the earnings of his wife. Naturally, therefore, they did not live together for long. The petitioner has been abominably used, and now it seems she has prospects of making a new start in life. The divorce will be granted.'

Gertie was thus foot-loose and fancy free, with a minimum of the unattractive publicity which was inclined to surround actresses' divorces in this period. Sure enough, Bert Taylor took the judge's hint; that summer he came to London and proposed marriage. Gertie accepted, though it was to remain a curious and ultimately unfulfilled engagement. For the next year or so, they were frequently to be photographed in each other's arms; on certain of these occasions Gertie would reveal to the press that she could hardly wait to become Mrs Taylor and that she was just longing to settle down and bring up his children in America as soon as the present production came to its close. On other occasions, beneath similar photographs, the caption would announce that regretfully Miss Lawrence and Mr Taylor had decided after all not to get married because, as Gertie would then explain at some length: 'I believe that the duty of a wife is to offer companionship to her husband. How can I, who must go to the theatre at night, be a companion to a husband who would be home from business at 5 pm? I would like to marry Mr Taylor very much, but I don't think it would be fair to him: he would expect me to retire, but I am now on the threshold of success for which I have worked for many years and I simply can't give it all up just for love.'

Being engaged, therefore, seemed to provide the ideal solution; it kept Bert tied reasonably closely to her without committing either of them to a radical change in their lifestyle. It satisfied the rather eccentric morality of the time, whereby a leading female star was expected to have some sort of male in close attendance, but it left Gertie free when Bert was not visiting London to carry on her own life, still indeed seeing Philip Astley in whom the flame was far from totally quenched, and the same applied to Bert. Theirs was, in other words, an 'open' engagement and as such was to remain reasonably successful for the next couple of years.

Early in January 1928, with *Oh, Kay!* still running successfully at His Majesty's, Gertie took another and very important, though little publicized, step forward in her career. Dedicated and devoted as she was to the theatre, she had already begun to realize that the life of a revue and musical-comedy star was inclined to be a little shorter than she might one day wish. Looking around her in the West End that winter, it was not hard to recognize that the stars who had lasted – the stars who were still working well in their fifties and sixties and even seventies – were not as a rule the song-and-dance brigade. If Gertie's star was to last, she would have to make herself into a straight actress too.

Her chance came when Charlot, her old protector and manager, agreed to stage, as a charity show for the Actors' Orphanage, for one Sunday night Owen Davis's Pulitzer-prizewinning American drama *Icebound*, about the old Maine family squabbling over money and a wastrel son. Gertie played plain Jane, the poor relation, 'far removed' said one critic 'from the quips and nods and becks and wreathed smiles which have made her famous in musical comedy'. There was no question of staging *Icebound* for any longer than that one Sunday night, and few papers bothered even to notice it next morning; but what Gertie had done, quietly and firmly, was to alert the ever-watchful eyes of London theatre managers to the fact that she was now open to offers of work in the straight theatre as well as in revue.

Then it was back to *Oh, Kay!* for the rest of the Winter and Spring of 1928, and by the time that show eventually closed Gertie had already had another script from George and Ira Gershwin. This was *Treasure Girl*, last and least successful of the 'smart' Gershwin scores of the 20s and one containing a song called 'I Don't Think I'll Fall In Love Today' which was intentionally or not, a remarkable summary of the current state of play concerning Gertie and Bert Taylor:

SHE: Just think of what love leads to:
           Maybe to marriage – maybe divorce.

HE: Into a jam love speeds two;
           It may be nature's course,
           But we mustn't be
           Like the other sheep.

SHE: Better far if we
           Look before we leap.

BOTH: Perhaps it's better after all
           If we don't answer Nature's call.

There was, however, no way of knowing, as Gertie once again packed her innumerable bags and set off for New York in the late summer of 1928, that *Treasure Girl* wasn't going to be another smash hit; indeed so confident was she of success, that she took Pamela with her, a maid, and two cars – a custom-built Bentley and, for when the traffic got really bad, a very small Austin Seven, which inspired one New York cop to shout as she drove past him 'Say lady, what do you do with it at night? Keep it under the bed?'

Bert was there to greet her on the quayside, where they gave one of their 'no we have no immediate plans for marriage' interviews to the assembled press. Gertie then established herself in a large apartment on Park Avenue and went straight into rehearsal. The score for *Treasure Girl* was by no means a poor one, including as it did 'I've got a crush on you', 'Feeling I'm Falling' 'Krazy for You' and 'Got A Rainbow', but something was wrong here and it was very possibly the plot. Gertie's private life may have been going rapidly from grandeur to grandeur, but there was something about her stage presence which still invited and indeed demanded sympathy for the 'poor little rich girl'. It was indeed Coward himself who was the first to spot the increasing gap between the lady Gertie thought she was and the lady she really was; that previous summer, following the run of *Oh, Kay!*, they had met up again in London just after Gertie had come back from a brief holiday on the French Riviera. She told him the stories of yachts, and parties, and grand friends, and then added that she would have to get back there as soon as possible, preferably in December or January, as she certainly couldn't stand the thought of ever having to live through another English winter. 'No, darling, I'm sure you couldn't,' agreed Noël, 'especially after all those childhood years in sun-drenched Clapham.'

Now audiences, too, wanted to reassure themselves that Gertie was never really as grand or as distant as she could somehow seem; they wanted to be able to warm to her, and *Treasure Girl* gave them no chance, telling as it did the story of a girl so avid for money and position that she would even double-cross her lover. Despite a strong supporting cast (led by Clifton Webb) and a lyrically good score, Broadway rejected *Treasure Girl* and two months later, wrote Ira Gershwin, 'we were all taken off to Cain's Warehouse' which was where scenery from Broadway flops was traditionally stored.

Too proud to return to London with news of her first real New York disaster, Gertie stayed on in New York hoping that something might turn up. What did turn up by about Christmas, was not another show (since in those days there were precious few mid-season openings and casting for the new season would not therefore begin again until the summer) but instead the offer of her very first film.

It came from Paramount, but not from Hollywood; instead, at their comparatively modest studio complex out on Long Island they were starting out on a picture first called *The Gay Lady* and then rapidly retitled *The Battle of Paris.* Initially the film had a good deal going for it, including not only the co-stars Gertie, Charlie Ruggles and Arthur Treacher, but the first two songs ('Here Comes The Bandwagon' and 'They All Fall In Love') ever to be written for the screen by Cole Porter. There was however not much of a script, indeed so little that the director threatened to resign. Held to his contract by Paramount lawyers, he returned to the studios on Long Island to discover that all the good daytime had been booked and floorspace was in such short supply that he and his company would have to work between eight at night and five in the morning.

Uncharitably described by one film critic as a 'floperetta', *The Battle of Paris* turned out to be a curious and now long-lost little musical comedy about a girl called Georgie who, struggling to make a living as an artist in pre-First World War Paris, falls in love with an American soldier and then takes up nightclub singing in an effort to secure his love. The plot here was something less than crucial, though one critic did wonder how, just before the

Armistice, Miss Lawrence had managed to assemble in Paris an entire male-voice choir from the American army, and another critic added that 'if all Miss Lawrence wishes to do is wear lovely clothes, then some plot device might have been found to alleviate the boredom of watching her steal dress after dress from mannequins in store windows.' But *The Battle of Paris* did at least give Gertie the chance to sing her way six numbers, and a note from Paramount's head office to its distributors said 'Sell strongly on songs and clothing of G. Lawrence', which they dutifully did. This may have been a less than spectacular or distinguished screen debut, but as such it was to be in almost perfect keeping with the rest of her film career.

By staying around New York, and commuting each morning to Paramount's Long Island sound stages, Gertie had the chance to keep her ear close to the Broadway ground and therefore to position herself carefully for the cream of the autumn show offers. Her unexpected and rather alarming failure in the last Gershwin musical indicated to her that a change of direction was called for. Rather than risk another musical, she was keen to try her luck in a straight play and rumour from England had it that Yvonne Arnaud had just opened there in a play which would perfectly suit Gertie on Broadway for the fall of 1929. It was a Viennese comedy called, in London, *By Candle-Light*. But as the adapter for New York of *Candle-Light* (as it became) was Gertie's old friend and author from *Oh, Kay!*, P. G. Wodehouse, there wasn't a lot of difficulty. Indeed when Gertie first saw the play, on her annual summer holiday in England after the filming of *The Battle of Paris*, she knew at once that it was the play in which she wanted to make her straight-theatre debut on Broadway.

Noël cabled when he heard of her plans, LEGITIMATE AT LAST. WON'T MOTHER BE PLEASED?

9

ENTER AMANDA

For the Broadway production of *Candle-Light* in the autumn of 1929, Gilbert Miller (who was both producer and director) decided to assemble a largely English cast, indeed so English that the three principals – Gertie, Reginald Owen and an up-and-coming matinée idol called Leslie Howard – did most of their rehearsing in London that summer and even played a trial week in Southampton before travelling down to the docks there and taking the boat back to New York. Wodehouse noted in his diary that his friendship with Gertie now became a little strained, largely because he was so confident of her success in his play that he chose not to hang around in New York but instead to travel on to California for a Hollywood scripting job instead. By the time he got back to Baltimore, where *Candle-Light* was now being tried out before American audiences, he therefore got 'a distinctly chilly reception from Gertie before being taken back into the fold'.

The Broadway opening was triumphant, and in their first week at the Empire Theatre they took just over $18,000 which meant a healthy $1,800 into Gertie's bank balance. Her reviews had admittedly been a little less than wonderful; the *New York Times* found her 'as charming and decorative as ever, but she turns on all the comic stops at once and overplays consistently'. Undaunted, Gilbert Miller hung her portrait up in the lobby of the Empire next to those of Ina Claire and Helen Hayes, and announced that Gertie too was now 'legit'.

Candle-Light had opened on Broadway at the end of September 1929; a month later, Wall Street crashed and though Gertie had never been much inclined to invest, the collapse of the Stock Exchange drastically affected her friendship with Bert Taylor: 'Bert was up to his ears in financial worries and responsibilities and in the circumstances it seemed impractical for us to marry. At least Bert said it was. I was free to marry him and I wanted to, just to prove that I loved him and not his money . . . I protested that I was willing to go on working to help things along financially, but that only hurt his pride more deeply. We were at a deadlock.'

So she carried on in the theatre, leading a somewhat less lavish private life than in previous Broadway seasons but still revelling in considerable public and private acclaim: 'her performance affected me' wrote Wodehouse later 'rather as his first perusal of Chapman's Homer had affected Keats . . . she had everything'; Burns Mantle noted that she was 'as graceful and accomplished in her first stage comedy as she was witty and charming in her many Charlot revues' and Brooks Atkinson added that she 'has the talent and the presence of the true comedienne'. To those who enquired what on earth the title had to do with a romantic comedy about a Hapsburg heir and a chambermaid (played by Gertie), Wodehouse replied simply that it came from an old Austrian proverb which, roughly translated, stated: 'choose neither women nor linen by candle-light'.

From that somewhat flimsy start they achieved 150 Broadway performances (rather more than a later Cole Porter musical version entitled *You Never Know*), presumably because the extramarital affairs of Viennese princes provided a welcome escape from the grim financial realities of New York in the winter of 1929–30. That Gertie's own spirits remained reasonably buoyant can be gathered from an Equity employment questionnaire she filled in at the time. To the query 'What are your stage ambitions' her answer was the one word 'Tremendous', and asked if she had ever done any writing she answered 'No, I always cable.' Her parents, she bizarrely noted, had been a celebrated double act known as 'The Moore and Burgess Minstrels' and her hobbies she added were 'Backgammon and moving apartments'. *Candle-Light* closed in the Spring of 1930, having made a star of Leslie Howard and a straight actress of Gertrude Lawrence.

Eager to stay in work, and there being no other plays on offer, Gertie then made a thoroughly unwise decision to go back into revue. The show in question was Lew Leslie's *International Revue*, a rare failure from the impresario of *Blackbirds* for which he had decided to counteract America's current introverted mood by importing a large number of foreign stars from Europe and South America. Despite songs by Dorothy Fields and Jimmy McHugh and dance routines by the great Busby Berkeley, not to mention Robert Conche (a Parisian child prodigy who played the violin and the concertina, conducted his own orchestra but soon disappeared forever from theatrical scene), the *International Revue* was less than triumphant. Anton Dolin had a success with his Apache dance and Gertie sang 'Sunny Side of the Street', 'Exactly Like You' and did a little dancing, but the first night dragged on until a quarter past midnight and even then there were six numbers still unplayed. Lew Leslie had apparently not noticed that a few weeks earlier something called *The Little Show* at the Music Box had revolutionized the whole shape of revue by making it brief and intimate. The unwieldy *International Revue* was still huge and therefore unfashionable.

It did however have one very happy consequence for Gertie. She decided after a few weeks that she would much like to be out of the whole affair, but lacking a good lawyer and unwilling to trouble Bert who still had his own preoccupations, she turned for advice to 'Pat' Dolin who recommended an already celebrated brother-and-sister partnership of New York showbusiness lawyers called David and Fanny Holtzmann. They soon discovered that Gertie's considerable troubles were not merely legal, but also financial. To extricate her from the *International Revue* was no great problem, but while doing so Fanny noticed that Gertie had not only never saved any money for her U.S. taxes, she had almost never paid any either. Somehow, through all the years of the Charlot Revues and *Oh, Kay!* and the other shows, because she kept criss-crossing the Atlantic, the taxmen had not yet caught up with her. When they did, Fanny realized, Gertie's debts would be massive.

But Gertie was never an imaginative lady, and therefore found it hard to grasp a problem that still seemed to lie somewhere in an uncertain future. There was always the hope that when the taxmen did finally catch up with her she would be back in London, or that in the current economic uncertainty of the United States, they might not even bother to extract a few hundred thousand dollars from an English actress still not resident there. Gertie was nothing if not optimistic.

Fanny, who was from now on to be her greatest admirer, adviser and manager, did manage to instil a vague sense of impending doom, however, and convinced Gertie there was only one thing for it. She was to get work, stay in work, spend nothing, and hope to God that by the time the tax bills began to come in she'd have saved enough to pay off at least some of them. That seemed to make sense, and when, therefore, André Charlot wrote making her an offer for his 1930 Revue, Gertie hastily accepted and signed a contract. No sooner had she done so than a script arrived for her in the post. It was a comedy by Noël Coward, and it was called *Private Lives*.

Private Lives happened for Gertie in a roundabout kind of a way; ever since their shared theatrical childhood, and all through their time with Charlot, Noël had promised his beloved friend that one day he would write her a full-scale show, not just another revue number here or there. Indeed when, in the summer of 1928, he had begun working on his first-ever operetta, *Bitter-Sweet*, it had been quite clear in his mind that Gertie was to be its star. But then, as the score developed, it became even more clear to him that it would need a singer with a considerably greater vocal range, and when a year later *Bitter-Sweet* opened in London it was with Peggy Wood in the lead, playing a role later created for Broadway by Evelyn Laye.

All this meant that Noël owed Gertie a show, and that was not a debt she was going to let him forget easily. Indeed when, in the autumn of 1929 while she was playing in *Candle-Light*, Noël had passed through New York on one of his many voyages around the world, Gertie gave him a farewell party and, he recalled later:

a little gold book from Cartier's which, when opened and placed on the writing-table in my cabin, disclosed a clock, calendar and thermometer on one side and an extremely pensive photograph of Gertie herself on the other. This rich gift, though I am sure prompted by the least ulterior of motives, certainly served as a delicate reminder that I had promised to write a play for us both, and I gazed daily, often with irritation, at that anxious *retroussé* face while my mind voyaged barrenly through eighteenth-century salons, Second Empire drawing rooms and modern cocktail bars in search of some inspiring echo, some slight thread of plot that might suitably unite us in either comedy, tragedy or sentiment. However, nothing happened. I was aware of a complete emptiness . . . and I resolved never again to make any promises that implicated my creative ability. They were limiting and tiresome and imposed too great a strain. I would write whatever the spirit moved me to write, regardless of whether the subject matter was suitable to Gertie Lawrence, Mrs Patrick Campbell or Grock; and in the meantime, feeling no particular urge to write anything at all, I closed Gertie's clock with a snap and read a book.

A few weeks later, however, Noël found himself at the Imperial Hotel in Tokyo awaiting the arrival there of his close friend and travelling companion

Jeffery Amherst: 'The night before he arrived I went to bed early as I wanted to greet him as brightly as possible at seven in the morning, but the moment I switched out the lights, Gertie appeared in a white Molyneux dress on a terrace in the South of France and refused to go again until four a.m., by which time *Private Lives*, title and all, had constructed itself. In 1923 the play would have been written and typed within a few days of my thinking of it, but by 1929 I had learned the wisdom of not welcoming a new idea too ardently, so I forced it into the back of my mind, trusting to its own integrity to emerge again later on when it had become sufficiently set and matured.'

A few weeks later still, by which time Noel was in Shanghai and bed with influenza, the idea re-emerged:

I lay sweating gloomily in my bedroom in the Cathay Hotel for several days. The ensuing convalescence however was productive, for I utilised it by writing *Private Lives*. The idea by now seemed ripe enough to have a shot at, so I started it propped up in bed with a writing-block and an Eversharp pencil and completed it, roughly, in four days. It came easily, and with the exception of a few of the usual 'blood and tears' moments I enjoyed writing it. I thought it a shrewd and witty comedy, well constructed on the whole, but psychologically unstable; however its entertainment value seemed obvious enough, and its acting opportunities for Gertie and me admirable, so I cabled her immediately in New York telling her to keep herself free for the autumn.

Considering that this was to be the greatest comedy of either of their careers, it would be nice to be able to report that Gertie immediately saw the considerable merits of *Private Lives*. In fact, she saw nothing of the kind and there followed a sustained sequence of telegraphic bickering between Gertie, still in New York, and Noël, whose round-the-world voyage had now got him as far as Singapore:

She cabled me there, rather casually I thought, saying that she had read *Private Lives* and that there was nothing wrong that couldn't be fixed. I had wired back curtly that the only thing that was going to be fixed was her performance. Now cables were arriving at all hours of the day and night, with a typical disregard of expense, saying that she had foolishly committed herself to Charlot for a new revue—could we open in January instead of September—could I appear in the revue with her, just to fill in—could I wire to Charlot to release her from her contract—that it wasn't a contract at all, merely a moral obligation—that it wasn't a moral obligation at all, but a cabled contract—that her lawyers were working day and night to get her out of it—that she would rather do *Private Lives* than anything in the world — that she couldn't do *Private Lives* at all. In her last telegram she remembered to give me her cable address which, had she done so sooner, would have saved me about forty pounds. I finally lost patience and cabled that I intended to do the play with someone else, and I heard nothing further until I arrived back in England.

By that time, Fanny Holtzmann had not only managed to persuade Charlot to tear up Gertie's revue contract but even more impressively managed to convince Charles Cochran (who was presenting *Private Lives* in London and had, as the producer, last presented Gertie just twenty years earlier as one of 150 children at Olympia in *The Miracle*) that in view of Gertie's impending financial troubles with the American tax people she should be given not only co-starring status in the play but also a cut of the management profits. It was thus not Cochran alone but 'Cochran-Coward-Lawrence' (or CCL as they were known on the posters) who presented *Private Lives*, and Gertie was better off to the tune of several thousand pounds.

Meanwhile, Gertie had retired to the South of France to learn the script, taking Pamela and her devoted friend Helen Downes to stay with her at the Cap d'Ail villa of the designer Edward Molyneux which she had rented, regardless of expense, for the summer. Other visitors were soon on their way down to join her, notably Noël and his new friend, the impresario Jack Wilson. Gertie was informed of this plan by a letter from Noël which read:

Mr Coward asks me to say that there was talk of you playing a small part in a play of his, on condition that you tour and find your own clothes (same to be of reasonable quality) and understudy Jessie Matthews whom you have always imitated. Mr Coward will be visiting the South of France in mid-July and he will appear at Cap d'Ail, whether you like it or not, with Mr Jack Wilson on the 20th. If by any chance there is no room at the rather squalid lodgings you have taken, would you be so kind as to engage several suites for Mr Coward and Mr Wilson at the Hotel Mont Fleury which will enable same Mr Wilson and Mr Coward to have every conceivable meal with you and use all your toilets for their own advantage. Several complicated contracts are being sent to you by Mr Coward on the terms you agreed upon — i.e. six pounds ten shillings a week and understudy.

Gertie made room at the luxurious Molyneux villa for Jack and Noël, principally by turning out her now twelve-year-old daughter who never forgave her; but there were other visitors who were allowed to stay on, notably the actor William Powell and the novelist G. B. Stern who thus became the first people ever to see *Private Lives* in rehearsal, as Noël and

Gertie pushed back the furniture in the sitting room and set about practising the balcony scene.

They didn't spend all their time rehearsing; once they heard that George Gershwin was staying at the nearby Hotel du Cap and made their way there. Also in residence at the hotel then was a young Simon Harcourt-Smith:

We had come down to Antibes, my mother to recuperate from an illness and I to study for an extremely stiff exam . . . occasionally 'G' Lawrence would pass my chair, deploying across yards of empty white tables in the hotel's vast dining-room a kind of moonlit charm that drew one's eyes again and again towards her . . . once she apparently told the manager that I seemed to be working far too hard. But we never spoke until Noël Coward came to lunch with her among the silent tables. I knew him slightly from London, and I could also claim a slight acquaintance with her other guest, no less than the composer George Gershwin . . . as the two men with G. passed me on the way to her table, Coward greeted me and Gershwin seemed to remember me. Later, at lunch, as my mother complained that the toast was cold, a waiter delivered us a message: would we join Mademoiselle Lawrence and her friends for coffee and brandy? Unfortunately, mother failed entirely to approve of Noël Coward. She had once attended a performance of *The Vortex* and was hardly persuaded that drugs were a suitable subject to be mentioned in a West End play . . . so despite my pleadings she mounted to her afternoon siesta while I guiltily made my way to my heroine's table. Theatrical gossip of a lively sort played over it: the air was scintillating with allusions which I could hardly catch. Then G. proposed that, as a protest against the *mistral*, an impromptu concert should enliven the afternoon . . . champagne was ordered and we proceeded in leisurely fashion towards the ballroom . . . George Gershwin slipped the last dust-cover off the piano and sat down before it . . . her face all animation, husky voice all caresses, G. went into 'Oh! Do, do, do what you did, did, did before, baby' and 'The Man I Love' and 'Someone to watch over me'. Noël sang 'They can't take that away from me' and 'S'wonderful' and then his own 'Half-Caste Woman' and 'Mad Dogs and Englishmen' while, through the chinks between the shutters, the sunlight slowly reddened . . . the next day I again flung filial piety and my studies for the moment to the winds and motored G. up to Eze in the hills for lunch . . . she began to sing 'Parisian Pierrot' and other enchantments I can no longer recall . . . then I motored her back and it was as if the day before had been stretched far beyond twenty-four hours. Thereafter, until she left for America at the end of the Thirties, we remained steadfast friends. She was singularly unaware of her genius, as she was of her defects.

One of those defects was a frequent tendency to overact, especially in comedy, and it was on this above all that Noël worked with her during that

Riviera summer. By the time they got back to London at the end of July, most of their scenes together had been pre-rehearsed and (with Noël himself directing and his regular designer Gladys Calthrop doing the sets) they went into full rehearsals with the rest of the cast. The other couple, in Coward's mixed marital doubles, was to be played by his lifelong friend Adrianne Allen (then Mrs Raymond Massey) and a young moustached Laurence Olivier. Their roles, Victor and Sybil, were considered by their creator to be 'little better than ninepins, lightly wooden and only there at all in order to be repeatedly knocked down and stood up again by Elyot and Amanda' who in the play have of course formerly been married to each other, are now on second honeymoons with their new partners, but seriously tempted to get together again.

Noël had approached Olivier because he knew that Victor had to be attractive enough to have become Amanda's second husband, and because he knew that to have a bad part played by a bad actor would be suicidal. On the principle that only a really exciting actor can play a bore without being boring, Noël told Olivier that the play would do him a great deal of good, especially as he was badly in need of a West End hit, having deserted *Journey's End* to go into a recent and disastrous *Beau Geste*. Olivier agreed, and later admitted that much of his comic timing and technique was gained from working this engagement with Noël and Gertie, though it very nearly didn't happen.

With *Private Lives* already well into its second week of rehearsal, the then Lord Chamberlain, Lord Cromer, who still had the power of British stage censor, announced that he was thoroughly unhappy with Act Two in general and the Elyot-Amanda love scene in particular. Considering that they were now supposed to be divorced and married to new and different partners, this seemed to him altogether too risqué for the public standards of 1930 morality, and his lordship added that unless the act was drastically rewritten he would regretfully be unable to give permission for *Private Lives* to be publicly performed.

Noël repaired instantly to St James's Palace, where he read the play, acting out all the parts in front of Lord Cromer, who was then persuaded that with some dignified direction the Elyot-Amanda love scene would after all be acceptable without any cuts.

10

THE POTENCY OF CHEAP MUSIC

On 18 August 1930 *Private Lives* had its world première at the King's Theatre in Edinburgh. It was the third time that Noël and Gertie had appeared together on stage, and they were only to work together once more (in *Tonight at 8.30*); yet theirs was perhaps the definitive light-comedy partnership of the century, and never better expressed than in this one play.

Private Lives almost certainly represents Coward's greatest claim to theatrical immortality. It is in many ways the perfect light comedy, arguably the best to have come out of England since *The Importance of Being Earnest* which preceded it by 35 years; and though at the time of its first production it seemed to many critics that *Private Lives* could only survive for as long as Gertrude Lawrence and the author himself played it, the comedy has in fact been consistently successful ever since, a guaranteed copper-bottomed audience-puller that has temporarily rescued countless local theatre companies from the throes of a bad season. Royalties received, and still being received today, by the Coward estate show that hardly a month passes without somewhere in the world someone deciding to revive *Private Lives*, and it was suitably enough the play which, in a 1963 revival by the Hampstead Theatre Club then transferred to the West End, launched in his own lifetime the 'Noël Coward Renaissance'.

Yet *Private Lives*, is a play that stands or falls by the way it is played. On paper, one discovers, there is almost nothing there: brief staccato lines, the occasional aphorism ('women should be struck regularly, like gongs') and duologues which take on a sparkling life of their own, nowhere better than in the second most famous balcony scene of all time:

AMANDA: How was the Taj Mahal?

ELYOT: Unbelievable, a sort of dream.

AMANDA: That was the moonlight, I expect, you must have seen it in the moonlight.

ELYOT (*never taking his eyes off her face*): Yes, moonlight is cruelly deceptive.

AMANDA: And it didn't look like a biscuit box, did it? I've always felt that it might.

ELYOT: Darling, darling, I love you so.

AMANDA: And I do hope you met a sacred elephant. They're lint-white I believe, and very, very sweet.

ELYOT: I've never loved anyone else for an instant.

AMANDA: No, no, you mustn't – Elyot – stop.

ELYOT: You love me too, don't you? There's no doubt about it anywhere, is there?

AMANDA: No, no doubt anywhere.

'Gertie and Noël looked so beautiful together [wrote Cole Lesley] standing in the moonlight, that no one who saw them can ever forget; and they played the scene so magically, lightly, tenderly that one was for those fleeting moments brought near to tears by the underlying vulnerability, the evanescence of their love.'

But the dialogue in this comedy of appalling manners is theatrically effective rather than naturalistic; there is virtually no action beyond a fight at the end of Act II and another at the end of Act III; there are no 'cameo' characters to break up the duologues except the maid at the end, and there is really no plot to sustain the actors if their comic talents start to fail them. *Private Lives* is in fact a technical exercise of incredible difficulty for two immensely accomplished light comedians.

After Edinburgh they toured Liverpool, Birmingham, Manchester and finally Southsea where one night the pioneer aviator Amy Johnson was to be found in the audience. Reviews on the tour had been generally excellent, though in this last week *Private Lives* ran into some high moral outrage from one critic who wrote: 'The play, with the exception of a certain amount of smart backchat, consisted of large buckets of stable manure thrown all over the great audience for over two hours. . . . Twenty years ago such a production would have been impossible . . . of course these four players may in their own private lives be quite moral and respectable. I know nothing about them, and don't want to.'

In London, *Private Lives* opened the new Phoenix Theatre in Charing Cross Road with a glittering high-society première on 24 September 1930: Olivier had spent the tour learning not to giggle on-stage, Adrianne Allen remembered 'supreme confidence – we all knew we had a hit' and Noël and Gertie 'enjoyed ourselves tip-top', though the general highspot was reckoned to be their moment at the piano with *Someday I'll Find You* and Elyot's remark about the strange potency of cheap music. 'Don't you just love it' asked Mrs Patrick Campbell sweeping into the dressing-room afterwards, 'when Noël does his little hummings at the piano?'

Reviews next morning were however mixed, more good than bad but none exactly raves; most critics offered something of the grudging, patronizing, qualified admission of enjoyment with which Allardyce Nicoll was later to dismiss Coward in his book *World Drama*: '. . . amusing, no doubt, yet hardly moving farther below the surface than a paper boat in a bath-tub and, like the paper boat, ever in imminent danger of becoming a shapeless, sodden mass.'

'Brittle', 'tenuous' and 'thin' were the recurrent adjectives first used to describe *Private Lives* in general and the Noël-Gertie partnership in particular, but there were also references to cocktails, evening dress, repartee and even irreverent allusions to copulation, thereby, noted Noël 'causing a gratifying number of respectable people to queue up at the box office'.

Private Lives fast became the most popular play in town, especially when it became known that Noël and Gertie had only agreed to play it there for three months before moving on to Broadway. For the two of them, life went on much as it had backstage during that first childhood run of *Hannele*; where in rehearsal Noël took a paternal interest in Gertie's work, in performance they reverted to brother and sister, a couple of loving, squabbling equals who, like Elyot and Amanda, found it difficult to be together and impossible to be apart. There were frequent rows: on one occasion Everley Gregg, playing the small role of the maid, came into Noël's dressing room to find him and Gertie in the middle of a full-scale fist-fight. 'Stop it, stop it,' she cried, trying to tear them apart, 'I love you both,' whereupon Noël and Gertie both rounded on her and threatened to sack her on the spot. But through all of that, Noël's deep devotion to Gertie remained unscathed; a few months later he was to write:

She has an astounding sense of the complete reality of the moment, and her moments, dictated by the extreme variability of her moods, change so swiftly that it is frequently difficult to discover what (apart from eating, sleeping and acting) is true of her at all. I know her well; better, I believe, than most people. The early years of our friendship set her strongly in my mind. I knew her then to have quick humour, insane generosity and a loving heart, and those things seldom change. I see her now, ages away from her ringlets and black velvet military cap, sometimes a simple, wide-eyed child, sometimes a glamorous *femme du monde*, at some moments a rather boisterous 'good sort', at others a weary, disillusioned woman battered by life but gallant to the last. She appropriated beauty to herself quite early, along with all the tricks and mannerisms that go with it. In adolescence she was barely pretty. Now, without apparent effort, she gives the impression of sheer loveliness. Her grace in movement is exquisite, and her voice charming. To disentangle Gertie herself from this mutability is baffling, rather like delving for your grandmother's gold locket at the bottom of an overflowing jewel-case.

Her talent is equally kaleidoscopic. On the stage she is potentially capable of anything and everything. She can be gay, sad, witty, tragic, funny and touching. She can play a scene one night with perfect subtlety and restraint, and the next with such obviousness and over-emphasis that your senses reel. She has, in abundance, every theatrical essential but one: critical faculty. She can watch a great actor and be stirred to the depths, her emotional response is immediate and genuine. She can watch a bad actor and be stirred to the depths, the response is equally immediate and equally genuine. But for this tantalising lack of discrimination she could, I believe, be the greatest actress alive in the theatre today.

It was said of Gertie, not only by Noël but by Laurence Olivier, Adrianne Allen and many others who worked with her later, that not only did she never give the same performance two nights running, but there was no way of knowing what she was going to do on the third night either. She was impressionable to a quite remarkable degree; one of her co-stars remembered taking her one non-matinée afternoon to a Maurice Chevalier film, only to have her play the entire evening performance like Maurice Chevalier. But even Noël, her greatest friend and sternest critic, had to admit that when she played Amanda, 'Everything she had been in my mind when I originally conceived the idea in Tokyo came to life on the stage: the witty, quicksilver delivery of lines; the romantic quality, tender and alluring; the swift, brittle rages; even the white Molyneux dress.'

True to the agreement they had made to play *Private Lives* on Broadway for Cochran, and with Noël still convinced that three months was the most he could ever play any one role in any one city without a kind of terrible boredom setting in, they closed at the Phoenix at Christmas, having played just 101 performances, much to the rage of those who had failed to get tickets. Noël was told that the day would come when he would bitterly regret his decision, though he never did and never (after Broadway) either experienced or expressed any desire at all to return to the role of Elyot Chase despite being told in print by Sir Cedric Hardwicke that it was 'unprofessional' to close a hit.

Unperturbed, the company set sail for New York (all but pregnant Adrianne Allen, who was replaced as Sybil by Olivier's then wife Jill Esmond) and opened at the Times Square Theatre on Broadway in January 1931. Walter Winchell reported that the opening night audience 'cheered long and loud when they weren't laughing in a lusty manner' and added that 'Miss Lawrence has never appeared to such advantage, nor has she ever captured an audience in New York as she did last night' but there was still considerable doubt about the play itself. Brooks Atkinson for the *New York Times* thought that 'though Mr Coward himself appears with competent agility in *Private Lives*, he has nothing to say and sometimes the nothingness of this comedy begins to show through the dialogue'. Burns Mantle for the *Daily News* was however more enthusiastic, and in any case a management decision to play again for only three months guaranteed capacity houses at all performances.

In the most memorable notice of all, it was the *Variety* critic who summarized the plot of *Private Lives*: 'Mr Coward and Miss Lawrence are a couple of cooing meanies . . . Coward seems kinda grouchy over their scrapping . . . he goes to the piano and starts to sing.' Nevertheless, the rest of the press reaction was good enough for Metro Goldwyn to put in an immediate and excellent offer for the screen rights. Coward accepted, but as neither he nor Gertie were then (or ever) to be considered genuine film stars, Leslie Howard and Norma Shearer were suggested, though when Howard proved unavailable, the role of Elyot went to Robert Montgomery. For Olivier too, the Broadway run of *Private Lives* led to Hollywood offers; he went straight out to California at the end of the run and started, albeit hesitantly, on a screen career.

One man who happened to see Gertie with Noël during those three Broadway months was her future husband, Richard Aldrich; though they were not to meet for another year or two, he recalled 'I can think of no two people who have given Broadway a more sparkling and memorable evening than Noël and Gertie in *Private Lives*. Each demanded the best from the other, and always received it; together they seemed to be the very essence of teamwork.'

Yet although Noël was happy enough during the run of *Private Lives* in New York, living in a little penthouse on West 58th Street and already hard at work on his epic *Cavalcade*, for Gertie it was a much less happy time. Once through the stage door every evening, things were as usual fine for her, as there was nothing she actually enjoyed more than playing a hit; but in the daytime she had to admit to herself that her life was less than wonderful.

The affair with Bert Taylor had cooled to the point where Bert had in fact got himself another lady, one who didn't expect him at the end of long and increasingly difficult days on Wall Street to wait dinner until she had played a two-and-a-half hour comedy. Confronted by Gertie, who had heard of Bert's new friend, he admitted her existence and added that if Gertie would give up the theatre he'd still happily marry her, despite the passing of a year in which he had lost most of his own money and what little she had ever given him to invest. The crucial question was not, though, one of money; it was simply whether or not Gertie loved him enough to give up the theatre for him and it was by now all too clear to them both that she did not.

The loss of Bert was however a considerable blow; as Noël told her backstage one night 'You think your heart is broken – it isn't, but your pride is very hurt' and that pride was at present almost all that Gertie had. As a result, the ending of the affair sent her into a kind of nervous collapse; rather than play *Private Lives* with anyone else (which he never had and never would), Noël sent her to bed and closed the theatre for a fortnight. They then reopened, played the rest of their promised twelve weeks, and handed over their roles to Otto Kruger and Madge Kennedy before sailing smartly back to London.

Gertie was leaving behind her, in New York, Bert Taylor and a mounting pile of debts; though the thousand pounds she had originally invested as her one-third share in the costs of staging *Private Lives* had already been repaid to her fivefold, her bill at Hatty Carnegie's alone was up above the $10,000 line and she was still spending, wrote Fanny Holtzmann, 'like an entire fleet of drunken sailors'. The unhappier she got over Bert and her failure to find any really successful kind of private life, the more she spent. Her generosity now bordered on the insane; once, at a counter in Cartier's, a woman came up to say how much she had enjoyed her performance in *Private Lives*. To the woman's amazement Gertie turned, bought the nearest bracelet in sight and pressed it into her admirer's hand before disappearing with a gracious wave into Fifth Avenue.

On the boat home to England in that summer of 1931, Miss Lawrence had a lot to think about. *Private Lives* had taken up a hugely enjoyable year of her life; it had consolidated her partnership with Coward (they were now and forever to be Noël and Gertie), made her some money, established her as a leading straight-theatre romantic comedienne, and been a lot of fun to do. But now Noël had other projects, ones that did not concern her, and she was again on her own.

Unlike him, she had no real control over her own professional destiny; Gertie couldn't write plays, or direct them. She had, like most jobbing actresses, to look at the offers which came along and try to pick the best of them. But she had no way of planning ahead, or of organizing her professional affairs any more clearly than she was able to extricate her private ones from looming financial chaos. She had, to misquote her own most popular song, no one to watch over her.

Not surprisingly therefore, on that boat home, her thoughts began to turn more and more frequently back to Philip Astley. It had been fully ten years now since he had launched her on London society, and more than three years since the Bert Taylor affair and her increasing devotion to Broadway had signalled an end to their intimacy. On the other hand, they were still deeply fond of each other, and there must have been moments now when Gertie began to wonder whether perhaps marriage might not be a good idea after all.

Fast approaching her 33rd birthday, she was in the uneasy position of being devoted to a branch of the theatre which did not require absolute devotion; had she been a Shakespearian, or any kind of classical actress or dancer, it is possible that the demands of those trades would have taken up so much of her time in rehearsal and performance that she would not have had much left in which to notice any kind of a void. But by its very nature the musical and light comedy theatre of the 1930s left rather more chance for outside activities. Now here she was, for instance, returning to England with absolutely nothing to do but revisit a mother and a daughter with whom she seemed to have even less in common than before, and wait for some sort of a script to drop through the letter-box for the following autumn. It was, she decided, high time to reconstruct a relationship with Astley and ease herself back into a social London life of the kind he and she had been living before the Charlot revues first took her to New York.

But that had been 1923. It was now 1932 and times had changed. For a start, Philip was not at the quayside to meet her. Unperturbed, Gertie moved smartly into the Savoy Hotel and waited for him to call and take her out for dinner, which he duly did. In order to tell her, as gently as possible, that he had just become engaged to Madeleine Carroll.

AMANDA: What's she like?
ELYOT: Fair, very pretty, plays the piano beautifully.
AMANDA: Very comforting.

II

NYMPH ERRANT

Within a matter of months, Gertie had lost the two men on whose arms and in whose beds she had spent most of the 1920s. She was alone again, and she was a lady for whom being alone was about the most terrifying prospect of all. Her greatest friend, ally and partner Noël Coward was a lifelong homosexual who had made it clear that professionally, too, they were to go their separate ways. He would of course write for her again after *Private Lives* (though in fact only once) but there was much else in the theatre that he fully intended to do without her.

Gertie's other early champion, André Charlot, had nothing more to offer Gertie than the chance to revive some of her earlier successes. Wisely she declined. It was, however, to be another two years before anything really worthy of her unique but uneasy-to-cast talent came along, and the fact that in the interim she threw herself into no less than four plays and three films (where recently she had been doing no more than one major show a year) is some indication of just how adrift her career had suddenly gone. It was also an indication of her desperation to stay in work, any kind of work, rather than face up to the collapse of her private life.

The first play she did back in England was a thoroughly curious and fairly disastrous Spanish farce which the Granville-Barkers had rendered into English as *Take Two From One*. As directed by Komisarjevsky (or 'Komanseduceme' as he was irreverently known to the drama students at RADA) this bizarre piece featured Gertie and Peggy Ashcroft at the Theatre

Royal Haymarket struggling for the affections of an understandably embarrassed Nicholas Hannen who concluded the play by jumping off the stage into a box, there to disappear from sight. The politest of the reviews called it 'an uneven farce', and the critic James Agate thought the scene where Gertie had to burst into the drawing room 'in the costume of an African savage', having spent several years captured by a tribe there, resembled nothing so much as 'a production number in a Cicely Courtneidge musical'. This was not intended as a compliment, and they were off within six weeks having received from *The Times* a sharp caution to the effect that 'it is time Mr Granville-Barker gets back to his work as a director and gives up interpreting minor matters from Madrid.'

Gertie herself, who treated her customers in a curiously regal way as if she were the archduchess of some middle European state and they her faithful subjects, merely noted that 'the audience did not like me in a role so foreign to the parts I had played.'

Within a month she had hastened over to another play, again at the Theatre Royal Haymarket where the management were keen not to lose her services. With this one, entitled *Can The Leopard?*, she had rather better luck, largely because it was a much better comedy and got her securely back onto home territory – a studio flat in Chelsea. The plot was not admittedly subtle, but it did allow for a certain amount of fun and the wearing of some lavish Norman Hartnell dresses. Gertie played a naturally helpless and untidy young girl-about-town who married a rather stuffy solicitor (Ian Hunter), spent six months trying to become a model housewife and then discovered that her husband had always preferred her untidy anyway, hence the full title quotation about leopards changing their spots. In the wake of *Private Lives*, most fashionable West End marital comedies were supposed to be about four rather than just two people, and so here the quartet was made up by Kay Hammond and Kim Peacock with Kathleen Harrison already starting to do her perennial comic cleaning lady. All in all it was a safe mixture, and it worked: *Can The Leopard?* lasted six months at the Haymarket and Gertie proudly noted that 'in the role I innovated a new fashion – an interesting streak of white hair swept away from the forehead. It caught on immediately and women began flocking to the hairdressers' for a "Riviera" bleach.'

At the end of the run Gertie herself flocked to the Riviera for her now annual summer holiday on Cap Ferrat. While she was still far from happy, while she had still found no one to replace Philip or Bert, and while her love life consisted at best of the occasional backstage encounter, she had at least had another West End success and was beginning to learn how to live alone again. Her mother was back at the house in Clapham, and her daughter Pamela was now a boarder at Roedean, the most expensive girls' public school in England:

Mother thought that was socially the right thing to do with me, and so we only ever met in the holidays. She was still a very social animal in the old 'Tatler' sense; she never read much, only ever took me to concerts when she knew somebody who would be there, and though she did occasionally meet up with intellectuals, she never really was anything more than a kind of adornment to their world. Through no fault of her own she had never really been educated, and whereas Noël Coward in later life painstakingly taught himself to think and to understand intellectual concepts, she never did. Her only real care was the theatre, and that on a purely practical, non-intellectual level. If you look at the theatre of her time, outside the Old Vic it really wasn't a very serious place and certainly the scripts that she was getting offered did not require a lot of intellectual analysis. They were jobs, and she did them as well as she could, often better than anyone else could, but they never really gave her the chance or the urge to use her brain, and as a result she seldom did. It was all froth.

We hardly ever got the chance to talk properly together, or to get to know each other, but when she did occasionally begin to unbend and unburden herself to me she would only ever talk about the theatre in terms of the struggle, the terrible need to stay on top, the awful fear of a flop which might mean you were finished. Success and the business of being Gertrude Lawrence were all she ever really thought about; having come up from the bottom, her whole ethos was based on not being poor. Her talent was for making bags of stones into bags of diamonds on stage, and that was a very real talent. In some ways she was a real innocent: 'invincible ignorance', the Catholic Church would call it. Her sophistication was always that of a little girl who dresses up in high heels and her mother's evening gowns: it was skin deep, and that perhaps above all was what made so many men like Philip, Noël, Bert, and later Douglas Fairbanks and Richard Aldrich want to protect her. She needed it, God knows.

For all those reasons, and above all because of an almost total change in the British and American theatre after the war, Gertrude Lawrence left virtually no heiresses: it would be impossible today to find an actress who much resembled her on stage or off, though traces of the Gertrude Lawrence stage presence were, interestingly, soon to be evident in the high-comedy career of her co-star from *Can The Leopard?*, Kay Hammond, who was to be, a decade later, the first actress allowed by Noël to recreate Amanda in *Private Lives* during its first West End revival.

And because there was nobody quite like her, in her own lifetime, Gertie found it often hard to know what she was supposed to be doing next. Her career was decidedly informal, almost to the point of shapelessness, but for all that a number of distinguished talents, by no means all musical, beat a path to her door. That summer of 1932 a script reached her at Cap Ferrat written by the man who, just twenty years later was as director to give Gertie her greatest and last Broadway triumph in *The King and I*. But at this time John van Druten was still purely a playwright, and the script he wanted her to read concerned a woman who, having been retrieved from the brink of suicide, then falls in love with an infinitely distinguished and already married and dying barrister.

Not perhaps the most cheerful of subjects, but *Behold We Live* already had a good deal of distinction attached to it: Gilbert Miller was to present it at the St James's, with a cast which was also to include Sir Gerald du Maurier as the dying barrister and Dame May Whitty as his mother. Gertie, sensing a touch of class, rapidly signed a contract and returned from Cap Ferrat to start rehearsal at the beginning of August.

Behold We Live was to contain, apart from van Druten, another link into her future in that it was to be Sir Gerald's daughter, Daphne du Maurier, who was to write Gertie's one postwar British stage play, *September Tide*. But the play that they were now working on filled them with a certain amount of gloom. Though there is no evidence that he actually knew it at the time, Sir Gerald was by now within eighteen months of his own death; still only on the very verge of his sixties, he had already grown tired of the theatre, perhaps also tired of life. Certainly, in Gertie's view, one of the reasons why Lady du Maurier was seldom seen around the theatre after the first night was that 'she could not bear to watch her husband night after night portraying his own destiny'.

But critics were not of course to know that, and reviews were somewhat mixed; on the one hand, thought Agate, this was a sentimental tale which would have been better done as a Hollywood silent called 'The Salvage of Souls'. On the other hand Ivor Brown wrote of Gertie's 'brave rejection of her sure-fire comedy techniques' and 'her fine grasp that keeps the play from sinking hopelessly into sentimentality'. Above all, many critics noted that she had at last begun to learn some vestiges of self-restraint on stage, and therefore had at last the makings of a good serious actress.

Behold We Live was therefore a worthy, rather than a hugely enjoyable, success, but the best thing about it was the discovery by Gertie and Sir Gerald of how much they had in common. Both at that time were in deep financial trouble, both viewed the theatre as a mechanical money-making function rather than a deep spiritual or intellectual calling, and (though she was little more than half his age) both had become considerably jaded about the way their own lives appeared to be going.

The result was an immediate and loving friendship which soon led them to work together by day as well as by night; during the run of *Behold We Live* Gertie's current lover, Benn Levy, was directing a film for Alfred Hitchcock's production unit at Elstree. It was, considering its Hitchcock-Levy pedigree, an oddly muddled comedy-thriller called *Lord Camber's Ladies*, but in it there were roles for both Gertie (as an actress in danger of being poisoned) and Sir Gerald (as a noble doctor). During the shooting, reported his daughter Daphne,

Gerald's dislike of film-acting increased tenfold, though no one would have believed it to look at him, with his pockets full of tricks and practical jokes that he let fly amongst the feet of cameramen, electricians and directors in a sort of desperate effort to relieve the tedium. Practical joking during these months developed to a pitch of positive frenzy, until both theatre and studio resembled another Bedlam. The nervy, highly strung Gertie was a boon companion in mischief, and the round-faced Hitchcock a surprising ally down at Elstree. It was a wonder that the picture was ever completed at all, for hardly a moment would pass without some faked telegram arriving, some bogus message being delivered, some supposed telephone bell ringing, until the practical jokers were haggard and worn with their tremendous efforts, and had lived so long in an atmosphere of pretence that they had forgotten what it was like to be natural.

But for Sir Gerald, as for Gertie, these jokes worked as a kind of safety valve which prevented either of them from having to face up to the reality of an unhappy present and an uncertain future. Their work was all they had; because they were in debt, there was no escape from it – even had they wanted one, or known how to take it and what to do once the escape was made. Gertie was now deeply into that tax trap still familiar and much dreaded by actors today. Hoping to find a way of clearing her debts, she threw herself into two other equally undistinguished films in 1932, making them all day while still working in the theatre by night.

The first of these ought to have been hugely distinguished and somehow wasn't; if ever a playwright, apart from Coward, was perfectly suited to Gertie's own brand of high comedy then it was surely the master of the country-houseparty satire Frederick Lonsdale. Yet curiously she and he were only ever once to be united, and then for an uninspired film version of his West End hit *Aren't We All?* Harry Lachman shot it in a month (with a cast which also featured Owen Nares, Hugh Wakefield and Marie Lohr) and though it was worth £2,600 to Gertie, it did her film career no more good than *Lord Camber's Ladies*.

Undeterred, she went on to make *No Funny Business*, a United Artists release for which she was reunited with two of her three co-stars from the Broadway *Private Lives*, Laurence Olivier and Jill Esmond. The film was a distinctly hackneyed rewrite of the Coward script, again to do with sudden Riviera meetings in the moonlight and the reawakening of dead marriages, though the plot was kept just far enough away from *Private Lives* to avoid charges of piracy. So too, alas, was the dialogue. 'Miss Lawrence conveys a certain vitality and assurance on screen,' thought the critic of the *Monthly Film Bulletin*, 'but she plays in a manner long outmoded.'

She was, in fact, too theatrical ever to work well in front of a camera and, though she was now the survivor of four films in as many years, not one of them had done her or its backers any real good whatsoever. Back in the theatre, where she belonged, 1933 was to be a vintage year.

As soon as the run of *Behold, We Live* drew to its close she went into rehearsal for *This Inconstancy*, a patchy and moralistic comedy by Roland Pertwee and John Hastings Turner. When the plot flagged, as it did quite badly in the second act, Gertie retreated to the piano and there sang a little song specially composed for the occasion by Ivor Novello; for the rest, she contented herself with wearing a series of sparkling Molyneux gowns and trifling with the affections of a husband (Leslie Banks) and two lovers (Hugh Wakefield and Nigel Bruce). 'Ultra Moderns In New Play' headlined the *Daily Mail*, while Agate thought that 'Miss Lawrence wears with consummate elegance backless dresses in a spineless part, and is as always immensely clever.' Too clever by half, thought another critic, recognizing amid the cocktails and laughter yet another sign of Britain's moral collapse, albeit one for once not written by Mr Noël Coward.

This Inconstancy kept Gertie gainfully employed at Wyndham's through the summer of 1933, but even though she was still filming by day her debts continued to mount up. In something approaching desperation she first took to writing some horrendously twee columns in the *Daily Mirror*, full of (largely ghosted) advice about how to keep a home spick and span and a husband happy, neither of which Gertie had ever had to think much about doing. Then, still in the hope of earning some extra money on the side, she agreed to go into partnership with Lady Diana Cooper and Felicity Tree in founding a Berkeley Square flower shop.

Known to their friends as Fresh Flowers Limited, and to their enemies as Faded Flowers Incorporated, the shop was a perfect microcosm of almost all Gertie's attempts at moneymaking. Though started with the best of all possible motives, quick clear profit, the shop rapidly became a white elephant, costing more to run than it could ever hope to make. Gertie had insisted that the walls were to bear frescoes by Oliver Messel, and that those of her friends who wished to send flowers to other of her friends but found themselves temporarily out of pocket were always to be given extended credit. Moreover Gertie herself naturally considered any flowers in her shop her property, having neatly overlooked the fact that at some point somebody somewhere would actually have to be paid for them.

By the middle of 1933, despite the shop, the *Mirror* column, the films and the plays, Gertrude Lawrence was actually in more debt than she had been a year earlier and there was by now but one hope: Fanny Holtzmann.

Hearing from New York of her English client's financial embarrassment, Miss Holtzmann began to cast around for another big moneymaker. Small films and straight plays were all very well in their way, but Fanny knew even better than Gertie that the big money lay in big shows, preferably long-running musicals. What Fanny needed for Gertie was not just another script but 'a property' and it didn't take her long to discover that Charles Blake Cochran, the impresario of *Private Lives*, actually had one.

He had recently bought the stage rights in a novel written by a young, and then very junior, keeper at the Victoria and Albert Museum by the name of James Laver. Called *Nymph Errant*, it told the simple but enchanting story of an English girl on her way home from school in Switzerland who falls in with a Frenchman and sets out with him on a series of adventures through which she travels wide-eyed, returning home at last totally unaware of what she has just narrowly escaped in the way of sexual and other misadventures.

Cochran originally intended this as a straight play, and had indeed given it to the actor Romney Brent for dramatization. Fanny, however, saw it as a musical comedy and approached Noël Coward with the request that he should write a score for it, and of course for Gertie. Noël replied that, though he was indeed planning to write something soon for his beloved old friend, it would be something totally of his own devising; he was not, he told Miss Holtzmann, a kind of hired hack who could be summoned whenever Miss Lawrence was in need of a vehicle.

Still determined that *Nymph Errant* was to be a musical, and strongly backed by Cochran, Fanny set out in search of an alternative composer. It did not take her long to track down Cole Porter, who read the book in a single evening and was at his piano by early the following morning.

What he had seen in *Nymph Errant*, according to his biographer Charles Schwartz, was:

. . . the story of an English lass hell-bent on losing her virginity in such offbeat places as a sheik's desert tent, the Parisian follies, a Turkish harem and a nudist camp. Cole created an extraordinary score for the show that not only kept pace with the heroine's global philanderings but added some wonderfully suggestive overtones of its own. Typical of Cole's breezy suggestiveness was the tune 'Experiment' with its admonitions to 'be curious' and to 'experiment'—presumably in things sexual. Also free-wheeling in approach was Cole's 'Si Vous Aimez Les Poitrines', a number glorifying the size and shape of Parisian women's breasts over other women's, including women in Poona, Bali, Spain and similar romantic Edens of the world. Sung in the show by Iris Ashley, as Madeleine, a well-endowed Parisian cocotte, the tune served as a titillating reminder to mankind that 'when zat feeling comes a-stealing' Madeleine was the one to 'call on'. Another tune that showed Cole at his wicked best was 'The Physician' a humorous anatomical inventory of the heroine's body from the viewpoint of an overzealous medical man who also happens to be one of the schoolgirl's long line of lovers. As recounted by Evangeline, the English schoolgirl played by Gertrude Lawrence, the song deftly enumerated all the parts of her body that the physician adored: her bronchial tubes, her epiglottis, her medulla oblongata, her pancreas and so on. Unfortunately, as the song makes very clear in the last line of the refrain ('but he never said he loved me'), the doctor was too carried away with the individual parts of Evangeline's anatomy to love her for herself.

Cole Porter himself thought that *Nymph Errant* was the best score he ever wrote, although apart from its three hits ('Experiment', 'The Physician' and Elisabeth Welch's great number 'Solomon') it remains among his least known internationally, largely because, at the time, the utter Englishness of the heroine denied the show an afterlife either on Broadway or on film. Indeed so unfamiliar is the show today that the sleeve notes for a recent re-issue of some of the songs solemnly announce it to be the musical version of 'Margaret Kennedy's celebrated novel *The Constant Nymph*.'

Though it was clear as soon as Porter began playing his score back in London to Cochran and to Gertie that they were now dealing with a considerably sexier version of James Laver's novel than had originally been contemplated, so delighted were they – and indeed Mr Laver – by Porter's scintillating score that they could hardly wait to get into rehearsal.

Gertie had another cause for celebration that summer of 1932: she had found herself a new lover – Douglas Fairbanks junior. She had also, she told Bea Lillie, taken a house in Berkeley Square: 'Well, dear,' replied Bea memorably, 'you'll just have to put it back again won't you?'

Pamela, meanwhile, was still in boarding school; so keen was Gertie to keep establishing her daughter's youth that Woollcott, reminded yet again by Gertie of Pamela's school, was heard to ask, 'And what classes does she teach there?'

12

YOUNG DOUG

I was still in my teens when I first met her, at the time of the first Charlot revue in New York [recalls Fairbanks] and developed a terrible crush on her, but Gertie, Bea and Buchanan were all caught up with much older friends, though they were very kind to me and got kind of used to finding me hanging around the stage door. A few years later, when the revue came out to California, I met them again at a party at my father's house, Pickfair. By this time I was older and had a moustache, and Gertie and I began to seem more or less the same generation. Then, at the very beginning of the 1930s, my father had got his divorce from Mary Pickford and I'd just got mine from Joan Crawford, and so the two of us came to London, at a time when Gertie was living on her own but seeing a lot of Eric Dudley, who used to escort her around town in the same way that Astley always had during the 1920s. Anyway she and I then began seeing a great deal of each other; she was ten or eleven years older than me, but she looked a lot younger, and I guess I must have looked a lot older. Increasingly she began inviting me to her parties and to meet her friends, and I found myself trying to nudge Eric Dudley out of the way so that I could have her to myself.

Dudley was very good-looking, dripped with charm, and both he and his brothers became good friends of mine, which made it all the more difficult to have to fight him for Gertie. She, of course, loved every moment of it; liked nothing better than having two men competing for her affections the way that Astley and Bert Taylor once had.

I don't think either Gertie or I ever seriously considered marriage, but we had some wonderful times together. She was very temperamental, very jealous, could be exhausting, moody, difficult—but also enchanting and alive and very funny. Later we tried to work together and indeed had one big stage success [*Moonlight is Silver*], but it was never easy to keep our professional lives and our private lives separate. In the end I had to go back to the States and we drifted apart, but some of my happiest memories of the 1930s are the months we spent together.

But she could be terrifying. Once we had a great row because I'd been seeing someone else, or anyway she thought I had, and she began throwing furniture at me, so I ran out in the street and jumped on a bus that was passing, and she just ran into the street after me and continued throwing things at the bus with me sitting inside pretending to the other passengers that I didn't know who she was. The bus got into Putney before I dared get off it.

Later, in the Second World War, Fairbanks also met up with Astley – one of the more curious aspects of Gertrude Lawrence's relationships was that many of her lovers tended in later life to befriend each other, presumably to compare notes on survival techniques after the whirlwind of Gertie's tempestuous friendship had passed them by.

Cochran was determined to spare no expense on *Nymph Errant*: he was already paying three creators (Laver for the original novel, Romney Brent for the adaptation and Cole Porter for the score) and he now brought in Doris Zinkeisen to do the sets and costumes, Brent himself to direct and, perhaps most intriguingly, a revolutionary young American choreographer on her first major musical theatre assignment. She was Agnes de Mille, niece of the great Hollywood czar, and she was soon writing home to mother instalments of a fascinating rehearsal logbook:

Cole Porter is a small, finely boned and fastidious little man with a round doll head like a marionette's (Charlie McCarthy), large staring eyes and a fixed and pleased expression that I rather think has nothing to do with his emotions . . . he barely speaks but, make no mistake, he is the most powerful person in the theater not excepting Charles Cochran. His rhymes are fabulous, male, female, middle word which I suppose could be called neuter. 'How do you do this?' I asked marvelling. 'It's easy,' he replied. 'It's just fun. Anyone can. Get a rhyming dictionary.' That's the answer, of course . . .

Our author, James Laver, is a bookish young man in a bowler, with a muted, slightly eighteenth-century air, the keeper of prints at the Victoria and Albert Museum. It seems he has his raffish moments, this play being one of them. I think it's silly, a mere excuse for good songs and Gertie's dresses . . .

Romney Brent has ability, and is by all odds the pleasantest person to work with I have yet encountered, as well as the most intelligent. Gertie on the other hand, although warm and charming, has been something rather special to deal with. In fact, I've left every rehearsal cursing with frustration. I finally asked Cochran if she really liked what I was giving her. He says she adores it. It dawned on me then that she actually thinks she is doing exactly what I ask. She never does eight consecutive bars twice the same way. She's more particular about her hats, I can tell you.

Gertie's art is built on instinct and improvisation. She disciplines her performance, I'm told, no more than her rehearsals, changing with whim and temperature and without warning. You expect Gertie downstage; she comes in centre back – even with the curtain up and a paying audience. You expect her to play *grazioso* and gently; she is *allegro vivace* and sharp. You expect her in a dark-green silk; she is in transparent gauze. But she's always fun, on and off stage, always . . .

Well, perhaps not always. On 16 September, Agnes de Mille was writing home from Manchester:

At dress rehearsal yesterday Gertie suddenly decided onstage that she hated her first act finale costume although, naturally, she'd been at all the fittings. Suddenly at that moment she couldn't abide it. She pouted and fretted and Cockie, instead of saying it was too late and to get on with her job, patted her on the cheek and said there, there, she'd have a new one on the next night. My heart turned over for Zinkeisen. If anyone had carried on in dress rehearsal about a dance this way! Zinkeisen was already making a pencil sketch of a new red velvet. The specifications were phoned to London and a messenger despatched on the next train with the drawing. Gertie will have it in time for opening. Throughout all this our author, James Laver, sat by admiring. Well, by God, so did I. Before openings, I'm told, Gertie goes to the theater with three or four outfits of her own for every scene and spends the day choosing. It distracts her from nervous horrors. It also gives the costume designer – who is never consulted – fits.

For James Laver, 'The combination of Cochran and Gertrude Lawrence was irresistible . . . on the [Manchester] first night of *Nymph Errant* I took Gertrude Lawrence in a taxi to the Opera House. She sobbed in my arms, crying ''I can't go on! I can't go on!'' But, of course, she did go on and in two minutes had the audience at her feet . . . I suppose I shall never be involved in any capacity in a more ''glamorous'' affair. Manchester had suffered an invasion of fur-coats and orchids and white ties. The Fairbanks party had taken a whole row of the stalls for themselves and their friends. The London critics attended in force and, when we got back to the Midland Hotel, the stairs leading up to the dining room were lined five deep with people clapping and cheering Gertrude Lawrence.'

For Agnes de Mille, more immediately involved in the show's mechanics than the author of its original book, it seems to have been a slightly less rosy world première:

The show began and it was, as I'd suspected, piffling. The Cole Porter songs are enchanting. The dances stopped the show, however; that's the God's truth . . . and Gertie. Ah, Gertie! As Frank Collins [the stage manager] said, 'She is like a racehorse. When the curtain goes up, her best foot is always forward. You can count on her as on the Queen. There will be no public error. She delivers. She leads the field. She breaks the tape', and also my heart a little, because it is never by any chance my exact work she is performing. Who cares? She sells tickets. She proceeds as I have told you by improvization. This may be rough on the play and the other actors but it means that her great nights are incandescent, and on this night she was pure magic. I've never witnessed the like—indeed I haven't. She was, as predicted, nothing like what she's been in rehearsals; the stage was nevertheless jumping with excitement. Acting shimmered. Gertie moves like a fish through shadows, the creation of her unexpected invention. She is funny, bright, touching, irresistible. When she walks, she streams; when she kicks, she flashes. Her speaking voice is a kind of song, quite unrealistic but lovely, and her pathos cuts under all, direct and sudden. Her eyes fill, her throat grows husky, she trembles with wonder. The audience weeps. She can't sing, but who cares?

The celebrations in Manchester that night involved not only the company of *Nymph Errant*; Fairbanks was there to be with Gertie, as was Noël with his usual acid-sharp advice about cuts needed before London, and so was Sibyl Colefax who seldom missed a party. Such was the American interest in *Nymph Errant* (both Cole Porter and Gertrude Lawrence being regarded there as fundamentally Broadway property) that an entire NBC radio crew travelled to Manchester to broadcast live from there a half-hour coast-to-coast programme about the making of the show. In the interests of drama, Cochran himself agreed to act out a little 'scene' wherein he calmed down a supposedly furious Romney Brent who wished to 'sack' Gertie for arriving late at a rehearsal. He also agreed to interview several of his 'young ladies' who were forming the chorus, and history was therefore made with the first-ever (if somewhat less than totally factual) trans-Atlantic backstage broadcast.

The only person who seemed less than thrilled by the arrival of *Nymph Errant* in Manchester was the father of its author: Arthur J. Laver, a local preacher and chapel steward, gave a lengthy press interview denouncing the show's immorality, though he did admit at the end that he hadn't actually been to see it himself.

There was, however, still a great deal of work to do before *Nymph Errant* was ready to face London audiences a month later: one of the singers got fired for sounding, said Cochran, 'like a Czarina vomiting' and a number that had gone rather too well (while not performed by Gertie herself) was moved to a spot in the show where it would be less of a threat to the star. A decade later, when the same thing happened with a Danny Kaye number in Gertie's *Lady in the Dark*, she had acquired the strength and self-confidence simply to leave the number where it was and rise above it – but not yet. 'Gertie', reported Agnes de Mille a week or so into their Manchester try-out, 'continues unpredictable. The other night she wore two dresses no one had ever seen. Also, she took off all her underpinnings for the Turkish scene, and the actor who was playing opposite her, on being confronted with his star virtually naked, was so surprised he had to leave the stage in order to recover himself. Gertie and young Doug [Fairbanks] thought this very funny.'

By early October they were re-rehearsing at the Adelphi in London and, though the box-office queues were unprecedented, or perhaps precisely because they were, a certain insecurity had begun to manifest itself backstage. Agnes de Mille wrote: 'The show is far from first-rate. The loss of morale in the cast has been profound and subtle. Cole Porter has disappeared, as I believe he always does under similar circumstances.' Tempers were now fraying; Cochran was (unusually) beginning to lose his nerve, and much to Miss de Mille's fury he even brought in another choreographer to insert some irrelevant tap routines. Then came the London first night, and Agnes de Mille stopped by Gertie's dressing room to wish her luck: 'She'd been closeted in there since ten in the morning trying on dresses without, by the way, either the permission or the assistance of the designer. Not even her secretary dared speak to her. She was making up in a state of manic euphoria. Beside her were young Doug's flowers, £50-worth. Two men had to lift the basket down from the stage door. The top roses brushed the ceiling . . .Then she handed me a present. A big box [containing] a milk-white vase from Asprey with a spray of absolutely exquisite pastel-coloured flowers made of feathers. It sounds tacky. It was enchanting – leave it to Gertie.'

For James Laver, out front-of-house, 'The foyer of the Adelphi Theatre was full of well-known faces, from Somerset Maugham to Elsa Maxwell, from Lady Lavery to Cecil Beaton. And at the Savoy afterwards the scenes at

Manchester were repeated. I suppose it was natural that I should have been made a little dizzy by all this, especially as my share of the royalties was rather more than ten times the amount of my official emoluments. The film rights were purchased by Twentieth Century Fox. I began to toy with the idea of giving up the Museum and living by my pen. It was as well that wiser thoughts prevailed for, in the following year, I paid out in income tax more than my entire earnings from all sources.'

Although the first night was a huge social success, the reviews for *Nymph Errant* next morning reflected some of the uncertainty that the cast themselves had begun to feel about the show. Critics generally much preferred Cole Porter's score for *Gay Divorce* (which Fred Astaire was then also playing in London) and accused him here of writing 'minor Noël Coward numbers'. Though ecstatic for Gertie, other notices referred to *Nymph Errant* as 'a sort of pantomime for intellectuals' and the critic of the *Observer* reckoned: 'The piece is doomed to failure; in sentiment, on which the English public singly dotes, it is as parched as a pea. And then again there is the deterrent of its unrelenting wit, the one quality of which the English public is uniquely shy. If it is rescued it will be because of "Solomon", a hot ditty bawled by Elisabeth Welch. This, though I hate it, is undoubtedly the hit of the show.'

A combination, however, of the advance bookings and word-of-mouth, which suggested that the show was in fact rather more enjoyable than many critics had indicated, got *Nymph Errant* off to a flying start at the Adelphi. After a week or two Agnes de Mille again dropped by Gertie's dressing room:

It is always a mass of flowers and there is always a bucket of iced champagne in the corner. 'Come in, darling. Come in,' she carols. 'Have some champagne,' her eyes moving beyond me to see if there were possibly a man in attendance. She never looks at me directly. I imagine she looks men in the eyes. But how can I be sure? She has never looked into mine or any woman's I've noticed. She fixes on men wholly, and although sweet and pleasant to women, is in the end oblivious to them. She is a coquette *par excellence*, and unfailingly successful. Many women, however, adore her. In her house in London every night at midnight is spread, I am told, a rich supper—pheasant, caviare, crêpes, roast beef and of course champagne. She gathers up whomever she wishes and takes them home. The staff are always ready. She lives on the scale of a duchess. She collects jewels as people collect gramophone records, and after every admirer's visit there is a fine new piece. The white ties and black tails flash in and out of her dressing room like blackbirds, and there have been near encounters and narrow misses. Gertie bubbles through it all, vastly amused, and the new pins and bracelets keep on appearing and being replaced. There was the tale of how on the opening night in a short-lived comedy drama, she found to her astonishment that all the stones in her stage jewelry had been replaced by real ones. There are rumours of Young Doug saying at breakfast to Gertie the other morning, 'Look out the window, Gertie,' and there, tied up in the Thames, was her new yacht right before her new house in Cheyne Row. None of this is to imply that she is anything less than a great big stunning star and deserving of all . . . Lawrence has bewitching, quicksilver grace, wit, prettiness, chic, and outrageous fun. Her energy is legendary. Her chic and fun have set the style in whatever city or place she graces.

Nymph Errant ran on at the Adelphi through the winter of 1933, achieving a neither spectacular nor shameful total of a hundred and fifty-four performances in a run of just under five months.

But it was during this run of *Nymph Errant*, which should have been one of the happiest of Gertie's career for she had seldom before and was seldom again to receive quite the same measure of personal (unconnected with Coward) acclaim in her own native city, that the difference between the way she was living and the way she could afford to live finally caught up with her.

For a long time now she had had a very high standard of living; though she had never lacked wealthy escorts (not only the Earl of Dudley but Ivor Guest, later Viscount Wimbourne, and the Marquis de Casa Maury were among those tactfully referred to at the time as her 'close friends') she had always taken a certain pride, rooted in her own childhood financial insecurity, in paying her own way. This arrangement meant that although she had no qualms at all about accepting, indeed collecting, rich gifts, it was usually she who paid her own very considerable household costs. She may have been (in Agnes de Mille's thoughtful analysis) a coquette, but she was seldom, if ever, a kept woman. She would cheerfully take diamonds, but cash would have been an insult and it was the cash which had long since run out.

For a while, she lived easily and happily on extended credit from everyone; she was after all a very big star, playing in a huge West End theatre in a show which was a popular if not critical success; shopkeepers and traders of the time were by and large an obsequious lot, eager not to lose customers especially if they happened to be famous and in a position to recommend their favourite retailers to others at their own exalted level of society. Miss Lawrence was known to have wealthy friends inside and outside the theatre;

true, her bills were seldom actually being paid but that time would surely come, and in the meantime it was always a pleasure to serve her, especially as she made a point of telling all journalists precisely who dressed her and in what.

That whole arrangement, which had lasted throughout the latter half of the 1920s and now well into the 1930s, fell totally apart one winter morning at the beginning of 1934 when the Inland Revenue let it be known that they were after Miss Lawrence for the payment of five years' back taxes on money earned on both sides of the Atlantic. There was at this stage no talk of bankruptcy, but occasional gossip-column references to Gertie's 'financial embarrassment' had the effect of alerting her many creditors to the fact that, if she was having trouble paying the Revenue, then she might also be having trouble finding the money for them. It was not long before some of them decided on some action of their own.

13

TONIGHT AT 8.30

'My mother never really understood the kind of financial chaos her affairs were in', recalled Pamela, 'largely because nobody in England ever dared to explain it all to her. Whenever her secretary or someone did find the courage to raise the subject Gertie would fly into terrible rages and so, to quiet her down and make sure she got to the theatre on time, they would simply have to let the matter drop. In the end it took an American, Fanny Holtzmann, to sort the whole thing out and by then it was very nearly too late.'

For the time being, however, life went on more or less as usual; true, the creditors were getting a little more restive, but there was still a sizeable salary coming in every week from *Nymph Errant* and the Inland Revenue had as yet done no more than request meetings with Gertie, most of which she managed to forget to attend. Aware that her only real hope of solvency now as always was to stay in constant work, the moment *Nymph Errant* reached the end of its faintly disappointing run in the spring of 1934, she decided to work for the first time with her beloved Young Doug in a play called *The Winding Journey* by Philip Leader, which opened in Manchester towards the end of May and somehow never managed to wind its way into London. As Fairbanks said: 'Neither Gee, nor I, nor Binkie Beaumont, who was presenting it for H. M. Tennent, thought it was not really good enough to risk bringing in to the West End, so a great friend of Noël's and Gertie's, the novelist Clemence Dane, was brought in to try and rescue it, but she said she'd rather start again and write us an altogether different play and that duly became *Moonlight is Silver.*'

But first there was the summer and Gertie, in recognition of her increasing financial problems, decided she would not be renting the usual villa in the South of France. Instead, she rented one on Majorca. Fairbanks remembered:

I didn't have any money then either, but I managed to scrape the fare together and I decided to surprise her, so I took the night boat over, got a taxi to Formentor, changed, shaved at the hotel and asked if there was an English lady renting a little cottage there. The manager pointed to the largest villa on the horizon, so I climbed the hill, rang the bell and waited. Gertie had said, back in London, that she was going there to be alone, to rest up after the winter and to think about her future. But when she saw me on the doorstep she went ashen, whispered 'Eric Dudley's here – get out,' and closed the door. Disconsolate, I made my way back to London; years and years went by, and long after the war I was sitting in White's one day reading the papers and Eric Dudley came in, so we began to reminisce about the past in general and specifically about that summer in Majorca, and I told him the whole story of my arrival there and then he too went ashen. He hadn't ever been to Majorca with Gertie. The question is, then, who the hell was she in that villa with? Now she's dead, and we shall never find out.

Back in London, Gertie and Doug began in the late summer to rehearse *Moonlight is Silver*, which Clemence Dane herself was directing with a strong supporting cast including Cecil Parker, Barry Jones, Alexis France, Helen Hayes and Martita Hunt. Given that kind of support and considerable public interest in the offstage affair of the two stars, the play could hardly fail, though a number of critics echoed Ivor Brown's feeling that '*Moonlight is Silver* is one of those plays which would stop soon after they began if the characters showed a grain of common sense.' It concerned a mining engineer (Fairbanks) who, returning home, is so convinced that his wife (Gertie) has been unfaithful to him that she ultimately decides to let him think she has. In the end, of course, her innocence is proved and all ends happily, but, without the benefit of a strong director, Gertie was apparently up to all her old overacting tricks again. According to *The Times*, 'Miss Lawrence may be a perpetual delight but in a play like this where the one need is for sincerity, she does tend to indulge her mannerisms at the expense of emotional power.'

Miss Dane had, however, borrowed a trick or two from her old friend

Noël Coward; when the action was in danger of slowing to near-standstill, Gertie would make her way over to the piano and croon a little number composed by the author and Richard Addinsell:

> Moonlight is silver,
> Sunlight is gold,
> We shall remember
> When we grow old . . .

The potency of cheap music was however on this occasion not quite enough; though the play was by no means another *Private Lives* it would probably have lasted a little longer than four months had Gertie not developed an abcess in one ear and had to leave the show. This news, by the time it had crossed the Atlantic, had somehow become considerably expanded: DEATH THREATENS GERTRUDE LAWRENCE headlined the *Chicago Herald* for 20 December 1934, and Gertie then had to spend much of her convalescent time writing to friends in New York that reports of her impending demise had been greatly exaggerated.

By the beginning of 1935 she was entirely recovered; Doug had been constantly by her bedside ('Among his many gifts to her,' reported one gossip column, 'have been diamond and platinum jewelry, a magnificent black sports car and, of course, the yacht which she has duly christened *Grateful*') and now the two of them were planning to work together again, this time in a film version of *La Bohème* to be called simply *Mimi*. It was, reported the film critic of *The Times*, yet another of Gertie's celluloid disasters:

On the stage, the chief charm of Miss Gertrude Lawrence is her extreme sophistication, her gift of making an amusing line sound wittier than it is, and her ability to take control of any situation. There is no reason why these talents should not have been reproduced on the screen, but in this film good care is taken to see that they are not . . . Miss Lawrence may be an extremely good actress but she has nothing at all to do with Mimi, who for one thing has consumption – and that is the last complaint from which any character taken by Miss Lawrence should suffer . . . the film is all very nice in its own uninspired way but the question which hung in the air before the lights went out is still there when they come on again – what has Miss Lawrence to do with it all?

But by early in 1935 Gertie had a great deal more to worry about than a few bad film reviews. Among the huge pile of unpaid bills which had been accumulating these past five years on Gertie's various London and New York desks were two from local laundries, known as the Mayfair Laundry and Cheyne Laundry. Together they totalled just under £50, and the only reason they had never been paid was that Gertie (whose weekly flower bill came to rather more than that) had simply never bothered. The owners of these two laundries, Mr William Cleghorn of Acton and Mrs Katherine MacLean of Church Street, Chelsea, now found themselves in the uneasy position of the child who in the Andersen fairy tale is the first one to remark that the King has no new clothes on. Being small local dry-cleaners, they had apparently not heard of the system whereby big stars of the period were allowed virtually unlimited credit with no questions asked. It seemed to them, after waiting a year or so for their money and still not receiving it, that the reason was probably because Miss Lawrence did not actually have £50, in which case she should surely be declared bankrupt. It was as simple as that, and they duly took out a writ. By 26 February, the whole of Gertie's complex financial affairs was in the hands of the Official Receiver. That morning the *Daily Mirror* reported:

Liabilities of £24,729 were disclosed at the first meeting held at London Bankruptcy Buildings of the creditors of Gertrude Howley, the actress professionally known as Gertrude Lawrence, residing at Cumberland Place, Regent's Park. Mr S. W. Hood, Official Receiver, dealt with ninety-nine proofs of debt, amounting to £6,802. The chairman reported that her assets were valued at £1,879. Further liabilities included a claim of £14,000 by the Inland Revenue in respect of the debtor's earnings while in America, and, apart from that claim, there were liabilities amounting to about £10,000 . . . the Chairman added that the debtor attributed her insolvency to having lived beyond her means and to the unexpected demand for Income Tax in respect of her American earnings, although she had already paid the full amounts demanded in America.'

In fact she hadn't, and there was to be a subsequent bankruptcy hearing when she returned to the USA; nor, if gossip-column reports of 'fabulous' jewellery had any truth at all, does it seem likely that Gertie's total worldly possessions only added up to £1,800. On the other hand, assuming she had not been too meticulous in having her personal possessions valued, it does seem likely that there wasn't much else. She had always lived in rented accommodation, had put the only insurance policy she ever bought in her daughter Pamela's name, and it is entirely possible that the yachts and cars invariably connected with her name in print had in fact been long-term loans from wealthy admirers rather than outright gifts. Jewels aside, then, she was at this juncture quite conceivably worth less than £2,000 and had no difficulty at all in seeing herself as a sudden Cinderella: 'When I came out of the court I had nothing, literally, but the clothes I stood in. Nothing else. My cars, my apartment, my jewels, even most of my clothes were immediately seized . . . Dorothy, my faithful maid, Mack, my dog, and I stood on the pavement outside the house . . . we had literally not a roof to crawl under. No money and no credit.'

But she was not left there to starve quietly with the dog and the maid on the pavement; her agent and manager at that time was Bill O'Bryen, who happened to be in partnership with Bill Linnit (later of the Linnit & Dunfee theatrical management) and it was Linnit who was duly persuaded to move in with O'Bryen, thereby vacating his flat in Albany for the use of Gertie plus maid and dog. She may have been poor, but she was no longer homeless.

Though she did not much care for the humiliation of the *Daily Mirror* 'Bankrupt Actress' headlines, as all her many other creditors now became considerably more importunate, in one sense the arrival of the Official Receiver had been almost a relief to Gertie. She had always lived in the belief that money was not something she should ever have to think about, and now here was the entire machinery of the British legal system proving her right. Her affairs were for the courts to worry about, and Gertie took the ever-optimistic view that at least her insolvency was at last in professional care, leaving her free to think about her career, which she had always found of considerably more interest than her debts.

That spring she went into an all-star Galsworthian stage epic at His Majesty's; called *Hervey House*, it was billed as the work of 'C. R. Avery' from behind which pen-name there soon emerged the distinguished American actress Jane Cowl. What Miss Cowl had written was a kind of latter-day *Forsyte Saga*, and the management gave it to a young director by the name of Tyrone Guthrie, who rapidly found himself having to tackle several bulls and at least one sacred cow. As Guthrie wrote later:

Hervey House was a fictitious ducal mansion in London; the story was romantic, set in the Edwardian era. There was the duke, very handsome; the duchess, equally handsome and very pure and good; the duke's mistress, very handsome and, to make up for not being very pure, very charming; the duke's secretary; 'character' aunts and uncles; a devoted lady's maid; a good old butler and dear God knows how many footmen, tweenies, grooms, gamekeepers and pantry boys. The scene changed at least fifteen times, from attic to basement of the great house. It had no particular resemblance to real life, but it was written with great verve and conveyed a rather charming admiration for the good old days and the good old English upper orders in a way which no English writer could have managed except tongue in cheek. We decided it would be an appropriate offering for King George v's Jubilee, done on a grand scale with a whopping star cast and lavish production. Nicholas Hannen was engaged to play the duke, with Fay Compton as his duchess and Gertrude Lawrence in the comparatively small but grateful role of the mistress. The cast was also to include Ben Webster, Margaret Rutherford, Alan Webb and Sebastian Shaw, but it was felt that certain alterations were necessary and I was despatched to America to discuss them with the author . . . I explained that His Majesty's Theatre was very large and that the management intended a lavish and spectacular production. Jane Cowl replied that a large theatre would kill her play, which was intimate. I queried the economic possibility of presenting in a small theatre a play with such a huge cast. She said they could double up, and with a pencil made an efficient plan for this on the tablecloth. I countered with the large number of sets. More plans were drawn, showing how it could all be staged with three good bits of furniture and some plywood screens. The tablecloth began to look like the plan of a maze . . . in the end I convinced her that it was the alterations or else no production, and the play was then a failure for just the very reason that Jane had foretold. It *was* a small intimate piece, which in my production was blown up to a size in which its charm was lost. The actors did well. The sets by Molly MacArthur were handsome but so complicated that, on the opening night of the try-out in Manchester, one of the actors got lost and flew about in a frenzy through room after room, pre-set on a turntable. The actors on stage, making up lines and pretending to look for their lost colleague in the garden, were startled to see him crawl through the fireplace.

But when Guthrie's production finally reached London the critics were respectful, especially towards Gertie's final scene as an old lady in a white wig 'showing just how gracefully she will still be delighting us in her sixties', a prophecy that was not alas to come true.

The theatregoing public however, not yet ready apparently for Edwardian nostalgia of this *Upstairs, Downstairs* kind, stayed away in their hundreds from *Hervey House*, which closed in the early summer after a run of barely six weeks.

Gertie, eager to escape the nervous demands of her creditors and the rather cramped confines of Bill Linnit's Albany flat, went down to Goldenhurst in Kent to stay for a few days with Noël at his country house.

There he was at last able to show her the basic lay-out and most of the scripts for a new and elaborate vehicle that he had constructed for their respective talents in partnership: a series of ten (nine survived) one-act plays ranging in mood from slapstick comedy through musical romances to high tragedy, in all of which they would both appear, playing them first in London and then in New York as alternating triple bills under the omnibus title *Tonight at 8.30.*

The success of *Private Lives*, followed by Noël's determination to do something to help his old friend out of her money troubles, had made him think long and hard about another way to bring himself and Gertrude Lawrence together again on stage in parts that would allow them to display their varied acting and singing talents to the best possible advantage. *Private Lives* had, in his view and that of many of the people surrounding him, proved that the combination of 'Noël and Gertie' conjured up a box-office magic which could be invoked again, given the right vehicle. But he needed to write something more than just another light comedy; he needed to write something that would be varied enough to let them both work in their highly individual ways, and also exciting enough to overcome the boredom that he found in nightly repetition of the same role. Given all these requirements, it soon occurred to him that three plays would be better than one and that, by the same token, nine would be better than three.

In the first quarter of this century, however, with a few distinguished exceptions to be found among the work of Bernard Shaw and J. M. Barrie, the one-act play had fallen on hard times; in the provinces some were still being presented, as under-cast and badly produced curtain-raisers, but by and large the *genre* had disappeared as the result of widespread managerial belief that the public would not come to see double or triple bills because they felt that they would somehow be getting less rather than more value for their ticket money. Yet for Noël, the one-act play 'having a great advantage over a long one (in that it can sustain a mood without technical creaking or overpadding) deserves a better fate, and if by careful writing, acting and producing I can do a little towards re-instating it in its rightful pride, then I shall have achieved one of my more sentimental ambitions.'

By the end of August, Noël had finished all of the plays and decided that, after rehearsing first with Gertie at Goldenhurst, where she also played him a mean game of croquet, they would then assemble a company in London under his friend John Wilson's management and open at the Opera House in Manchester in mid-October. Then, after a nine-week provincial tour and a brief Christmas holiday, they would open in London at the Phoenix (scene of their triumphant *Private Lives* six years earlier) in the January of 1936.

During the various provincial, London and Broadway runs of *Tonight at 8.30* the sequence and arrangement of the plays was altered frequently in a kind of permanent repertoire, and even the title went through such pragmatic local variations as *Tonight at 8.00*, *Tonight at 7.30* and, for matinées, *Today at 2.30*.

The triple bill that launched the whole endeavour in Manchester consisted of *We Were Dancing* followed by *The Astonished Heart* and then *Red Peppers*. Of these, the first was really no more than a curtain-raiser, an acid little comedy about Gertie deciding in the cold light of dawn that she would not after all be eloping from her marriage to run off with a marvellous lover of the night before; the second was a psychological drama (later filmed by Coward with Margaret Leighton in Gertie's role) about a suicidal relationship; and the third was the one which, though the least ambitious, was to become in many ways the most popular and successful of all the plays in the cycle.

In *Red Peppers* Coward managed, with satire tinged by a certain sentimental nostalgia, to recapture the precise flavour of tatty music-hall acts struggling to survive on bad touring dates. Not only the back-stage bickering of Lily and George Pepper but also their appalling musical numbers ('Has Anybody Seen Our Ship?' and 'Men About Town') suggested that Coward had a very sharp eye for the decline of the old 'Halls', and with a faint feeling of guilty delight Gertie realized that she was here going to be allowed to mock precisely the kind of seedy touring life she had been living with Walter Williams back in 1921:

LILY: I'm sick of you and the whole act. It's lousy anyway.

GEORGE: The act was good enough for my Mum and Dad, and it's good enough for you.

LILY: Times have changed a bit since your Mum and Dad's day, you know. There's electric light now and telephones and a little invention called Moving Pictures. Nobody wants to see the 'Red Peppers' for three bob when they can see Garbo for ninepence!

GEORGE: That's just where you're wrong, see! We're flesh and blood we are — the public would rather see flesh and blood any day than a cheesy photograph. Put Garbo on on a Saturday night in Devonport, and see what would happen to her!

LILY: Yes, look what happened to us!

GEORGE: That wasn't Devonport, that was Southsea.

LILY: Well, wherever it was, the Fleet was in.

GEORGE: If you think the act's so lousy it's a pity you don't rewrite some of it.

LILY: Ever tried going into St Paul's and offering to rewrite the Bible?

14

GROSS EXTRAVAGANCE

While Gertie continued to work with Noël first on the rehearsals and then the tour of *Tonight at 8.30*, her creditors had a series of private meetings in order to establish what could be salvaged from the wreck of her accounts. A list of her assets published in the summer revealed: 'Jewellery worth £300, a bracelet costing £500, a mink coat now valued at £50, furniture and fittings worth £500 and ''a certain amount of pawned jewellery which has still not been redeemed'' ', though whether that list represented Gertie's total worldly assets or merely those she was prepared to have on public discussion remained a moot point. At all events she was now a declared bankrupt: 'Gertrude Lawrence', announced the *Daily Mail* in a sob piece, 'once a chorus girl, once a musical comedy actress, now a firmly established star is appearing in the Theatre of Tragedy – London's bankruptcy courts. She ascribes her failure to having lived beyond her means; to heavy domestic expenses; to ill health [sic] and to a demand for Income Tax on her U.S. earnings.' Smaller print revealed that Gertie now had no less than £16,000 worth of jewellery in pawn, and that her pre-tax earnings for the years 1932–35 had totalled £19,000. Her problem, she said, was that though her average annual income was now £6,700, yet her annual expenses 'including payments to daughter and parents' were just over £10,000. Somebody, said Gertie in one of her more memorable utterances of this period, would have to do something about it all.

As usual it was left to Noël to get the whole thing into a somewhat more cool and clear perspective; during rehearsals for *Tonight at 8.30* he was asked by the two Bills (Gertie's then managers Linnit and O'Bryen) if he and his own friend and manager Jack Wilson would join them in a united attempt (after one of her more costly shopping sprees) to explain to Gertie the facts of a bankrupt's life. They all agreed to meet for supper one night. 'Gertie', predicted Noël, 'will be in one of her three moods. Either she'll be very angry and break all the furniture, or she'll be very tearful and make it all wringing wet, or she'll just sit there with her hands on her lap and say that she doesn't understand any of it. I only hope to God she pretends not to understand.'

In the event, she simply failed to show up at all.

Halfway through the first week of *Tonight at 8.30* in Manchester, Coward brought in the second of his three triple bills; this started with *Hands Across The Sea*, a light comedy about Gertie as a London socialite faced with the sudden and total confusion of the arrival in her front hall of two colonial guests and a Maharajah who might possibly have religious objections to the comedian Douglas Byng. It was designed primarily as a vehicle for Gertie, and years later Coward found he still could not think of the play 'without remembering the infinite variety of her inflections, her absurd, scatterbrained conversations on the telephone, her frantic desire to be hospitable and charming, and her expression of blank dismay when she suddenly realised that her visitors were not who she thought they were at all. It was a superb performance in the finest traditions of high comedy, already now over and done with forever, but as far as I am concerned never to be forgotten.'

Coward always denied that the characters portrayed by Gertie and himself were based on Lady Edwina and Lord Louis Mountbatten, both of whom were close friends and not easily fooled by the denials. 'Noël gave us a couple of tickets for the first night,' Lord Louis said forty years later, 'which I always thought was the very least he could have done considering that he got a whole play out of us.' It did not, however, hurt the friendship, and a few years later Noël was to pay Lord Louis an altogether more dignified compliment by portraying him as the noble Captain D in his classic film of the war at sea, *In Which We Serve*.

The second play in this cycle, *Fumed Oak*, was set in an altogether different social milieu, and had Noël as the down-trodden, brow-beaten suburban husband Henry Gow who, in a worm-will-turn final scene, finds the

Public and private lives:
(left) with Leslie Howard in *Candle-Light*, 1929, and (below) with Noël Coward in *Private Lives*, 1930.

ABOVE AND RIGHT: Noël and Gertie in two of the nine plays that comprised the three evenings of *Tonight at 8.30*, 1936: 'Family Album' and (below) 'Shadow Play'.

OPPOSITE: Two of the three films Gertie made in 1932: with Gerald du Maurier in *Lord Camber's Ladies* and (below) with Laurence Olivier and the body in *No Funny Business*.

As Liza, the *Lady in the Dark*, in Moss Hart and
Kurt Weill's revolutionary Broadway musical, 1941.

Star in battledress:
Gertie as a driver for the
American Red Cross and
(below) later on a naval tour
of the Pacific.

Gertrude Lawrence as Mrs A.:
(left) with Richard Aldrich at the time of
their marriage and (below) at the Cape
Playhouse in Massachussetts.

OPPOSITE:
ABOVE LEFT With Raymond Massey at
the time of their Broadway *Pygmalion*,
1946.

ABOVE RIGHT Her last London
appearance, in Daphne du Maurier's
September Tide, 1949.

BELOW Her first and last Hollywood film,
The Glass Menagerie, 1950.

WARNER BROS. STUDIOS
WARDROBE TEST
FOR
'GLASS MENAGERIE" 368
OF
GERTRUDE LAWRENCE
AS
"AMANDA"

WARDROBE CHANGE # 1 ALT.

WORN IN { SET
SCENE 10 THRU 15

'Shall We Dance?' with Yul Brynner in her final
Broadway musical, *The King and I*, 1951.

courage to walk out on Gertie as his altogether awful wife. Then the last of the three plays in this second *Tonight at 8.30* sequence was a return to elegance, a romantic musical fantasy called *Shadow Play* in which Noël and Gertie, impeccably dressed, danced in the moonlight to the echoes of *Private Lives*:

SIMON: Well, here we are

VICKY: My name's Victoria.

SIMON: Victoria what?

VICKY: Victoria Gayforth.

SIMON: What a silly name.

VICKY: I adore it.

SIMON: That's because you're sentimental.

VICKY: Fiercely sentimental – over-romantic, too.

SIMON: Dearest darling.

VICKY: The wedding went off beautifully, didn't it?

SIMON: Brief, to the point, and not unduly musical.

VICKY: Didn't mother look nice?

SIMON: Not particularly.

VICKY: Oh, Simon!

SIMON: It was her hat, I think – it looked as though it were in a hurry and couldn't stay very long.

VICKY: Was that man who slapped you on the back your uncle?

SIMON: Yes, dear – that was my uncle.

VICKY: I'm so sorry.

SIMON: He ran away to sea, you know, when he was very young and then, unfortunately, he ran back again.

Overpowering charm was exuded through a rather transparent account of a marriage being retrieved from the brink of collapse, but *Shadow Play* (though by no means the most interesting of the plays) retains a certain technical fascination for Coward's use on the stage of such highly cinematic techniques as flashbacks and disconnected scenes played very quickly in pools of light to make up the theatrical equivalent of a *montage*.

These then were the first six plays of *Tonight at 8.30*, and alternating them, Noël and Gertie toured the British provinces throughout the autumn of 1935. Meanwhile, from London in November came better news of Gertie's financial affairs. The *New York Times*, which had taken a keen interest in the

case, reported on 8 November under the headline ACTRESS FREED FROM
BANKRUPTCY that:

Stage and screen star Gertrude Lawrence was today freed from bankruptcy,
subject to an undertaking to pay £50 per week out of her earnings until all her debts
were cleared. In the course of a public hearing, she admitted that at one period she
had received about five times as much in gifts as she had earned on the stage. Chided
by a frowning Official Receiver for 'gross extravagance', the actress said that part of
her financial woes were due to expenditures in entertaining the friends of an
unnamed former fiancé and in spending money on a trousseau which was never used.
Miss Lawrence's attorney said she admitted 'gross extravagance' and that though she
had nothing left now but her earning power, she was determined to pay off all her
liabilities. Mr Registrar Mellor noted that Miss Lawrence was a distinguished
actress, and added that extravagance was to some extent a question of degree. One
did not, he concluded, expect people in the dramatic profession to be as careful in
their expenditure as those in other classes of life.

And so, at £50 a week, Gertie slowly began paying off her debts; she was
not, though, best pleased when her now seventeen-year-old daughter Pamela
turned up in the chorus of Cochran's *Follow The Sun* and announced to the
press: 'I have done this to help Mummy. I hate the life she leads, and I want to
get her out of it. What she needs is a long vacation somewhere sunny, with no
money troubles. Deep down in my heart, I don't believe Mummy really likes
stage life all that much.'

Like it or not, and most other evidence suggests that she did, Gertie was
now committed to the London and New York runs of *Tonight at 8.30*.
Typically, she had also decided that the £50 a week which had to be repaid to
her creditors was not going to involve her cutting back any further on her
living standards. She would merely have to earn it on the side, by filming
during the day and doing cabaret stints after the shows at night.

The *Tonight at 8.30* tour had proved extremely profitable (taking just over
£26,000 in nine weeks) and towards its end Noël had slipped in a seventh
play, *Family Album*, an enchanting little mock-Victorian musical comedy
about a missing will, in place of *We Were Dancing*, with which he had never
been altogether happy. At the beginning of January 1936, therefore, the first
two sets of *Tonight at 8.30* plays opened in consecutive weeks at London's
Phoenix Theatre to a rapturous reception from first-night playgoers among
whom were the then Prince of Wales and Mrs Simpson.

Reviews varied from the disappointed to the besotted, but the general feeling was that here was something for everyone; true, Agate reckoned that the score so far was 'for the first trio of plays, 1 dud 2 wows; for the second, 1 wow, one semi-dud and one dud' but at least no one could now accuse Noël or Gertie of a lack of versatility. The plays offered them countless opportunities for virtuoso musical and dramatic solos and duets which they clutched with both hands, and the whole venture seemed dedicated to the proposition that there was now really nothing in the theatre that this partnership couldn't handle. 'I wonder', mused one playgoer after sitting through all six plays at consecutive matinée and evening performances in one day, 'what they are like on the high wire'.

But early in the London run of *Tonight at 8.30* (which Noël had warned would again only be for three months pre-Broadway) the death of King George V was announced; he had come to the throne only a few months before Noël and Gertie had first met, and his reign had spanned their entire professional careers. All theatres were of course closed on the night of his death, and the atmosphere of deep mourning in which they reopened made the jokes about bereavement in *Family Album* seem in execrably bad taste; it was therefore hauled out of the repertoire and replaced by *We Were Dancing*.

Gertie meanwhile, determined to make the extra money required for her bankruptcy settlement, had signed with Alexander Korda, the only Czar of the British motion picture industry, to play the somewhat frenetic role of the housekeeper to Charles Laughton's *Rembrandt*. Daily she would commute to the studios, taking, she noted proudly, 'the five-thirty a.m. workmen's train to Denham, filming all day and then returning to the Phoenix to do three plays every evening.' No sacrifice was apparently too great if the money still owing was to be repaid in full (which it ultimately was), though Sir Alexander's nephew, Michael Korda, reports that life on the set was less than easygoing:

Charles took a vivid dislike to the presence of Gertrude Lawrence . . . since she enjoyed exchanging dirty stories and theatrical gossip with Alex. It seemed to Laughton that Gertie Lawrence was taking up too much of Alex's time and attention and that Alex was snubbing Laughton by paying court to her. Her voice, he complained, got on his nerves, she talked out loud and laughed in an irritating way while he was preparing his scenes. Finally Laughton had Vincent [Korda] place a pair of soundproof screens around him whenever she was anywhere near the set, and he would retreat there to sulk whenever he heard her voice.

Gertie doubtless objected to the fanatical seriousness with which Laughton approached his work; Noël, though equally dedicated, was a lot more 'fun' to have around. Nevertheless, when a few months later the reviews appeared for *Rembrandt*, Gertie emerged from them with considerably more distinction than ever before in her screen career.

To play three shows a night and make a film by day was however a strain even on her robust health and energy, and shortly after shooting was completed on *Rembrandt* she duly collapsed with laryngitis. Noël insisted (here as six years ago in *Private Lives*) that he could not possibly play without her, and the Phoenix Theatre was duly closed until she recovered her voice. Never in his entire career did Noël ever play a role he had written for Gertie with any other actress, even for a single night. She, however, once played *Tonight at 8.30* without him: her co-star, in a revival several years after the war, was to be Noël's great and good friend Graham Payn and both were to work then under the Master's own direction.

Despite the laryngitis, Gertie was now in reasonably cheerful shape: the money was pouring in from both *Rembrandt* and *Tonight at 8.30* (from which she was getting not just a salary but also a royalty, since her friend Robert Montgomery had invested in it on her behalf) and she began to think that at last she could see, if not a way out of the woods, then at any rate a decent-sized clearing.

When the Phoenix reopened, Noël brought in the remaining two plays of his original scheme so that, with the reinstated *Family Album*, they could now offer customers three complete triple bills. These additions to *Tonight at 8.30* were a little high-society burglary sketch written in the Lonsdale vein called *Ways and Means* and, infinitely more intriguing, a railway-station romance for himself and Gertie called *Still Life*, which ten years later he was to expand into the screenplay for David Lean's classic film starring Celia Johnson and Trevor Howard, *Brief Encounter*.

With the repertoire at last complete, *Tonight at 8.30* ran on at the Phoenix until the end of the third week in June 1936, to achieve a total of just over 150 sold-out London performances. Ivor Brown, summing up for the *Observer*, noted that Coward, 'the man who used to write very slight long plays, has now composed some very full brief ones' and the legendary actor-manager Sir Seymour Hicks, in the audience at the very last performance, was so impressed by Noël's achievement that he insisted on presenting him with one of his own most treasured possessions, a sword which had once belonged to Edmund Kean. Noël kept it, proudly, for thirty years and then handed it on to Sir Laurence Olivier on his formation of Britain's National Theatre Company.

For Noël, the stage partnership with Gertie had again been an absolutely magical if intermittently tempestuous affair; their acting together was still part of a greater private relationship in which the audience were being allowed almost vicariously to participate for an hour or two each night, and though there was never real competition between them there were occasional rows, caused usually by Noël's determination not to let Gertie drift off from the top of her form or resort to any of her old tricks of overacting. During February he had cabled to Jack Wilson in New York: EVERYTHING LOVELY STOP CRACKING ROW WITH GERTIE OVER 'HANDS ACROSS THE SEA' LASTING SEVEN MINUTES STOP HER PERFORMANCE EXQUISITE EVER SINCE.

In March, by which time it had been agreed that Wilson would also present the plays on Broadway the following autumn, another cable from Noël, this one in mock-fury, ran: VERY SORRY FIND MY ENGAGEMENTS WILL NOT PERMIT ME APPEAR UNDER YOUR BANNER IN AMERICA UNLESS I GET A FURTHER 58 PERCENT OF THE GROSS FOR ARDUOUS TASK RESTRAINING MISS LAWRENCE FROM BEING GROCK BEATRICE LILLIE THEDA BARA MARY PICKFORD AND BERT LAHR ALL AT ONCE.

Gertie knew, however, that she was among friends and was determined not to waste a moment of their summer break between closing in London and opening on Broadway. This year there would be no villa in the South of France or even Majorca; instead, she immediately signed on for a cabaret season at the Café de Paris and agreed to make another film for Korda at Denham. This, though a much less expensive and ambitious affair than *Rembrandt*, was to give her one of the most rewarding of her screen roles. Called *Men Are Not Gods* and directed by Walter Reisch, who had been Korda's assistant back in the Vienna of the early 20s, the film told an intriguing tragi-comic tale of an actor (Sebastian Shaw) who, while playing Othello on stage to the Desdemona of his real-life actress wife (Gertie), decides to strangle her so that he may be free to marry Miriam Hopkins. Rex Harrison also turned up as a reporter, and the film achieved an interesting sub-Pirandello confusion of stage reality and actual reality. Best of all, it cast Gertie as an actress, gave her the chance to have a creditable stab at Desdemona (her only ever Shakespeare) and allowed her to be what she always anyway was on screen which was theatrical. Only this time the critics, taking due note of the plot, praised rather than blamed her for it. If there was a moral here it was perhaps that she should have played more actresses on screen – and maybe on stage, too.

But Gertrude Lawrence was only ever to make one more film, and that in Hollywood fourteen years later; for now it was back to the theatre, back to *Tonight at 8.30* and back to Broadway, where to her horror she found precisely the same sort of bankruptcy demands awaiting her as those she had only recently escaped in London. Again there was a rash of unfavourable press headlines of the BANKRUPT ACTRESS variety, but at least on this side of the Atlantic she now had the constant support and advice of her lawyer Fanny Holtzmann who rapidly negotiated for her the same kind of deal that she had been given in London – a couple of years to pay off the debts at around $150 a week to be drawn straight out of her salary. This however presupposed that she was to stay in more or less constant work, and she already knew that Noël had therefore agreed to play *Tonight at 8.30* for twice his usual three-month season. This was just as well, considering that shortly before she left England Gertie had bought herself a country house and small farm in Buckinghamshire, which had the unlikely and uncharacteristic name of 'Mopes'. It fell, as usual, to her long-suffering agent Bill O'Bryen to try and explain to her that although a lot of money was now coming in, a great deal more still had to go out in repayment of debts before she could be considered free to indulge in such extravagance. By way of a reply, Gertie sent him a cable from New York: REFERENCE MOPES KINDLY ASCERTAIN COST OF INSTALLING SWIMMING POOL.

With the kind of logic that had always hallmarked Gertie's conduct of her private life and affairs, having for the first time ever just bought herself a house in England she was only once to visit her native country again for more than a matter of weeks, and then only because a play happened to keep her there for a short time.

Apart from that and the occasional English holiday, from the Broadway opening of *Tonight at 8.30* in November 1936 through to her New York death a little less than sixteen years later, America was to be her spiritual, professional and private home. True, she may neither have known nor have planned that at this time, any more than she ever really knew or planned anything more than about a week in advance unless others organized it all for her; but she was now and forever more to be a Broadway baby.

15

BROADWAY BABY

The end of *Tonight at 8.30* in London meant not only the end of the 'Noël and Gertie' partnership in England but also the end of her Fairbanks affair. Press reports were now linking his name with Dietrich's, but there was more to it than that, as Fairbanks recalled later:

In the end, I guess we just decided amicably enough to go our separate ways. There had always been other men in her life, just as there had been other women in mine, but I shall always be grateful for the time that we spent together. She was a very funny woman, you know, and that is still kind of rare; but she was also a great star and that to her was a full-time job. Sometimes we used to escape for a weekend, taking the boat and maybe Pamela and the dog and going off up the Thames for a day or two, and I was always very keen to stay unrecognized, but Gertie after a few hours would begin waving to people on the bank, not people she actually knew but people she wanted to know her. She really loved being recognized, noticed; I think she needed it. She was never one of those actresses who disappear out the stage door after a show in an old coat and a headscarf; her exits from the theatre were as carefully choreographed and arranged as any of her stage exits. She was always 'on', maybe because that was all she knew or understood. She didn't like being alone, almost never was; I don't think she perhaps wanted to find out too much about herself, and she certainly wasn't a lady who needed time to think. I don't remember her ever thinking much.

But she could be wonderfully waspish: years after we broke up I'd married Mary Lee and we were both given house seats by Gertie for *The King and I*, so we went backstage afterwards and Gertie put on this terribly regal, condescending performance, patting Mary Lee's cheek and saying, 'Oh you dear little thing, I'm so glad Douglas married you,' and then solemnly taking out of her jewel case some pin that I'd given her and handing it to my wife. I don't think she much cared for her old flames getting married, even if she didn't plan to marry them herself.

Tonight at 8.30 opened on Broadway at the National Theatre in November 1936; in those days, before either American or British Actors' Equity had placed any restrictions on the transatlantic movement of casts, Jack Wilson's management managed to import the entire London company and they were therefore able to open the nine plays on three consecutive nights. After the second, wrote Brooks Atkinson for the *New York Times*:

Noël Coward and Gertrude Lawrence, being tired of the plays they presented on Tuesday, put on three more at the National last evening expecting to keep interested in them until tomorrow when the third bill is scheduled to go on . . . No student of the drama will ever grind out his doctor's thesis on Mr Coward's contribution to thought on the basis of the current one-act panels, nor will anyone but Mr Coward and Miss Lawrence ever give them much vibrancy on stage, for they are personal vehicles . . . but although Mr Coward has written his miniatures with skill and acts them admirably, it is Miss Lawrence's triumph and further proof that one who seemed not long ago to be merely an amusing hoyden has now become a brilliant actress.'

'Expert razzle dazzle' added the *Post*, and Burns Mantle noted: 'Coward and Lawrence fans were so happy to have their favourites back that there was a welcoming demonstration at the evening's close. Mere outsiders looked on and marveled a bit . . . nothing very serious happens in these plays and nothing dull tarnishes any part of them.'

This New York première was preceded by a Boston and Washington try-out, and it was in Washington that Noël had decided, as a joke, to send Gertie a good-luck telegram signed Fiorello La Guardia, then Mayor of New York. Accordingly he dictated it over the phone, ending with the signature:

OPERATOR: But are you really Mayor La Guardia?
NOËL: No.
OPERATOR: Then you can't sign it Mayor La Guardia. What is your real name?
NOËL: Noël Coward.

OPERATOR: Are you really Noël Coward?

NOËL: Yes.

OPERATOR: Then in that case you may sign it Mayor La Guardia.

Their New York opening was eventful, and not only because of the crowds who turned out to welcome them back to Broadway; Lucius Beebe, then a reporter with the *Herald Tribune*, agreed, as a publicity stunt for a Fifth Avenue jewellers, to wear in his lapel a diamond gardenia worth fifteen thousand pre-war dollars. During the first interval it was stolen, not in fact for publicity purposes, by a kleptomaniac English lady of noble birth who only returned it to the store after considerable police persuasion.

Soon after *Tonight at 8.30* opened at the National, news from London about the abdication of King Edward VIII caused Noël and Gertie to issue on behalf of their company a brief and dignified statement of unswerving loyalty to the crown and its new inhabitant, but privately they were both more than a little disturbed and depressed: 'I refuse to give that woman any publicity,' Gertie had earlier told reporters. As Prince of Wales, Edward VIII had been a good friend to Gertie, and in private life he had stood for a section of English high society to which she and Noël eagerly attached themselves as soon as they were able to escape their own more humble beginnings. The King's abrupt departure from the throne for the woman he loved seemed to them both unforgivably unprofessional and, worse still, it appeared to fragment a social order whose members had until now found no reason to suppose that it and they would not be secure for some years to come.

It would be an exaggeration to suggest that Gertie's decision from now on to live and work in America was consciously prompted by the events of December 1936; unconsciously, however, she may well have been made aware that the old pre-war England, the England where she had struggled to the top of the social and theatrical heap, was fast coming to its close. As far as America was concerned, she had been born, not in a London suburb, but in a Charlot revue, and she was beginning to think that maybe she liked it better that way.

Tonight at 8.30 ran on through the winter to capacity audiences, but then, in March 1937, the strain of playing nine separate roles in as many plays within a repertoire that often entailed acting no less than six of them consecutively on matinée days began to take its toll of Noël just as, a year previously in London, it had of Gertie. At first he only missed a couple of nights but then, three days after he returned to the cast, he broke down again directly after a performance and this time his New York doctor refused to let him go back to the theatre for at least a week.

On 5 March, therefore, Gertie was able to send a postcard from Atlantic City to her daughter, back in England and now known as Pamela Gordon since she had taken the first half of her father's Gordon-Howley surname, and was intent on some sort of a stage career:

Darling PG: Noël was suddenly stricken with laryngitis on Saturday last, so we've closed the plays for a whole week and your old Mum packed a grip, picked up the dog and with Dorothy [her maid] running behind made for Pennsylvania Station and the witching waves as fast as her 38-year-old legs would carry her. The dog? Oh yes, he's new, a present from Schyler Parsons, who now breeds them – he's a black miniature schnautzer, the dog I mean not Schyler, and great company. So here we are with our noses full of brine and my heart and eyes filled with the longing to see the white cliffs of Southampton again.'

After a few more weeks of the run, she and Noël were both determined to be back in England in time for the 12 May Coronation of King George VI in honour of which occasion Gertie had all of her jewellery dipped in gold: 'I shall always be glad,' she wrote later, 'I saw London again during that Coronation summer. It was wonderful—a last burst of splendour before the storm burst.'

She had no intention of staying there long though. As the run of *Tonight at 8.30* drew to its close, the ever-present Fanny Holtzmann made it clear to her that though the bankruptcy problems were receding fast, they were as yet by no means cleared and she would have to keep working as constantly as possible for at least another year. It was, therefore, no good waiting around on the off-chance that Noël might have another good idea; something had to be lined up for the autumn, and since there were now many more demands for her services coming from Broadway than the West End, the feeling was that she should consider doing a new show there for the 1937–38 season. In fact, the one she chose was so successful that it carried her through on Broadway and on a long subsequent coast-to-coast tour until the very beginning of 1939.

The play was *Susan and God*, and it was the work of a pioneering feminist American playwright called Rachel Crothers whose scripts are, in 1980, only just beginning to emerge again from the undeserved neglect in which they have languished for more than four decades. Born in 1878, Miss Crothers had her first one-act play produced in 1902; but though she was to live until 1958, *Susan and God* was in fact to be the last of her twenty-three full-length dramas. It told the story of lovable, feather-brained Susan Trexel who returns from a European vacation full of the news that she has been converted to a fashionable and wonderful new religion – the religion of love. Subsequent events, involving an alcoholic husband and a repressed daughter, suggest however that what Susan needs is not a new religion but a new understanding of those closest to her. 'God is here – inside us' is the play's final message, and it was topical enough to give Gertie the greatest success she ever had in a straight play.

Meanwhile the film of *Rembrandt* had opened in America, where critics were inclined to pay much more attention to Gertie's part in it: 'As the shrewish housekeeper who becomes Rembrandt's mistress and later second wife,' wrote the *New York American*, 'the former song-and-dance girl Gertie Lawrence shows that she has developed into practically perfection as an actress among actresses', and when, a few weeks later, *Susan and God* opened at the Plymouth on Broadway, Brooks Atkinson added: 'Entertaining, diverting, beaming Miss Lawrence keeps the drama either bubbling or boiling. She bursts into the play like a breath of fresh air . . . spirited, witty, dynamic acting that is superlatively keen and alive – if ever there was a virtuoso performance, this is it.'

With that kind of attention and adulation being paid her, Gertie did not need much encouragement to stay firmly in America; though Noël had thought of *Susan and God* that 'only the title is right', he was being proved wrong at the box-office, where the play was working well on a whole series of different levels. For those who wanted the old Gertie, here she still was, dressed in a series of stunning fabrics, coping lightheartedly with the problems of a tricky family. For those who wanted something more serious, here was a dramatic sobbing-breakdown ending; for those who wanted something more topical, here (as the *New Yorker* was the first to realize) was a thoughtful, if satirical, attack on the greater lunacies of the Oxford Movement and its discovery of 'the new religion'. Here, in fact, was something for everyone, as Gertie carefully explained to her audiences in a programme note:

People who see me in the role of Susan Trexel in Rachel Crothers' grand play may be inclined to think that, because the world is so filled with Susans, I might be like her in real life. While I believe wholeheartedly in many of this flighty character's beliefs, I hope that I may never stand out in life as the self-centred person she outwardly represents across the footlights . . . but I can say without reservation that my role as the woman who has 'found God in a new way' is one of my favourite tasks of all time on the stage. This is no trivial theme that Miss Crothers has spread across the three acts of her work, and if I didn't believe in the final redemption of Susan I couldn't make you believe in her, in spite of yourself. I do believe in *Susan and God* and I want you to also. Because there is a little bit of Susan in all of us.

In more modern terms, *Susan and God* is an attack on encounter groups and, as such, needed all of Gertie's flamboyant stardom to get past the distaste of those fashionable New York theatregoers who were already deep into the pre-war equivalents of such gatherings. But, in fact, the play itself was – at least by the time Gertie had finished with it – considerably more about Susan than about God and, as John Mason Brown noted:

All the skill which Miss Lawrence scattered so profusely through the various playlets of *Tonight at 8.30* she now consolidates to give the most complete and scintillating performance of her career. Only rarely does she broaden her values in the manner of musical comedy; for the most part her acting of the silly, selfish, insincere and colossally selfishly glittering worldling is as brilliant as it is acid. It is a pleasure to hear her stretch out certain words as if they were taffy; to follow her ever-expressive gestures and graceful body; to respond to the full breeziness of her impersonation; and to watch her as from time to time she wrinkles her nose as if she were sipping from an unseen glass of very bubbly champagne. It is even more pleasing to note how she has grown as a comedienne and to recognize the integrity of her performance.

With praise like that ringing in her ears, Gertie played *Susan and God* happily enough through to the spring of 1938 on Broadway and then, for John Golden's management, embarked on a tour of no less than twenty-seven cities, twenty-four of which duly gave her their keys. Ultimately she played *Susan and God* on radio, in a pioneering NBC television excerpt in August 1938, in a wartime New York revival at City Centre and, for one performance only, at the underground Broadway Temple on Broadway and 174th Street to which she had been invited by Dr Christian Reisner whose policy it then was to have distinguished stage stars perform scenes from their current successes at the end of his equally dramatic sermons.

Reviews on the road were almost equally ecstatic: 'Times there are,' wrote the critic of the *San Francisco News*, 'when you think you are watching Ina Claire; at others, you are certain she's Lynn Fontanne, and sometimes you even start to think she's Billie Burke. But, as the show gets under way and Susan becomes more and more familiar, you realize that you are seeing only Gertie Lawrence, brilliant, nervous Gertie, one of the most delightful comediennes of our time.'

By the time she got to Chicago in November of that year, she had become an American resident and the flags were still being put out. As the Chicago *Tribune* critic wrote:

Even in these lean years, the Gods do still smile upon the Chicago stage every now and again. The prospect of Miss Lawrence's return here after a lapse of fourteen years had created a suspense in the breasts of Chicago theatregoers that was nothing short of tantalizing. When she played here before in *Charlot's Revue* she was a breezy *ingénue*, brought up in the hard school of children's pantomimes and vaudeville tours throughout England's least refreshing centres of culture, and at that time only recently acquainted with wit and culture on their higher levels. Now she has returned to us a world celebrity – and justly so. There is no use trying to avoid being carried along by her inexhaustible vitality, by the high excitement of her enthusiasm and freshness, still completely unspoiled after months and months in the same role. For Gertrude Lawrence is one of those rare actresses in whom the unexpected always seems desirable after it has happened, and the wayward always seems inevitable.

But now that her professional life was back on course with a vengeance, her private life still left a good deal to be desired. Since the ending of the Fairbanks affair there had been no regular man in her life and she was beginning to admit to herself an increasing feeling of loneliness. Noël was working back in England and, though she had made several American friends, they were for the most part new friends, unable to share with her memories of an English past which was no less important to her now that it was over. Fanny Holtzmann alone began to recognize something of what was going on behind the now rather strident vivacity of Gertie's public image. That summer, while she was having a brief holiday in Bermuda, news had come through that back in England her daughter might be about to become engaged to an Indian army officer. Almost nothing Pamela ever did much pleased her mother, but when she wrote indignantly of this to Fanny, the reply was more to do with her own life than Pamela's: 'Oh dear, I do wish the right man would turn up for you and fill your own life. You have reached the top rung of the ladder professionally – now give the private life of Gertrude Lawrence a chance. Your life has been no bed of roses, and while you are still young and beautiful and the most envied woman in the world, I hope that the new season may hold more than professional glory for you.'

But somebody less besotted with her than Fanny might have taken a cooler estimate: Gertrude Lawrence that summer celebrated her fortieth birthday, and precious few men, especially of the dashing and glamorous type liked by Gertie, were either free, willing or able to invest themselves in marriage to a tempestuous theatrical superstar who had already frequently admitted that the stage was always going to be the most important thing in her life.

16

TO THE CAPE

When the tour of *Susan and God* finally ground to a halt early in the spring of 1939, Gertie could still see no pressing reason to return to London or her new Buckinghamshire farmhouse. The Charlot management had by now totally collapsed and, though there were occasional expressions of interest from the Cochran office, no specific vehicle for her seemed even on the horizon; Noël meanwhile was working on a revue for Bea Lillie and, though there was no question of a rift in their relationship, they were now on opposite sides of the Atlantic. Both Noël and Gertie remained, as always, utterly confident that they would be working again together soon, but precisely because of that confidence there was no sense of urgency. Six years had, after all, separated *Private Lives* from *Tonight at 8.30* and there was no way of knowing even then that 1939 was to mark the end of an era.

The one person, apart from Gertie herself, to take a passionate and constant interest in her career was Fanny Holtzmann, and that in itself constituted a good reason for staying in or around New York. 'Fanny's star client,' wrote her biographer Edward Berkman, 'in every sense was Gertrude Lawrence. Lawyer and client were an extraordinary pair, linked by vitality, humour and a kind of mutual envy. To Fanny, as to half the males of the English-speaking world, Gertrude Lawrence was the epitome of alluring sophistication . . . she was the Fanny that Fanny herself never thought she could be . . . poised and self-assured. Gertrude in turn was awed by Fanny's law degree, her negotiating finesse and her prestige . . . to Fanny it was

obvious that Gertrude needed total control . . . she could not be permitted small purchases any more than an alcoholic could be permitted a small
drink.'

And all that Gertie now had was Fanny; the relationship with her daughter
was getting progressively worse, for reasons rooted deeply in Pamela's
childhood:

She had never really been around long enough to be my mother, but suddenly
when I got to be about twenty she began taking a lot more interest in me, as if she
suddenly thought of me as a younger sister and found that relationship easier to deal
with. She didn't care for me trying to become an actress; she wanted me to settle
down, to make a 'good marriage', to have lots of children, as if somehow in that way
I could make up for all the things she had never managed to do with her life. But it
was already too late for us to get along. She desperately wanted to be proud of me, to
be able to boast about me to her friends, but she never really filled me with
confidence. Once she came backstage to see me after a show I was doing on tour and
told me that my performance reminded her of Nellie Wallace. I think she wanted to
put me off the stage as fast as possible, and in some ways she succeeded. For years I
blamed her for my failure as a person, though on reflection I now don't think it was
actually entirely her fault; I think I inherited also a kind of hopelessness from my
father. But Mummy and I both desperately wanted to get to know each other, to get
to like each other, yet we never managed it. She wanted the best for me, wanted me
to be a kind of golden girl, and I just wasn't cut out for that.

Despite the fact that Fanny Holtzmann was now having most of Gertie's
earnings paid straight into her office, then giving her client a weekly
allowance in the hope of keeping her finances at long last on a reasonably even
keel, Gertie was still (thanks to chequebooks and the miracle of charge
accounts) managing to live and to spend in some style. Like royalty, she now
seldom had to carry money herself; once, faced with a seventeen-dollar
purchase to be made at Woolworths, she told the amazed girl behind the
cosmetics counter to charge it. 'There are no charge accounts at
Woolworths,' replied the girl; 'But then how,' demanded Gertie in genuine
astonishment, 'have you all managed to stay here in business so long?'

Gertrude Lawrence was, in the practised eye of the showbusiness
columnist Radie Harris, 'the only stage star I'd ever met who managed always
to live like a movie star—butler and all.'

Pamela meanwhile, during an Atlantic crossing on the *Queen Mary*, had met
a young American doctor by the name of Bill Cahan:

She and I became good friends, first in the summer of 1938, when I was on vacation from medical school and touring England, and then again in New York a year later. The Munich crisis persuaded Gertie that Pamela would be safer living with her in New York, and after a while it became clear that we were seeing a great deal of each other, so I was summoned by Gertie to a meeting where she could look me over as a prospective son-in-law. In fact we didn't marry until 1941, by which time Gertie herself was also married, and, although we managed to be friendly, she wasn't best pleased at having her daughter marry a guy then only earning fifteen dollars a month as an intern. Pamela had also been seeing a lot of a Canadian army officer and I think Gertie would have been a lot happier with him as a son-in-law. Her ambitions for her daughter did not include marriage to a penniless medical student.

Sadly, neither the marriage nor Gertie survived long enough to see Dr Cahan move into his present eminence as one of America's most distinguished cancer specialists.

Even before Gertie finished the long tour of *Susan and God*, she knew precisely what she was going to do next; another long tour. The play this time was *Skylark*, a new comedy by Samson Raphaelson, who was the first to acknowledge in print his debt to his star:

It is a very odd experience, after having five plays on Broadway and having every one of them presented almost precisely as they were first turned in to the producer's office, to become the author of a show which is freely acknowledged to have been rewritten three full times . . . *Skylark* had already achieved narrative existence as a serial in the *Saturday Evening Post* and Knopf liked it well enough to print in book form . . . but as soon as I began to work on the stage version [as both author and director] with Gertrude Lawrence, I realized how much more resourceful and witty and vital the central character could be, and had to be, if she was to play it . . . Miss Lawrence is a light-giving switchboard, and no one can know the extent of her patience and the fullness of her contribution as an actress to the remaking of *Skylark*.

Work on the play started early in 1939 during the closing weeks on the road of *Susan and God*, and they continued working on it right through that summer, playing stock dates all over the country until they were confident enough that they had at last got it right enough for Broadway. *Skylark* was in fact a fairly inconsequential little comedy about the neglected wife of a money-mad advertising man. Donald Cook and Glenn Anders were the two men in her life, a young Vivian Vance was the other woman and though the play was, as John Mason Brown tactfully put it, 'not the kind of drama which need fear winning the Pulitzer Prize,' Gertie with her usual unerring eye and instinct for a star vehicle had found another winner here. 'Watching Miss Lawrence,' added Brown, 'is always entertaining. Joy spills from her eyes. her smile is beguiling. She moves with uncanny grace, is charming to look at, dresses smartly and has a voice of velvet which she can wrinkle as amusingly for laughter's sake as she does her upturned nose. Even when she is led into overplaying, when she reverts suddenly to her musical comedy past, and is misguided by the generous abandon of her acting into treating a comedy scene as if it were a black-out sketch, she does not lose her fascination. Hers is no ordinary personality, neither is hers a skill commonly encountered. Her performance may get out of hand at moments, but such uncomfortable moments when they do occur prove no more than air pockets encountered during an otherwise delightful flight.'

But even Gertie knew that *Skylark* had to be stronger before she could risk it on Broadway, and in the company's search for a series of summer homes where they could work on it they eventually landed up on Cape Cod at the Cape Playhouse in Dennis, Massachusetts, then being run by a young American called Richard Aldrich:

It was our policy at the Playhouse to bring there the greatest stars available, on the theory that the summer people would willingly pay Broadway prices for the best that Broadway had to offer . . . what the Golden [management] office requested for Miss Lawrence's two weeks' stay at the Cape was a cottage by the lake, sufficiently near the Playhouse for convenience but distant enough for complete privacy. Besides generous accommodations for herself and for guests she might care to invite, the star would need rooms for a personal maid and a secretary, garage space for her town car and grounds for Mac, her West Highland terrier. I was instructed to place an order with a florist to keep the vases in Miss Lawrence's cottage filled with fresh flowers, preferably lilies, her favourites. The Playhouse commissary should be at pains to see that Miss Lawrence's refrigerator was well stocked with a list of delicacies that ranged from avocados and caviare, and sweetbreads through melons, quail, pâté de foie gras and rainbow trout. Nothing in my previous experience with stars had prepared me for anything like this. Jane Cowl had exhibited no such delusions of grandeur. The previous season Miss Ethel Barrymore had arrived by bus – and in the middle of the night, unexpectedly, before we could prepare an appropriately gala welcome for the First Lady of the American theatre . . . what, I thought darkly, did Gertrude Lawrence think a summer theatre was? And who did she think she was? I could tell her in less than ten words: a spoiled, pampered actress with a prima donna complex.

It was ultimately explained to an indignant Mr Aldrich, largely by Gertie's now ever-faithful gossip columnist Radie Harris, that most of these requirements were in fact the Golden office's idea of what a star might need rather than Miss Lawrence's own personal requirements. The night she arrived there in person, it was pouring with rain:

The train drew to a stop [wrote Aldrich later] and people began tumbling out of it, hurrying for shelter from the storm. A white-coated porter swung off the step of one of the cars and stood at attention. I watched a trim young coloured woman descend, carrying a jewel case in one hand and what was patently a make-up case in the other, followed by another woman carrying a supercilious white terrier. Porters began handing down piece after piece of handsome luggage until they grew into a sizeable hillock on the platform. We advanced to the car steps regardless of the pelting rain. Then, with a timing I mentally applauded, a slim, golden-haired figure appeared at the top of the car steps.

This first encounter on his home territory (they had met once before, backstage in London some years earlier) was not, however, the greatest of successes for the couple who were to remain husband and wife from a year later until Gertie's death in 1952. She found him 'passably polite but not overimpressed with me', and he found something uneasy and irritating in her constant cheerfulness. Later that night, at a surprise party given to welcome Gertie to the Cape by the author of *Skylark*, Aldrich found himself 'an awkward anachronism on the edge of the swirl of which Gertrude was the centre. Once or twice I felt her glance on me. It was puzzled, and a trifle pitying.'

As they rehearsed and played *Skylark* on the Cape that summer of 1939, Gertie found herself increasingly drawn to the rather 'Boston Brahmin' figure of Aldrich; feeling himself no part of her Broadway world, he tried at first to stay out of her way until bullied by Radie Harris (who knew something of Gertie's considerable loneliness at this point in her life) into taking her out one night after the show: 'Gertie had had glamorous lovers in the past, but now she had reached that stage of her life when she needed, as she plaintively sang, ''Someone to Watch Over Me''. She felt that she had found him in this solid New England rock. Like all stars of her magnitude, Gertie scared men off. They would see her on stage and think ''Who am I to invite this magical creature out unless I can take her to supper at El Morocco or the Stork Club?'' So she would sit alone in her dressing room while the young kids in her company would rush off to their dates.'

135

By the end of the *Skylark* season on the Cape, it was clear to Gertie and Richard—and even to a few members of the company—that they might have something going for them. Both had, however, been married unsuccessfully once already, and neither was about to rush into another partnership without some careful thought. Aldrich stayed on the Cape to manage the rest of his theatre's summer-stock season there, and Gertie returned to New York to open *Skylark* that autumn at the Morosco.

Her home country, one she had not seen since the end of the Coronation summer two years earlier, was now at war with Germany; but Pamela was safely with her in New York, both her parents had died peacefully in the previous year, and there were (whatever she would tell the press about her 'agony' at being out of England in its hour of need) precious few links tying her back to Britain. Her life was now a Broadway life, and she spelt it out that autumn in mind-bending detail to a reporter from the New York journal *American*:

My day starts at 8 a.m. This usually shocks people when they hear it. The popular impression is that every actress sleeps until noon. So why do I get up so early? Well, I've loads to do. I have to exercise to keep in good physical condition, and then a quarter of an hour for massage of feet and ankles to keep these useful appendages slim and unweary. Then, breakfast in bed. But no ham or eggs or marmalade or pancakes. Just fruit and coffee. Next, the morning mail . . . fan letters, letters about plays, business matters and lastly of course social correspondence. I have a secretary to help me, but even so dictating an answer to every single letter takes oftentimes until noon. Of course, personal letters I answer by hand. Then, while my secretary is typing, I relax before lunch by arranging flowers. They are my passion, and I love to have all my rooms simply filled with them, and order big boxes of them fresh every day. My favourite colour is white. When these are all beautifully arranged in bowls and vases, it's usually lunch time. If there is half an hour to spare, my secretary and I play a game of chess. This is not only a splendid game but teaches you to concentrate. Lunch, which follows this busy morning, is a simple meal of vegetables and salad. Afterwards I sew for awhile. I enjoy making old-fashioned samplers, but usually there is not a very long time for this quiet occupation before my producer's representatives call. They visit me every day to discuss the problems that naturally arise in every production. After they leave me there are usually some new scripts to be read. After this I take Mackie my Highland terrier for a walk, thus giving both of us the necessary daily exercise. If I have shopping to do or visits to make, this is the time I do it—but always when I'm playing I make it a rule to be home in time for two hours' rest before going to the theatre, relaxing before the evening's work and making up for too brief sleep at night. I don't like to eat before I go to the theatre. After the performance I am usually very hungry, and I have a big meal usually with friends, for if I eat alone I seldom eat enough. It's well after midnight before I am home again and ready to go to bed. And this is what people call a glamorous and romantic life. There may be glamour and romance about certain phases of it, but let nobody imagine that it isn't mostly hard and tireless work. I travel too much to have a real home, and I always say that a new play takes a year off one's life.

If, up there on the Cape, Aldrich was reading all this, it is not perhaps altogether surprising that it took him until the following spring to propose marriage. Marriage to Gertie, he had already discovered, would also mean marriage to Mackie the dog, Dorothy, the English maid and companion, Corinne Turner, the nurse who often looked after her health and diet on tour, Carrie, her dressing-room maid and Hazel, who was Carrie's assistant. Then, of course, there was still Fanny Holtzmann, plus Jack Potter, who was Gertie's touring manager, not to mention Pamela, whom Gertie bullied Aldrich into taking along with him on a long Mexican journey that autumn. Nevertheless, their friendship flourished through that winter while Gertie was playing on Broadway in *Skylark*; Aldrich had now taken over sole management and ownership of the Cape Playhouse, and Gertie had promised that in the brief holiday between the end of the Broadway run of *Skylark* in April and the start of a four-month nationwide tour she would open his 1940 season with a week of *Private Lives* for which her Elyot was the celebrated English actor Richard Haydn. She told Aldrich during that week that she would also marry him, preferably on her forty-second birthday, American Independence Day, 4 July 1940.

It cannot be said that many of Gertie's friends behaved well over her marriage to Aldrich; though undoubtedly a man of the theatre, indeed one of the very few to own and manage one that was virtually his own private property, this was still a summer-stock theatre on Cape Cod, and Cape Cod was still a long way away from Broadway, let alone the West End. Either not knowing or not caring about the desperate loneliness that had begun to overtake Gertie as she moved into her forties, most of her oldest friends reacted in utter bewilderment to what they saw as the rather boring and infinitely stolid image of her prospective husband. Gertie herself had few doubts: 'It was as though he combined in one person the different things I had found and admired in Philip Astley and in Bert Taylor. He was Boston and Harvard, and had been a banker, but above all he loved the theatre. He was the first man in my life who understood what my career in the theatre meant to me – the first man who really understood me.'

Noël, on the other hand, took the view that she had married him under the mistaken assumption that he was a member of the wealthy Winthrop Aldrich clan, and Constance Collier merely added, 'Poor man – he thinks he's marrying Miss Lawrence and will wake up to find he has married Myth Lawrence.'

It rained the night of the wedding – just as it had on the night of Gertie's first arrival on the Cape a year earlier – and they were married in Aldrich's own cottage there with only her maid and couple of his friends as witnesses. Fanny Holtzmann was not present, but had ensured before the ceremony that all Gertie's legal and financial affairs were to remain in her own, rather than Aldrich's, control. From Noël there came a telegram:

> Dear Mrs A
> Hooray Hooray
> At last you are deflowered;
> On this as every other day
> I love you. Noël Coward.

A week later, back in New York just before setting off on the rest of her *Skylark* tour, Gertie happened to run into Otto Preminger who had been directing up on the Cape and knew Aldrich. As Preminger recalls, 'He was an attractive but very conservative and serious man, while Gertie was very outspoken and bubbling over with a delightful sense of humour. . . . She said laughingly, "I bet you didn't expect me to marry that man." I was taken aback and protested. I told her I thought he was an admirable choice and hoped they would be very happy. "Happy or not," she shrugged, "it doesn't matter. I needed roots and he is a very firm root." '

17

THE PRINCESS
OF PURE DELIGHT

It wasn't only Gertie's friends who were dubious about her marriage; Richard Aldrich's mother, a conservative and puritan old lady who was already having trouble enough getting used to the idea of her son as a divorcé and, perhaps worse still, the manager of a theatre, when asked for an opinion about the new marriage replied memorably, 'We will not mention it to anyone, and naturally none of the people we know will mention it to us.' It says a good deal for Gertie's singleness of purpose that, having decided to make the marriage work, she also managed eventually to win over the entire Aldrich clan including even Richard's sons by his previous marriage, one of whom was to write in later years perhaps the most sensitive and loving of all press tributes to her.

There was now considerable debate as to where precisely Gertie's future should lie; true, she was committed to a new American husband and the end of the *Skylark* tour which might have seemed straightforward enough. But this was the middle of 1940, a time when all English patriots were being called home and when those who had decided to stay away, especially in Hollywood, were being attacked in the British press for having 'Gone with the wind up'. Gertie, sensitive still to public reaction in her own native land, though surely aware that she was unlikely to be fighter pilot material, decided first that her duty was to go to the aid of her country in no matter how vague or unspecified a capacity.

It took, therefore, a combination of her new husband and the British

Ambassador in Washington to point out to her that while there was virtually nothing she could do in London that was not already being done there by somebody at least as suitable for the task, there was perhaps a certain amount that she could do for her country by remaining in America. As Gertie was still a British subject and citizen, though now also able to take out American papers because of her status as 'Mrs A', she could usefully fund-raise for the British war effort in every town the *Skylark* tour took her to, and that was precisely what she then proceeded to do.

She also began sending parcels to friends and distant relatives back home. Though the 'Bundles For Britain' campaign had not yet started, Gertie had always been a compulsive parcel-poster and a lady with a deep understanding of what constituted useful and acceptable gifts. Soon after her marriage she discovered that Clay Smith, her first great patron and the man who had discovered her on tour and got her into the chorus of her very first London revue, was now penniless and blind and living in an old folks' home in Illinois. She at once despatched him a large number of silk shirts from Sulka, and when Richard painstakingly pointed out that woollen shirts would probably be more useful, Gertie explained that they were not talking about usefulness. They were talking about the past, and about luxury, and about something that would impress Mr Smith's acquaintances in Illinois; usefulness was, even in 1940, not everything.

After a twelve-day honeymoon, Gertie departed for a five-month tour of *Skylark* that would take her out to California and the Midwest while Aldrich remained on the Cape to run his theatre; this was not, as he later noted, either the best or the easiest way to start a marriage, particularly as they were both in highly theatrical environments where jealousies spread easily. Gertie, for example, was not best pleased to discover that one of his summer stars up on the Cape was to be Tallulah Bankhead, while Richard found himself faintly uneasy about press reports of what a wonderful time Gertie was having in San Francisco, where the press club gave her the honorary title of 'Scoop', one with which she was frequently to sign letters from then on, and even published an entire special edition of a local paper in her honour.

Though the *Skylark* tour still showed no sign of being grounded, they had now begun to do one-night stands in small cities ('nine states in nine days' was Gertie's proud boast in September) and between train calls she was also helping to organize the evacuation of sixty children from the English Actors' Orphanage (of which both she and Noël were on the management committee) to Canada. Aldrich, Fanny Holtzmann and various other members of the entourage were also roped in to help, and eventually the children landed safely in Montreal and were then bussed to various American homes, thanks to another friend of Gertie's who ran a Chicago transport company and had also answered the call when it came from her. Few ever had the courage to refuse it.

The strain of the one-night stands, and of the Orphanage manoeuvre, left Gertie in a state of physical and mental exhaustion which, though new to her now, was to recur with ever-increasing frequency in the twelve years that she had left to live.

Still feeling guilty about being out of England, especially as the war news from there was now getting worse and worse, Gertie continued back in New York on her frantic round of 'war work': fund-raising at every possible opportunity, speaking at charity lunches to rich American women who still, it being fully a year before Pearl Harbour, failed to see what the British troubles had to do with them, and generally trying to make herself as useful as possible, even if that did just mean giving endless newspaper interviews about the need for solidarity and hands across the sea. It was a minor public relations job at best, and Gertie knew it, but that at least was better than doing nothing at all.

She still had with her the complete staff including her maid Dorothy, who on first arrival in New York had been asked what she would most like to visit and had replied, ''Strip teas''. What, enquired Gertie in some displeasure, did her maid already know of Minsky's? Nothing, it transpired; Dorothy had just heard the phrase and thought it might be nice to get a cup of a tea and a scone while watching some nudity.

By now the Orphanage children had been safely settled into the Gould Foundation just outside New York where, somewhat to Gertie's dismay, they were treated throughout the war with such care and devotion in conditions of such hitherto undreamt-of luxury that, when the war ended, a number of them showed an understandable reluctance to return to England.

Gertie had, meanwhile, had more than enough of *Skylark* which she had after all been doing on and off but mainly on since March 1939, and there was something very much more exciting in the offing, though to grasp it she had to get embroiled in a nasty Equity row with the Golden management, who seemed to be expecting her to tour for them forever. She had, in fact, toured for the best part of a year, before and after the Broadway run, and an indication of her recent war work comes from an interview she gave the *Kansas City Times* in September 1940. 'I think,' she told their reporter, 'that Great Britain will be invaded, perhaps with horrific loss of life: but mark my words the Germans will never win. Their greatest mistake was in bombing Buckingham Palace. The British will never stand for that. So far the Allied Relief Fund that I've organised on Cape Cod has sent 2,000 knitted garments, a ton of powdered milk and fifteen hundred dollars for a mobile canteen to Britain. We're starting now to raise another hundred thousand dollars but whatever we British do on this side of the Atlantic can never be enough. I keep thinking of Bea Lillie and the others who are over there giving performances for the soldiers right now.'

But Gertie now had one very good theatrical reason for staying right where she was. For several months past an old friend of hers and Noël's, known to Gertie as 'Mossyface' and to the world at large as Moss Hart, had been paying regular visits to a psychoanalyst, partly as the result of a broken engagement to Edith Atwater but mainly as the result of an increasingly desperate feeling that though with George S. Kaufman he was one half of the most successful playwriting team on Broadway (*Once in a Lifetime*, *You Can't Take It With You* and most recently *The Man Who Came To Dinner*), by himself he was nothing. The psychoanalyst not surprisingly recommended some work away from Kaufman, and the first fruit of that spectacular recommendation was a musical about psychoanalysis which Hart wrote, with music by Kurt Weill and lyrics by Ira Gershwin, and called *Lady in the Dark*. His own account of the genesis of this production was published in the Sunday drama section of the *New York Times* a week before the show finally opened on Broadway in January 1941, and so unbeatable an account is it of both Gertie and the *Lady* that it is quoted here in its entirety:

It seems like yesterday, but I'm afraid it was a good fifteen or sixteen years ago that I stood shivering outside the stage door of the old Forty-eighth Street Theatre, waiting for Katharine Cornell to come out. I had pawned my overcoat that night, for a first glimpse of Katharine Cornell and *Candida*, and, though the wind that whistled down the alley was a cutting one, I was set upon making a memorable evening complete by a starry-eyed look at the star herself. Finally, when it seemed that I must perish with the cold, the stage door opened, and, silhouetted against that magic and wonderful background of light that only stage doors glimpsed down an alley on a winter's night possess, stood Candida herself.

Though she has since denied any recollection of it, I could have sworn Katharine

Cornell smiled directly at me, and if she didn't whisper, 'You must write a play for me some day' as she brushed by, you have only my word against hers, and the word of a shivering, smitten, and stage-struck young man of eighteen is the one to take, I assure you, or the theatre of the future hasn't a chance. At any rate, that is what I blissfully chose to believe I had heard as I rumbled home on the subway that night, and that, fantastically enough, was the real beginning of *Lady in the Dark*.

For some two years ago, while we were trying out *The Man Who Came to Dinner* in Boston, I once again stood in an alley waiting for Katharine Cornell to come out of a stage door and, though now it was a warm autumn evening and the play was *No Time for Comedy*, when the stage door opened finally there stood Candida again. Then it was I decided I must keep my word to that young fellow of eighteen and an hour or so later as we sat and listened to Benny Fields sing 'Melancholy Baby' as only Benny Fields can, I said, 'Kit', (see how wonderful the theatre is), 'I'm going to write a play for you right away. I'll catch you in Philadelphia – end of March – and read you the first act.'

But by the end of March, with the first act completed, it was apparent to both Miss Cornell and myself that *Lady in the Dark* was not the play for her. Originally conceived as a straight play with recurrent musical themes, it had grown musically to such Frankenstein proportions it was now a little out of her province. We both decided that of a Saturday night in Philadelphia.

Then on a Sunday night I went to a rehearsal of a British war relief party for which George Kaufman and I were to do an act, and Gertrude Lawrence, among others, was there to rehearse her bit.

It was a rather old fashioned boy-and-girl number that she was doing, but as I watched her sing and dance I knew that here, irrevocably, was the Lady of *Lady in the Dark*. After the rehearsal finished I asked Gertie to come and have a snack with me at the back room of the Plaza, and as we drank our beer I asked her point-blank if she wanted to hear my new play. She was charming and, from even the little I told her, it seemed nothing could be more exciting than the prospect of playing Liza Elliott. She was, as a matter of fact, searching wildly about for a play for the new season and would give me an answer immediately. It was all too wonderful and just Fate, that was all, just Fate. When could she hear it? Tomorrow afternoon? Fine! We arranged a meeting then and there. Had I but known that my life with Gertie was just beginning, it would have been much simpler to have taken a slight overdose of sleeping pills that night and either miss the appointment next afternoon or never to have awakened. But I didn't know it, and the next afternoon, all unaware, I read Gertie the first act in her apartment.

Her apartment is a delightful spot, and Gertie herself, over the teacups afterward, was thoroughly enchanting. She had liked the play. I could tell that. And she literally was the part as she walked about the room talking about it. It was more than exciting, she kept repeating. It was an adventure in the theatre and something she had always hoped for as an actress. Yes, of course she had liked the play and the part – she was mad about it. But her astrologer, reading her horoscope only the week before, had said, 'Do nothing until April seventh,' and since he had also more or less told her that a new play would fall into her lap almost to the minute I had appeared, it would be flying in the face of Providence to do anything but wait until then. Besides, she wanted very much to hear the completed script, and since I worked very fast, why didn't I go down to my farm and finish the play? April 7 was still two weeks away. I could surely finish by that time and she could then say yes to me and her astrologer with a clear heart.

I battled vainly for a half hour or so and then gave in. Cursing Gertie's astrologer all the way down to Pennsylvania, I holed myself in at the farm and worked steadily until the sixth of April. That morning there was a call from Gertie. Was the play finished? Just. And I was coming in that very night to read it to her. 'Wonderful, darling,' said Gertie, 'it's all working out beautifully, because I've just had a cable from Noël and he arrives tomorrow morning. Isn't that wonderful?' It was, I agreed, but what did Noël have to do with it? 'But don't you see, darling,' cooed that lovely voice, 'it all works out! My astrologer said to do nothing until 7 April and I never do anything without Noël's advice and here he is arriving on the very day! You must read the play to Noël and if he says ''yes'', I'll do it. It's all working out beautifully. Bless you, darling!'

I groaned as the receiver clicked. Noël Coward was coming over on a war mission for Britain, and I rightly knew that the last thing in the world he desired was to have a play read to him. Certainly the last thing I wanted to do was read it, but I had already taken some measure of my Gertie and I suspected that was what I was going to have to do. I also realized with that clearheadedness for which I am not noted that Gertrude Lawrence was by no means doing the play as of this nasty moment, and the next morning, bright and early, I called Noël. Noël, as always, was unpredictable, infuriating, and a tower of strength. He made no secret of the fiendish delight he took of the spot I had manoeuvered myself into, but he agreed, busy as he was, to hear the play the next afternoon. It was a nervous lunch we had at my house the next day, and as we went upstairs to begin the reading you could have bought all of Freud and psychoanalysis from me at a very nominal sum.

I began badly and knew it, but as I finally dared look up after the first scene Noël just said, 'Fine,' very quietly and I did pretty well with the rest of it. His comment, at the end, was short but sweet to my ears. 'Gertie ought to pay you to play it,' was what he said, and, the matinée of *Skylark* being just about over, off we both went to tell Gertie the glad news. Gertie's reception of it was typical. 'Bless you, darlings,' she said, and though no mention of an Equity contract was even whispered, I was happy enough to accompany Noël to see the Lunts and let them be the first to know.

Only a slight cloud dimmed an otherwise bright horizon, and that little cloud was placed there by Mr Coward himself. 'Uncle Moss,' he said as I left him at his hotel, 'now your troubles are really beginning.' 'But Gertie said yes, didn't she?' I insisted. 'That's just the point, my boy,' he replied, 'Gertie said yes!' and he dashed through the doors before I could grab him.

That was early April. Late in July I was spending a brief two days at Woollcott's Island trying to catch my breath, when Noël Coward arrived. He had seen Paris fall, been to bombed London and back since our last meeting, but it was not of the war he spoke as he stepped out of the launch and we shook hands. 'Gertie signed the contract yet?' he asked quickly. 'No,' I answered miserably, and the amount of emotion I apparently managed to get into that one word sent him roaring with pleasure up the path and into what I can only describe as a tribal war dance. But I am getting ahead of my story. Oh, far ahead.

I waited a polite two days for Gertie to read and digest the finished script and then I called her. 'Darling, I love it,' she said, 'and now we must read it to Fanny Holtzmann.' 'Who's that?' I asked with a sense of impending disaster, 'and why must we read it to her?' 'Fanny is my lawyer and business manager. I never do anything without her, darling! We'll be at your house tomorrow for lunch at two. Bless you, darling!'

The next day Fanny Holtzmann came into my life. I say 'came into my life' because in the following weeks and months all of the life that I had lived before – my boyhood, my first loves, everything I had ever done, any place I had ever been, I could only dimly recall. I could only remember that at two o'clock I must see Fanny Holtzmann and be sure to have enough sleeping pills by my bedside that night.

It is a sore temptation to set down here a life-size portrait of Fanny Holtzmann, but for one thing Fanny is a little larger than life, and for that reason quite unbelievable, and for another, I shall probably do a play about Fanny some day and I do not like to waste ammunition. Suffice it to say that Fanny is a small, delicate, mouselike creature given to wearing floppy hats in the spring and creating a first impression of wistful helplessness. Helpless, indeed! Fanny is about as helpless as the Bethlehem Steel Company and as delicate as Jack the Ripper. At any rate, I read the play again – this time with Kurt Weill and Ira Gershwin playing and singing the score, and Fanny liked it. 'We'll have it all settled by the end of the week,' said Fanny blithely, as she and Gertie left and as Ira, Kurt, and myself happily congratulated each other.

The next day negotiations began with Fanny Holtzmann. I say 'began', but that is not really the proper term – 'carried on' is what they were, amid Fanny's various other activities, such as bringing over boatloads of child refugees, running the war for England, and making constant calls to the British Embassy. I would leave after a two-hour session, limp and bedraggled, only to be called to the telephone fifteen minutes later, no matter where I was, for at least a forty-five minute conversation. Fanny is a telephone girl and how the British Embassy ever stood up under it I still have no idea. And then, a few days after that, the terms of the contract were finally settled. Gertie was to receive for her services in acting in *Lady in the Dark* my farm, the Music Box Theatre, Sam Harris's house in Palm Beach, half of Metro Goldwyn Mayer, a couple of race horses, and five thousand dollars a week. The contract was finally drawn. Gertie, Fanny assured me, would sign it tomorrow. But, the next morning, after the first good night's sleep I had had in a number of weeks, I was awakened early, and it was Fanny herself on the telephone. By some strange coincidence, Gertie had gone off to Dennis to play a week of *Private Lives* in summer stock, and there would be some slight delay. For once, I talked a little longer than Fanny did, and insisted somewhat rudely that I had had enough of Fanny and Gertie and that unless Fanny went up there and brought back a signed contract the following Monday the whole thing was off.

How the British Embassy would get along without her during the three days she was away, Fanny did not seem to know, but, finally, she agreed to do it, and with a gaiety born of complete despair I went down to the country, having first taken the precaution of dispatching Louis Schurr to Hollywood to sound out Irene Dunne and find out if she was available for a play. Monday came and also a call from Miss Holtzmann. Had she brought the contract back with her? No, she had not, nor would she give me any explanation until we could meet privately. I agreed to come into town and meet her that afternoon, but before I left, a telegram arrived from Gertie which explained something of the delay. She had been married the night before to Richard Aldrich, and I suppose it was utterly beyond her to sign two contracts at once. Bitterly, I wired Richard Aldrich whom I had never met, 'Congratulations and are you sure Gertie said yes?' I decided that, come what may, I would not go up to Dennis and read the play to Richard Aldrich, and while I waited for Gertie to get over the shock of having said 'yes' to something, word came from Hollywood that Miss Dunne was definitely interested and would give me an answer by the next afternoon. That news gave me courage.

I got Gertie on the telephone. As always, I was completely disarmed by that warm, delightful voice and overcome almost at once by a sense of guilt that I was pushing this charming creature into making some hateful decision. But I had lived through three months of this deadly charm and now I managed to shake it off. I told Gertie about Irene Dunne and that she must either make up her mind now, over the phone, or this was the end of it. There was a little silence at the other end of the wire and then, in a voice of complete surprise, Gertie said, 'But, darling, I said yes months ago, didn't I? Whatever are you troubling your little head about? I am coming into town on Monday—let's have lunch at Voisin's and I will bring the contract with me all beautifully signed. Bless you, darling.' Well, I did not quite believe it, but there was nothing else I could do, so I wired Louis Schurr to cancel all negotiations in Hollywood and appeared as bright and cheerful as I could for lunch at Voisin's.

Gertie made her entrance in a little while like a breath of salt Cape Cod air. She was brown and healthy and brimming over with great good spirits, and though I kept eying her handbag hungrily, I had not the gumption to say "Give me that contract" until we had had a few cocktails. Then I did. And almost jumped out of my seat when Gertie said, 'Darling, the most awful thing has happened. I left it in Cape Cod and Fanny is drawing another one this very minute. We will have it for you the day after tomorrow.' 'But you are leaving for the tour of *Skylark* day after tomorrow,' I said. 'Are you sure to have it?' 'Of course I am, darling,' said Gertie. 'It's all worked out beautifully, hasn't it?' And she was off to Elizabeth Arden's, where I would have given anything to have been the masseur and pummeled the hell out of her. Day after tomorrow finally came, and with it that inevitable call from Fanny Holtzmann. Yes, the contract was all signed just as she had told me it would be if only I had a little patience, and she would meet me at the Music Box Theatre at two o'clock and deliver it herself as a gesture of good will. I was there promptly, and so was Fanny, but after one glance at the contract my heart sank. Gertie had signed it all right, but had not initialed any of the additional clauses, so that the contract was completely useless. This was at two o'clock and at three o'clock Gertie was leaving for Los Angeles. I knew that unless that contract was properly signed before she got on that train the jig was up. Where was she, I demanded to know. She was at the final rehearsal of *Skylark*, Fanny explained. And I could not possibly go over there and have her sign it because that kind of thing upset her. I hollered back that I had been pretty upset too, but Fanny remained adamant. Finally it was agreed that Jack Potter, Gertie's personal manager, would somehow sneak into the rehearsal and grab Gertie as she came out, have her sign the contract properly, and bring it to me at Essex House, where I had an appointment to work with Gershwin and Weill. This was the end of July, mind you, and Gertie had said yes in March.

All three of us, Weill, Gershwin and myself, paced about the room nervously waiting for the telephone to ring. Finally it did. It was Fanny. Gertie had signed the contract all right, but it appears we had rushed her into this so fast that she had forgotten one important clause which must be inserted now – the play must open at the Music Box or the whole thing was off. 'Fine,' I screamed into the receiver, 'the whole thing is off. I will be here for fifteen minutes longer, and if that contract is not here by then just tear it up.' Ira Gershwin, that sweet, simple soul, thought my behavior had been a little rash, but by this time I would not have cared if Zasu Pitts had played *Lady in the Dark*. And, as a matter of fact, in fifteen minutes our troubles were over for the contract arrived, all properly signed – signed beautifully, as Gertie herself had phrased it.

Not quite over. I must confess that I approached the first rehearsal of *Lady in the Dark* with some misgivings. The play, a difficult one, had to be put on the stage and be ready for an opening in Boston in only three weeks' time. It was the first play I was to direct myself, and, all in all, it was rather a frightening task. Though I had no sense of panic about it, I felt that if Gertie conducted her professional life in the same haphazard and scatter-brained way in which she conducted her business life there would be real trouble ahead. I privately decided that the first time Gertie came late to rehearsals and the first sign I noticed of any dawdling and shilly-shallying I would go right to the mat with her and fight it out, for, when rehearsals begin, the actress is trapped quite as much as the producer and author and at least you fight on even terms.

My fears were groundless. From the first moment of rehearsal Gertie was the very antithesis of her contract-signing self. A brilliant and intelligent actress I knew her to be, but what I did not know was that she was also a perfect angel once past a stage door. Sensitive and kind and completely conscientious, I would have to drive her out of the theatre at night, and there was one element of a working relationship with Gertie that I have never experienced in working with any other actress. That element was fun—rehearsals were unalloyed fun. That is the only way I can explain how we ever did so difficult a job as *Lady in the Dark* in so short a time. In three weeks Gertie made, by her shining good nature and her own special magic, what would have been an otherwise torturous task fun to do. And those four months, while Gertie made up her mind, were completely blotted out by the joy of those rehearsals and the final opening in New York.

All in all, only the pleasant things now remain of my life with Gertie, but next year I am writing a little play—without four revolving stages. In fact the play has no scenery at all. It is to be done on a bare stage with no actors. Just lights. And if she ever says yes again—Gertrude Lawrence.

18

LADY IN THE DARK

Hart's efforts were not in vain: *Lady in the Dark* proved to be among the greatest of both his and Gertie's successes and is now beginning to be recognized (along with *Pal Joey*) as one of the two great pre-*Oklahoma!* pioneers of the modern Broadway musical. Given that it brought together, for this once only, the many and varied talents of Moss Hart, Ira Gershwin, Kurt Weill and Gertrude Lawrence (not to mention Victor Mature in his first starring role and a show-stopping appearance by a young unknown called Danny Kaye) it is perhaps not altogether surprising that the show has become something of a legend to those who saw it.

Gertie played Liza Elliott, a successful magazine editor whose problem is that she 'can't make up her mind', in the words of one of the show's best-known songs (others included 'My Ship', 'Princess of Pure Delight' and Kaye's 'Tchaikovsky'). Liza's indecision spans her own magazine covers and her own life, and in order to help her (the show was once going to be called *I Am Listening*) the psychoanalyst has her describe her many and various dreams, which then form the basis for four major sequences in the show – the glamour dream, the circus dream, the childhood dream and the wedding dream. Weill himself called these Broadway innovations 'little one-act operas which continue the story in musical fantasies while the realistic story stops'.

Gertie was only ever to do one more musical, *The King and I*, and that a decade later; for now, the importance of *Lady in the Dark* lay in the way it

149

stretched her talents for singing, dancing and acting to their limits. This was a hugely ambitious show, and one that for Richard Watts of the *Herald-Tribune* established her as 'the greatest feminine performer in the American theatre'. It also made a star of Danny Kaye; at the suggestion of Max Gordon, Hart had been to see Danny in cabaret at La Martinique and wrote for him the role of a silly circus photographer who was to jump from a wooden horse and sing the Gershwin-Weill 'Tchaikovsky', which contained in twelve lines the unpronounceable names of fifty real-life Russian composers from Caesarciu through Stchertbatcheff to Kryjanowsky. On the first night in Boston, remembered Kaye: 'Applause came bounding over the footlights. I was still bowing and smiling and bowing when the awful realization hit me that the great Gertrude Lawrence was also on stage, waiting to sing a number called "Jenny". And I knew that, when a star is waiting, the worst crime in showbusiness is to delay her entrance. I bowed all right – but I wanted to bow right out. I was well aware that greater men than little ham me had been fired for hogging the show. The audience may have liked me, but I was close to being a great flop with the management.'

Watching from out-front that opening night in Boston were a select band of the show's creators, plus Pamela and her prospective husband Dr Cahan, plus the director Otto Preminger:

Moss had invited me to attend the Boston opening. We stood together in the back of the theatre. Gertrude Lawrence, the star of the show, was sitting on a swing when Danny Kaye entered. Kaye was, until then, a night-club performer. This was his stage debut. He had to sing a song especially written for him, and he did it brilliantly. The audience applauded and cheered until he repeated the song, and then stood and cheered until he did it again. Gertrude Lawrence sat on the swing the whole time waiting for him to finish and to follow with her song 'Jenny' which, during rehearsals, had been considered the hit of the play. Moss whispered to me, 'We'll have to move Gertie's song. It is not fair to have her follow Kaye.' But Gertie had made her own plan while watching the long noisy ovation. She had rehearsed her number singing it on the swing with full voice. But now she decided that would not give much contrast to Kaye. So she waited through all his encores and the noisy applause until the audience was quiet. Then she got off the swing, walked slowly to the footlights, and whispered her song. After the bedlam that had preceded her, it was stunningly effective. The audience applauded and cheered her with even greater enthusiasm than Danny Kaye. Thanks to Gertie's showmanship it did not prove necessary to move the number.

Because she had managed to live up to his success, Gertie and Danny Kaye remained on reasonably good terms, though it was not an altogether easy relationship as Kaye recalled: 'One night, while I was singing "Tchaikovsky", the audience's attention seemed to wander for the first time. Glancing over my shoulder, I saw Miss Lawrence nonchalantly waving a red scarf. It was a good-natured theatre "incident" and in turn I plotted my equally good-natured revenge. While she was singing, she was startled by an unexpected laugh because I, sitting astride my wooden beast, was doing a little mugging in the background. The lovely Miss Lawrence turned around and raised an arched eyebrow at me. I received the subtle reprimand with a slight bow, and after that we called it quits.'

Success overcomes many problems; John Mason Brown thought *Lady in the Dark* 'little short of miraculous', and in the *New York Times* of 24 January 1941 Brooks Atkinson wrote: 'All things considered, the American musical stage may take a bow this morning . . .Moss Hart's musical play uses the resources of the theatre triumphantly and tells a compassionate story magnificently . . . the music and the splendors of the production rise spontaneously out of the heart of the drama, evoking rather than embellishing the main theme . . . as for Gertrude Lawrence she's a goddess; that's all.'

Lady in the Dark rapidly attracted other fans: Eleanor Roosevelt declared it 'the best show of this or many another season' and Orson Welles told Gertie in a telegram after the première 'YOU ARE EVERYTHING THE THEATRE LIVES BY'. It was also to give Gertie her longest-ever run: she finally gave it up three years later, having played three entire Broadway seasons (the last at 'popular prices') and toured it through every major city in the continental United States. Had it not been wartime she would also doubtless have brought it to London, where the show has never yet had a major professional production.

Kitty Carlisle, who later married Moss Hart and was herself to star in a postwar revival of *Lady in the Dark*, had declined to be Gertie's standby for the original production but remembers tales of her stripping off all nail polish and cutting holes in her underwear in an effort to overcome the heat of a New York theatre. She also recalls her husband having to tell Gertie to cease mugging during Victor Mature's big scene, and instead to sit perfectly still on stage during it without moving a muscle:

Gertie agreed, and Moss went along next night to watch the improvement.

Gertie kept her promise. She didn't move a muscle. The only trouble was, just before Mr Mature started on his scene she had lit a match. So there she now sat, motionless as promised, while the flame slowly started to burn down the match towards her fingers. Guess what the audience watched that night? So then the message went around backstage that Gertie was not to be allowed any extra props whatsoever, until one night she went to the stage manager who was Moss's brother Bernie and said that a friend of hers had sent in a bunch of violets, and as the friend was going to be out front that night could she please have the flowers in a vase on her desk during the show? Bernie thought about it, decided there was nothing that even Gertie could do to distract anyone with a bunch of violets, so they duly appeared on her desk and during Mature's big scene she very slowly and very deliberately ate every single one. Another night she took to doing dog barks all through Danny's number.

So *Lady in the Dark* was not plain sailing even on Broadway, as a somewhat acid report in *Variety* (published six months after the show's original opening) indicates:

Miss Lawrence first developed bronchitis in April, rented a suite in a hospital and spent all the time she wasn't on stage or organising Bundles for Britain taking great care of herself. Still, numerous performances had to be cancelled. Her part is one of the longest and most wearing the theatre has ever had, and in addition grippe arrived early and came to stay. Then Miss Lawrence decided she had to vacation from 14 June to 1 September. A number of the cast including all three male leads were then lost: Victor Mature to Hollywood, Bert Lytell in search of a better role and MacDonald Carey also took a film. Their loss was serious enough, but it was Danny Kaye's defection that caused the most Hart-burn . . . as soon as he became temporarily at liberty because of Miss Lawrence's vacation he was offered five times his present salary to join a Vinton Freedley show. What else is a young fellow with a wife to do? The result is that when the show returns this fall to New York it will having nothing but Miss Lawrence, part of the investment still to pay off, and all of its profits still to be made.

In the end they were, thanks to Gertie's determination to carry on until necessary, even if that was to be 1943.

In the meantime she spent part of that first holiday from *Lady in the Dark* playing for her husband at the Cape Playhouse in one of her earlier London successes, *Behold We Live*. The old Gerald du Maurier role was now being played by Philip Merivale, then newly married to Gladys Cooper, who had a curious amount in common with Gertie, ten years her junior, though the two actresses seldom actually met. Both had been co-stars of du Maurier's, both were lifelong friends of Noël Coward, both had comedies written by him for them, and both were professionally noted for a kind of on-stage *insouciance* as beloved by audiences as it was loathed by other actors. True, Gladys could not sing, but then there were those who claimed that Gertie could not sing much either. Both were possessed of an attitude to work which seemed a great deal more casual than, in fact, it was; both were above all and forever determined not to be caught taking themselves or their chosen professions too seriously, and it is more than likely that had Noël written as often for Gladys as he did for Gertie then her career might have taken a somewhat different turn.

At the Cape that summer Gertie and Richard Aldrich began to get themselves acclimatized to the idea of being a married couple; since their wedding a year earlier they had spent a great deal more time apart than together, and in fact the war and Gertie's career combined to separate them for much of their married life.

Despite her earlier illness, however, Gertie's energies showed no sign of flagging; she joined the Cape Cod Canners' Association, naming the new Aldrich house there The Berries in honour of her devotion to the local cranberries. She also financed and inaugurated the Gertrude Lawrence Mobile Lending Library and Gift Shop, which was in fact an old ambulance with the insides torn out and replaced by bookshelves. This, complete with its own driver, then toured Cape Cod for the benefit of the thousand or so coast guards stationed at lonely outposts along its shorelines.

She also found time that summer to play host to a couple of the evacuee boys from the Actor's Orphanage, and to organize her daughter's wedding to Dr Bill Cahan: 'Pamela and I were married quietly on the Cape, and she then went to work as a secretary for the British-American Ambulance Corps while I was still on fifteen dollars a month; but Gertrude by this time seemed reconciled to having me for a son-in-law. She'd invite me to very glamorous American Theatre Wing parties, and made me feel like I was a member of her family, albeit maybe a rather distant one.'

That autumn Gertie went back into *Lady in the Dark* on Broadway and was still playing that there on 7 December 1941. Dr Cahan remembers: 'I was with Pamela at my parents' house that Sunday when the phone rang at lunch-time and it was Gertrude saying ''Have you heard the radio? Turn it on'', and of course it was the news of the Japanese attack on Pearl Harbor. I got into the Air Force as a physician, Richard got into the Navy and our war had started.'

Gertie threw herself rapidly and eagerly into the new role of Navy wife; now that America and her husband were both in the war she felt a good deal easier about not having returned to England earlier, and took to organizing a Happiness Ship which was to be sent over to England that Christmas packed with gifts for victims of the Blitz. Meanwhile another minor row had broken out over *Lady in the Dark*, this one concerning a singer called Hildegarde who had managed to rush out recordings of the show's hit songs ahead of Gertie herself; in reprisal, though it was hardly their fault, Gertie refused to sign a limited edition of the score which was to be sold off by the composers for profit. Ira Gershwin, ever ready with the right lyric for the right occasion:

> Gertie made her mind up in '41
> That because of Hildegarde she'd been undone.
> She got even by the autographing she forebore;
> So — no limited edition of the vocal score.

Ira's feelings about Gertie remained reasonably charitable; he had plunged himself into *Lady in the Dark* initially to assuage his grief over the death of his brother George (with whom he had of course written Gertie's *Oh, Kay!* fourteen years earlier) and she assured him that George was 'watching over' their new success, though their friendship took a subsequent beating when she, playing the same show night after night, began to tire of some of the lyrics in *Lady in the Dark* and demanded new ones. Ira, rightly and understandably, refused the request.

Hollywood, meanwhile, had heard of *Lady in the Dark* (though Gertie was not to play it in California until 1943) and had sent an urgent request that Gertie agree to be screen-tested. 'On no account agree.' came the advice from Fanny Holtzmann, 'I urge, plead, pray, beg, implore you *never* to submit to a test here or anywhere. Tests are what the word connotes — for others; you are *you* — *Gertrude Lawrence*, first lady of the Drama — a Goddess! To submit to a test means that you go into competition in a Hollywood projection room or the drawing-room of any fat-bellied producer after he has been well fed at dinner. These uninformed producers then compare you with some Mary Glutz who has no acting ability but whose sweater appeal stands out because she is seventeen years of age.' Paramount, unperturbed and undeterred, went ahead with Ginger Rogers, though as they neglected to include in the film at least one song ('My Ship') which explains a great deal of the plot, audiences left the cinema somewhat bemused.

In June 1942 *Lady in the Dark* closed its second Broadway run and, in the holiday before starting a massive winter tour, Gertie returned to the Cape, to play Julia in her beloved Noël's *Fallen Angels*, a part she was sadly never to play on home territory or anywhere that the Master might have been able to see it. The rest of that summer she spent decorating The Berries, inaugurating the Gertrude Lawrence branch of the American Theatre Wing which was to entertain soldiers stationed however temporarily on the Cape, and driving for the Red Cross.

Then it was time to set off on the tour, a journey that was not undertaken lightly. Richard Aldrich remembers: 'Gertrude's departures for a tour always followed an established ritual, in which each member of the court had an assigned role. With Jack Potter as chief dragoman, the party assembled at the house. Hazel was custodian of the make-up box. Dorothy had the overnight bag and picnic basket. Turner attended to Mackie and his luggage. The other fifty odd pieces, including a case filled with the blue silk sheets and special fine blankets for Gertrude's berth aboard the train, were the chauffeur's affair.'

Gertie was thus still living in considerable style, wartime or no wartime; her financial affairs had at last sorted themselves out, not because she was spending less but simply because she was earning more. For *Lady in the Dark*, Fanny had managed to negotiate her an unheard-of $3,500 a week and that applied to the tour as well. Travelling coast to coast for the author she now described as 'Boss Moss' Hart, she began to feel like a member of the Barnum and Bailey outfit: 'One nighters, split weeks, constant dashes for railway stations, making sure all the children in the show are still with us, trying to get increasingly rare cabs to the theatre, eating at drugstores, worrying about my voice.'

'Always alike, you singers,' the House Manager at Pittsburgh had said to Gertie in perhaps the greatest of the many tributes she now received as a matter of course, 'You, Flagstad, Lily Pons, Grace Moore, always worrying about your voices.'

The myth that Gertie was a frail and delicate creature took some bashing on this ten-month grand tour, during which she only ever missed two performances. In the opinion of one critic, asked about rumours of her failing health, 'Vitamins should take Gertrude Lawrence.'

19

MRS A.

When the tour ended Gertie went back to Broadway to play a third and final season there of *Lady in the Dark*; that she was now again up to her old overacting tricks is clear from a number of reviews noting that the musical appeared to have 'considerably broadened in emphasis' during its long tour. But by now nobody much cared; the show had a few more dollars still to make, and would then be quietly laid to rest while Gertie went back to her new home on the Cape for the summer, there to fight off press rumours that her marriage was already in trouble and to consider the best way of getting back to England to entertain the troops.

Being an American Navy wife was all very well in its way, but Gertie was still aware that her old friends from the revues, Noël, Bea and Buchanan, were a great deal more involved in the war effort than she was and this troubled her considerably. Throughout all her years in America, perhaps indeed because of them, she had retained a fierce, if vague, patriotism for Britain.

That autumn she went to work regularly in New York for the Red Cross and the Stage Door Canteen, but she declined any offers from Broadway in the hope that there would be a call from ENSA, an abbreviation colloquially understood to stand for 'Every Night Something Awful', which was in fact the Entertainment National Service Association. When the call failed to come, largely one suspects because ENSA already had plenty of entertainers on home territory without going to the additional trouble of shipping one over from America, she took to doing a weekly radio show for Revlon instead.

This was by all accounts an eccentric affair: radio was then very big business indeed and the idea here was that, in the interests of Revlon, Gertie would host a 26-week series (at ten thousand dollars per show) for what was then known as the 'Blue Network'. This 'Revlon Revue' featured Gertie doing highlights from her stage successes, from *Lady in the Dark* all the way back to *Skylark*; it also featured her in conversation with such guests as Uncle Aleck Woollcott and Moss Hart, and introducing guest stars in scenes from their current stage or screen hits. Morton Gottlieb, then a young Broadway publicist, was also somewhat involved since his firm was representing the show's producer Charles Martin. Later Morton was to work up at the Cape Playhouse:

From the first moment I met Gertie in September 1943 I never saw anything negative in her; she may not have been the best mother in the world, and there were indeed those who didn't find her easy to get along with, but to me she was never less than marvellous. Charlie Martin had already done the Lux Radio Theater and he was brought in to launch her in radio, and very early on she recognised in me somebody who knew something about how to get her in print, and there was nothing she ever loved better than publicity. The more stunts I thought up for her, the more she delighted in doing them; it was a marvellous relationship, and it went on for years both in New York radio and later up at the Cape. She was a publicist's dream; nothing was too much trouble as long as it was going to get her name into print. She had a kind of addiction to newsprint.

The radio series started with massive publicity as a half-hour show that was going to be a formless, sophisticated 'evening in Gertie's dressing-room.' Robert Benchley just happened to be there, and Ray Milland, and Dorothy Kilgallen typing out her column, and Moss Hart just dropped by, so then they went into a four-minute condensation of *Lady in the Dark* using every single song but not quite finishing any of them. It was a wonderful exotic *pot pourri* and then Benchley began doing his own little sequences; during the second show they even did *Private Lives* in five minutes. The reviews were marvellous, New York critics liked it, but the trouble was that nobody else did, so they rapidly had to shift the format towards doing half-hour condensations of movies, much more like the old Lux shows had been. Sometimes the shows were based on original scripts, one even went on to become a movie, and then she'd still find time to talk to guests like Orson Welles and James Cagney and Joe Cotten and Walter Pidgeon and Paul Muni, all of whom would also play scenes from their current movies with her. Ironically, while Ginger Rogers was out in Hollywood trying to become Gertrude Lawrence, in New York Gertie was turning all Ginger's old movie musicals into radio shows.

Out in less sophisticated climes, however, the Gertrude Lawrence Show was still proving something of a failure; sadly, reading her reviews forty years later, it is clear that she was just ahead of her time. Critics blamed her for leading 'too casually' into the commercial breaks and for conducting conversations with actors that were 'altogether too informal'. Had she lived on into the television era, Gertie might well have hosted a good chat show in the Dinah Shore tradition. As it was, she contented herself with persuading Bernard Shaw to let her do a half-hour version of *Pygmalion* (in itself no mean achievement), though her old friend Noël proved less co-operative about her new career on the radio. Asked by an ambitious producer if he would prepare for Gertie a script based on the life of Bernhardt, he wired back: TERRIBLY SORRY UNABLE WRITE LIFE OF SARAH BERNHARDT FOR GERTRUDE LAWRENCE AS BUSY WRITING LIFE OF ELEANORA DUSE FOR BEATRICE LILLIE. Nor was he about to let Gertie do his new comedy *Blithe Spirit* as a radio show, though she was still desperately keen to work with him again. On 12 January 1944 she wrote to him from New York:

I have not been home in almost seven years and am longing to get back for some War Service . . . after that why don't we do a play together either here or there? Oh Angel, do let's; it has been so long since *Tonight at 8.30*. We could finance it again ourselves, and be back once again hand in hand for the curtain calls. You know what might be fun for a change? A really smart mystery drama, very chic and funny. You've never tried one of those, have you? Everybody loves a good mystery and you could write us a corker. Darling please do it; it could start at the home of a very rich woman (me) who lends her living room out to First Aid classes and the victim would then turn out to be a real corpse or something like that. Ever so exciting and I really am much better on stage nowadays and jolly calm. Do let's.

The idea of a Coward-Lawrence mystery thriller, presumably on the lines of *The Thin Man* film series, was intriguing but did not entertain or engage Noël, and no more was ever heard of it.

Virtually Gertie's entire family were now involved in the war; Richard was serving on a destroyer called the *Maddox* (which Gertie rapidly adopted, crew and all) and her daughter Pamela was with Moss Hart's *Winged Victory* company, of which the resident physician was her husband, Bill Cahan. For

Gertie, this made it all the more imperative that she too should get into full battledress and entertain the troops, preferably somehwere in Europe.

At last the call came from ENSA. Waiting in New York only long enough to inaugurate Fiorello La Guardia's new City Centre with a two-week revival of *Susan and God* for which the cast now included a young Doris Day, Gertie started to organize her concert tour for allied troops in Europe. Her diary for 5 May 1944 read: 'Three suitcases have been bought and all proved too heavy to keep my air weight down to the fifty-five pounds allowed. I have packed and repacked a dozen times . . . new songs have been written, orchestra parts made, dance routines rehearsed, taxes paid, visas and exit and re-entry permits all procured.'

At last she got herself a clipper on 16 May and a few hours later was reunited with Richard, now serving in Southampton with the U.S. Navy amphibious forces. Gertie arrived on the same flight as Ernest Hemingway, and was caught by one amazed photographer descending the steps of the plane clutching the great author by one arm and holding two dozen eggs in the other, the latter a gift for her beloved English secretary Evie Williams.

She moved smartly into the Savoy – the war had not changed many of her old habits—and from there set about organizing the Gertrude Lawrence Unit which was soon to set off on tour through England, France and Belgium. D-Day, 6 June 1944, found her still playing the south coast of England but within a month she was at the head of one of the very first ENSA units to play in France after the Normandy landings, an achievement which got her onto the cover of *Life* magazine a few weeks later. Conditions there were not good, but they were at least no worse than she had found them a few days earlier in London. From her diary:

Sunday night. Am in bed at the Savoy, 10.00 p.m. Alert just gone. Wonder if it's Hitler's dirty flying bugs again? The window in my bedroom is broken from the blast concussion. But part of Cherbourg is ours tonight; so who cares? 1.00 a.m.: Three of the bloody things have just fallen outside. You hear the beastly droning; then it stops; then it explodes. The whole hotel shudders and my curtains blow into the room from the blast. 1.50 a.m.: one more has just blazed over and dropped with a terrific bang near by. The Strand seems to be the popular target for tonight. Next door a couple are making love. Here comes another! And now it's raining hard to make things harder for the A.R.P. rescue workers. That couple must be fatalists. Wouldn't Hitler be furious at their complete unconcern? There's another. That makes six around here up to now. And our Combined Air Forces are supposed to have been hammering at the robot bases every day. Seven. More rain. Quiet next door now. Eight. What a night. Haven't heard a shot from our guns, but I don't see how they can spot them. The projectiles seem just to come over like fireworks on the fifth of November. Nine. Now it's two-fifteen. Not much lull. The Krauts must be having a gleeful evening across the Channel. This kind of warfare costs them no pilots. I wonder if Hitler has it all arranged so that he can sit at home and push a button that fires the wretched things? Ten and eleven. Two at once that time. Now they are coming in pairs. It's no use trying to sleep in a tin hat and it looks pretty silly, especially when one is alone, so I shall just have to sit up and record this my first real experience of being blindly blitzed by robots. It really is a strange and utterly helpless feeling—not one sound of a plane of ours overhead, or any attempt at gunfire; just these oncoming, droning, phantom missiles loaded with destruction. My room is on a small courtyard, so I can see nothing, but the explosions have been very violent. Much damage must be being done. Being Sunday, and this a business section, there may not be too many casualties but the property loss will be great . . . I was just going to write 'all over for tonight' but here comes Charlie again, making it a round dozen since one o'clock. How many more? I suppose this is a reprisal for Cherbourg.

Seventeen bombs fell around the Savoy that night, and not surprisingly Gertie suddenly found herself thinking back twenty-six years to the night of another air raid over London, the night when she had rushed out of the Vaudeville stage door after a performance of *Tabs* and realized that she was about to give birth. But with Pamela now safely in California filming *Winged Victory* Gertie completed her ENSA tour (in a company which by now included Margaret Rutherford and her old Charlot understudy, Jessie Matthews) and then collapsed; an attack of dysentery in Normandy, together with the shock to her already taut nervous system of front-line battle conditions, had proved too much for her.

She had however done her duty by ENSA. The drama critic Felix Barker, aware that she was in already poor health, noted in his diary:

8 September. Etretat, Normandy. Gertrude Lawrence and her company are going to play in the Casino again, as in this weather it is hardly feasible to perform in a field. We've put in all our own lighting and curtaining to cover the bizarre interior set for our show and theirs, and the ENSA company, which played here yesterday, in the dimmest gloom, were very pleased. . . . G. Lawrence, back from America after her tour, was in tremendous form. What can one say of her show and performance? That it was great and she tremendous? Well, the supporting company was average

and she won a triumph out of what looked like defeat. Either from experience of
troop shows, or from an idea of her own, she made the initial mistake of playing
down to her audience. Almost, one could see her saying to herself, 'I have to deal
with a bunch of unsophisticated, braw Highlanders. I must fire every gun I've got.'
and so, during her first number, we were treated to a full salvo of every trick she
knew. But the braw Highlanders, who'd been under fire before, were not
impressed. In fact, they thought it rather grotesque. For a ghastly five minutes one of
the greatest artists of our stage looked like getting a grouse straight from the moors.
But she was too clever for that. A Cockney number, a couple of wise-cracks at the
expense of officers and padres, a lovely number from *Lady in the Dark*, and she was
back. By the time she was smashing over 'All's Well, M'moiselle', the whole
audience was with her and the show ended in one of those red-white-and-blue, First
World War, Tipperary-type finales. . . .

Once her show had gone down well she was delightful, and was very sweet
afterwards when I told her how sorry I was that I hadn't put up grey curtains instead
of blue, which clashed with her dress – insisted that she hadn't *noticed*! But of course
she must have done, and was just being gracious.

In our show at that time there was a skit I had written – of all things – about a
temperamental ENSA star touring in Normandy entertaining the troops. Gertie had
somehow heard of this and said she was determined to see it. She and the company
gave up their dinner to see the whole show. Elliot ('Bunny') Playfair was in his best
form as Madame Rusticana screaming down the phone at Basil Dean, furious that
some other performer is also going to France. I changed the tag of the monologue
from her imperious demand, 'Who is Gracie Fields?' to 'Who is Gertrude
Lawrence?' and she was delighted.

I was relieved because the whole thing was very near home and I was frightened
that Gertie would see the sketch as an extremely impertinent slap in the face. I tried
to take out some of the offence when I went out to compère the introduction, but I
needn't have bothered. She was marvellously complimentary.

By the autumn she was safely back on Cape Cod, already writing an
account of her ENSA touring for the autobiography which was soon to be
published as *A Star Danced*. She also found the time to tour briefly for Gilbert
Miller in a curiously disastrous war play called *Errand For Bernice* which
opened in Buffalo that November and closed on the road without ever
reaching hailing distance of Broadway.

But with the war still not yet over, and her autobiography now completed,
she decided the time had come to sign up again; not this time for ENSA but for
its American forces-entertainment equivalent the USO, which promptly sent

her out to Hawaii and from there on to Guam at the start of a long tour of Pacific naval bases with a concert performance of songs from *Lady in the Dark* and *Nymph Errant* and *Oh, Kay!* On her way home from this, passing again through Honolulu, she was persuaded by Major Maurice Evans that the troops might also like something a little more nourishing in the way of entertainment. Evans and she therefore put together a production of Noël's *Blithe Spirit* for which Gertie of course played the ghostly Elvira.

Noël had always seen Elvira as an extension of Amanda in *Private Lives*, and had Gertie not been playing *Lady in the Dark* on Broadway when his comedy first opened she would doubtless have been offered it. As it was, he was less than delighted to find her turning up in a Hawaiian production without his express approval:

'Perhaps I should explain about *Blythe Spirit*' replied Gertie by airmail, cheerfully mis-spelling its title. 'I had just come back from a gruelling island tour, tired and disheartened; I knew the men now wanted plays instead of just songs. They'd already had Boris K. in *Arsenic* and Moss Hart in *Man Who Came To Dinner*, and they were yelling for *Private Lives* but the USO wouldn't pass it for troop consumption. *Skylark* wasn't good enough and *Susan and God* would never have got past the Chaplains on account of its title and topic; I could hardly do a potted version of *The Lady*, and *Tonight at 8.30* needed too many sets and versatile players. But the men badly wanted a play with me, and Milly Natwick agreed to fly out and repeat her Madame Arcati so John Hoyt and I went ahead and staged it. We did it jolly well, too; hope you don't mind. Love Gert.'

If Noël did mind still, it was now anyway too late as Gertie was back on Cape Cod celebrating the imminent end of the war and publication of her book *A Star Danced* which was, she announced proudly, 'all my own work' though some thought they could discern traces of the pen of Fanny Holtzmann. She travelled the length and breadth of the United States selling it, thereby pioneering the 'author tour' that was to become a feature of postwar publishing but remained at this time an almost unknown adventure.

Back on the Cape, however, the Aldriches were in considerable trouble; many longer-lasting and more securely-rooted marriages had been endangered by the war, and theirs was now on the verge of a total break-up. Aldrich himself, back from the Navy, found that he had no real career to return to; true, there was the possibility of restarting his management of the Cape Playhouse for the summer of 1946, but that remained a part-time affair.

His ambition to become a full-time theatre manager in New York looked unrealistic, and in the meantime he was finding to his horror that after a distinguished war he was now nothing more than 'the uniformed husband of the successful star and author Gertrude Lawrence. I did not like it.'

Gertie, having always had, like her Amanda in *Private Lives*, 'the emotional stability of a shuttlecock', was finding certain attractions in other men; nothing very serious or long-lasting, just reflections of a need to remind her husband that 'married or not I'll see whom I like, when I like and where I like. I don't need anyone to manage my life for me. I did it pretty successfully for some years before I ever heard of Richard Stoddard Aldrich.' They had now been married for five years and been together for less than one.

Aldrich took to quoting Browning's *My Last Duchess* ('She had a heart too soon made glad, too easily impressed . . . Oh sir, she smiled no doubt whene'er I passed her; But who passed without much the same smile?') and Gertie, never at her best in literary contests, took to long silences. Eventually, at the insistence of the inevitable Fanny and various neighbours up at the Cape, they decided to give themselves a year to see if their marriage could be saved before reaching any decision about a divorce. At any time in her past, it is hard to believe that Gertie would have waited that many weeks, let alone months, before heading to a lawyer. But she was now forty-seven, older if not necessarily wiser, and long before their year was up the marriage had been patched together again.

Meanwhile, Fanny was busy getting on with Gertie's stage career; it had been more than four years since the opening of her last success, *Lady in the Dark*, and with the ending of the war Fanny took the view that there was not a moment to be lost. If her star client was to move untarnished into the postwar era, then it was no use her hanging around in the hopes of another big musical or harking back to the now long-dead days of revue. She would have to remind both her public and potential casting directors of her talents as a straight actress too, since that was inevitably where the most theatre work still lay. As Noël had unaccountably never got around to writing the comedy thriller Gertie had asked him for, and now seemed highly preoccupied with retrieving his own career from a sudden post-war slump, Fanny turned to that other well-known playwright George Bernard Shaw.

Even he proved no match for Fanny. The two had first met in the early 1930s during one of Fanny's periodic English visits; from that time on, notes Edward Berkman, 'playwright and lawyer enjoyed a lively friendship' and it was through Fanny that Gertie had managed to get permission to do an abridged *Pygmalion* on her half-hour radio series. That was just the beginning; now Fanny had a still more ambitious idea. She had seen the Leslie Howard-Wendy Hiller film of *Pygmalion*, indeed had made Gertie go with her to a special New York screening before the première. Gertie hadn't much cared for the 'old chestnut' but Fanny was already off on the idea of a musical: 'If an audience will listen to you in *Lady in the Dark*' she told Gertie, 'singing about psycho-analysis, then surely they won't mind you dancing with a grammarian. This can be the biggest musical of all time.' *My Fair Lady* was of course thirteen years later to prove Fanny had been absolutely right; sadly, however, Gertie never lived to see that, and Fanny had no part of it because at this time Shaw would not contemplate a musical. Fanny persisted, and asked if Gertie could do *Pygmalion* straight; she was, wrote Fanny to Shaw, 'no longer the musical comedy actress of the old days but an accomplished dramatic star.'

Shaw evidently had his doubts. 'I know,' he wrote back to Fanny, 'all about Miss Lawrence in her professional aspect. *Pygmalion* is worn to rags, and filmed.' Finally, however, crumbling under a barrage of letters from Fanny, he gave his consent to a 1945 Broadway production of *Pygmalion* to star Gertie. In the interests of helping save the marriage, Fanny also took the view that Aldrich should be involved in the production, and so it was staged under the aegis of a pioneering, non-profit theatre group he had joined called Theatre Incorporated. The rest of the casting was done somewhat informally, as Raymond Massey relates:

Dick Aldrich came to my place on 80th Street and told me about the planned *Pygmalion*. 'We'd like you to direct, or play Higgins. What would you rather do? Shaw would rather have you direct.' . . . Nevertheless, without hesitation, I said to Dick: 'I'd rather play Higgins.' He told me, 'You'll be co-starred with Gertie Lawrence. Have you any suggestions about a director?' 'Cedric Hardwicke is the ideal director of any of Shaw's plays,' I said. 'Shall we see if he's free?' I called the Château Marmont in Hollywood and got Cedric at once. 'Cedric? It's Ray here, Ray Massey. Are you busy? Good' (He says he's in the middle of re-reading a Trollope but is open to offers.) 'There's a production of *Pygmalion* here in New York with Gertie Lawrence and me. Would you like to direct?' (He says yes, of course, he'll direct and George Melville Cooper is there with him and would like to play Doolittle).

So that was more or less that. They tried out in New Haven and progressed from there to Broadway where they opened at the Ethel Barrymore in December 1945 and lasted 179 performances, thereby breaking the house record for a non-musical. Directing Gertie, Hardwicke found that, 'She has a touch of the divine spark, but it is totally undisciplined. She has an incandescent quality and almost always overacts: when she enters, the stage becomes visibly brighter. Gertrude and her audiences have always had a passionate love affair.'

By now though, that affair was beginning to show slight signs of cooling; a number of critics were less than happy about her Eliza, including a young Ronald Bryden, who found it:

. . . genteel and slightly lachrymose, where she should have been like a spitfire; but all I can really remember is the tea-party at Mrs Higgins's, where Eliza displays her new vowel-sounds. Exquisitely gowned, her back like an arrow, she moved around the central ottoman like a dancer. It was a pleasure to watch her sit, get up again, stretch her arm out for tea. But there was nothing in the performance to write home about, nothing you could really write down at all. That may have been the mystery about her. The actors that critics write about best are those whose effects bear analysis; who offer a vividly thought-out impersonation, a lucid, communicable approach to a whole role. The notation for Gertie's kind of acting does not yet exist. In the cerebral sense, she was scarcely an actress at all. She moved like a dancer, and probably thought like one, with her body. When it was amused, she was witty; when it was functioning with perfect control and economy, she was beautiful; but all it left on the retina of memory was a line, fading like the trail of a firework on the air.

American critics also had reservations about this production: 'New *Pygmalion* Lacks Old Punch' headlined one critic while another merely added 'Shaw Survived'; still, John Chapman for the *Daily News* thought Gertie 'reborn' and George Freedley for the *Morning Telegraph* found her 'lovely if a little hard to hear'. Undeterred, they played on at the Ethel Barrymore until the middle of June and then (with Dennis King replacing Ray Massey who had a film to make) planned to spend the winter of 1946 and most of 1947 on a lengthy *Pygmalion* tour which took them as far as Mexico City. Gertie, though now getting increasingly physically exhausted, was resigned to these back-breaking tours on which she had always made the bulk of her American money. Others, in the old cliché, may have been *tours de force*; Gertie was forced to tour, and remained throughout her American years the Queen of the Road.

═══ 20 ═══

QUEEN OF THE ROAD

Back in New York, Fanny was still determined that Gertie should do the musical of *Pygmalion*; she continued to deluge Shaw with requests, eventually suggesting that the obvious man to adapt it for her would be Noël Coward. This finally produced a furious response from Shaw; 'My dear Fanny: Stop cabling crazy nonsense. What you need is a month's holiday. Noël could not possibly interfere in my business. My decision about *Pygmalion* is final: let me hear no more about it.'

Fanny conceded; if her client couldn't do a musical version of *Pygmalion* could she at least do an hour-long NBC television version of his *Great Catherine*? Shaw agreed wearily, and a year later Gertie did just that, with Micheal MacLiammoir co-starring.

Meanwhile she returned to the Cape before starting her *Pygmalion* tour, and for their reopening season at the Playhouse there that summer of 1946 the publicity manager was Morton Gottlieb:

Within six weeks I managed to get two entire layouts in *Life* magazine, one on Gregory Peck, who'd gone up to work there, and one on Gertie rehearsing with the young apprentices. By the following year *Life* had an edict that no Cape Playhouse publicity was to be allowed into the magazine and I took that to be a kind of personal challenge, so I devised a feature on summer activities, and we had the company from the Playhouse fight a water-pistol battle with the people of Dennis, only the pistols were filled with local cranberry juice. Anyway, over one side of the pitch I had a big sign saying 'Cape Playhouse' and over the other side I had a big sign saying 'Dennis', and when that picture appeared in *Life* with Gertie as the umpire there couldn't be much doubt about where she was working.

Richard had that New England delight in making money at the theatre, but he used to find all the publicity and Gertie's everlasting exuberance a little embarrassing, even though he could see how much good it was doing his Playhouse. The Cape did, though, give her a kind of security, and that perhaps she'd never found before.

Between 1946 and 1950 Gertie was to do one play every summer on the Cape; in 1946 it was *The Man in Possession*, though she also gave them a week of her Eliza Doolittle to celebrate the reopening. Eliza was meant to be her sole contribution to the season but, as Arthur Sircom (who directed nine of the ten plays that Gertie was to do at the Cape between 1939 and 1950) recalled, things didn't work out quite that way:

We offered *The Man in Possession* to several good actresses, all of whom refused it on the grounds that the real star role there was the man's; Gertie agreed in the end to step in, and we started rehearsals keeping quiet about the fact she was in the cast but announcing that a Finnish-English actress called Alexandra Dagmar would appear in the play in her American debut . . . people were used to seeing Gertie backstage around the theatre so that didn't cause any suspicion, and we refused all interviews for 'Miss Dagmar' on the grounds that she was too busy learning her lines. The Boston critics, curious about this unknown actress, all came to the opening night and in the second act Gertie finally made her entrance. She glided on to the stage down a flight of stairs, brandishing in her hands a perfume atomizer. For a moment there was a stunned silence, then a gasp from everyone in the audience, then someone let out a whoop which caused a roar of laughter, and this started an ovation which lasted for minutes . . . Gertrude took this in her stride at first, but, as it didn't let up, she started to feel foolish. Rather than just stand there with egg on her face she flourished the atomizer about, resorting to every trick she could think of . . . she sprayed her hair, her shoes and a lot of the rest of her; then she sprayed the cushions on the sofa and the actress on stage with her; finally she aimed it at the audience and gave them a few whiffs . . . then she gave such a sparkling and captivating performance that she had everyone starry-eyed.

By her marriage to Aldrich and her residence on the Cape each summer, Gertie had given a kind of star-studded respectability to the straw-hat circuit of summer theatres around there. In return, the Cape Playhouse gave her the chance to lark around, play her incessant theatrical practical jokes, and generally recapture some of the fun she'd first had as an understudy for

Charlot thirty years earlier. It was, as she once said, 'so much more jolly than stuffy old Broadway' and she even inaugurated a policy whereby big stars could play the Cape in shows with their own daughters, a policy of which both Helen Hayes and Gladys Cooper promptly took advantage.

Pamela's marriage to Dr Cahan was collapsing as fast as many other wartime marriages; Gertie's relationship with her son-in-law had turned somewhat sour, though intriguingly he was to be the last person to see her alive. At this time, however, Gertie was not altogether surprised to hear from Pamela that she and her husband were separating:

To which news she responded by telling me that I was being very foolish since I was neither beautiful, nor talented, nor leaving him to go off with someone else! All of which was brutally true. I told her that I was thinking of going home to England as there wasn't anything to tie me to the States. She was terribly pleased, and envious . . . not only about that, but she seemed, at that moment anyway, to envy my escape from matrimony.

I did not return to England until a few days before *The King and I* opened in New Haven. The night before I left I spent with her in her apartment on West 54th Street.

I think that night we spent together was the nearest we ever got to being really intimate friends, and it is not just with hindsight that I recall how terribly unwell she seemed to me at that time . . . which of course I put down to the strain of rehearsals. She must have been ill and in pain very much longer than anyone will ever know. She was that sort of person. Her commitment to the theatre and her responsibility to the public, *her* public, was *everything*.

But there was now to be no turning back; America was Gertie's home, her life and her career and though she would occasionally still murmur about a desire to see England, reports filtering back to her from there had already indicated that England immediately after the war was no longer her England, no longer the England where she and Noël and Charlot and Cochran had ruled the West End. There was no real home for her to go to there. Home was now a house called The Berries on Cape Cod and typically Gertie then made the best of it, 'the best' starting at that time with a massive paint-and-redecoration job.

Pygmalion was toured through the United States for the rest of 1946, and then in early 1947 Gertie took it on into Canada; there, finally, the show closed and in May she was unemployed and suddenly very frightened. It was too late to start anything new that season on Broadway, too early to go to the Cape; Aldrich by now had developed a flourishing theatrical management on Broadway, but was carefully avoiding any professional contact with his wife. Even Fanny had nothing to offer. The best that anyone could suggest was that Gertie should take a holiday, which she then did, paying only her second visit to London since the summer of the Coronation, nine years and a world war ago.

She did not care for what she saw; London in May 1947 was still a fairly bleak place. Noël was doing a revival of his *Present Laughter* with Moira Lister, other friends seemed to have all died or disappeared or settled into a married life which left precious little room for nostalgic meetings with pre-war West End stars. Girls she had known in the chorus at the Vaudeville, Gertie noted acidly, were now Duchesses while she was still 'coping on the good old Cape'. Worst of all, nobody made her an offer of work. Nor could she understand how if England had just won the war everybody there still seemed so badly off; in Paris (which she also visited) there was at least a thriving non-rationed black market where anything could be had at a price. Gertie never understood why London couldn't be run like that.

Soon enough she made her way back to America and the summer season on the Cape, having first left instructions with Noël and Binkie Beaumont, now the head of the H. M. Tennent theatrical organization, that any possible scripts were to be sent to her for the following autumn. A number of possibilities were in fact discussed, including new plays by John van Druten and Emlyn Williams, neither of which seemed to be absolutely right for her return to the British stage after an absence of an entire decade. Rattigan had also written her a play but that had been pre-empted by the Lunts and turned into *Love in Idleness* (in London) and *O Mistress Mine* (in New York).

On Broadway there did not seem to be much for Gertie either; keen perhaps to do another musical, she thought long and hard about what eventually became the Nanette Fabray role in *Love Life* by Kurt Weill and Alan Jay Lerner, who had just had a huge Broadway success with *Brigadoon*. Gertie's eventual verdict was that 'the Virgin Mary herself couldn't hold that show together' and instead, after a brief season on the Cape doing *The Lady Maria*, she decided to take to the road in a revival of *Tonight at 8.30*.

Noël himself was less than enthusiastic about this project, but pressured by Gertie and Fanny Holtzmann on the one side and Jack Wilson on the other, and knowing that another of his most constant friends Graham Payn was to play his old roles in six of the original plays, Coward finally agreed that they should go ahead. Rehearsals were however deeply uneasy, leading up to a final split in the Coward-Wilson relationship and to Noël himself taking over the production and indeed standing in for Payn when the latter went down with 'flu in San Francisco: 'I flew down to the theatre, started rehearsing at 1.20 and was on at 2.30, proud of the fact that I didn't dry up once. Performance not bad; company and audience thrilled, but it was all rather exhausting.' It was also the last time that Noël was ever to appear on a stage with Gertie.

The tour eventually reached New York where *Tonight at 8.30* played a brief and not terribly successful season at the National Theatre in February 1948; the general critical feeling was that the plays themselves had 'lost their jauntiness', 'become hopelessly dated' and misplaced their verve since the first production on Broadway twelve years earlier: 'It is not that they have mellowed with age like wine,' wrote Louis Kronenberger, 'but that they have puckered and wrinkled like cocoa.' For Graham Payn, in his first starring roles on Broadway, the memories of Gertie are of:

. . . Her immense kindness and patience and skill. Her career wasn't going terribly well at this time, and I think perhaps she knew there was a kind of desperation in going back to milk an old pre-war success like this one. Fanny Holtzmann got the whole thing going because there wasn't anything else on offer for Gertie at the time, but Gertie treated the whole thing very conscientiously and all through the long tour we used to go down to the theatre every night a couple of hours early and rehearse some of the numbers. Yet she was a strange lady, you know; somebody once went to stay with her at her house on Cape Cod, right by the sea, and complained of feeling tired and Gertie in all seriousness said, 'Oh yes, it's the altitude.'

She was still in good health then, though she used to get very exhausted after the show, and she was marvellously good with me, felt she had to look after me a bit because she, after all, had done the shows before and I hadn't. Also I was maybe a little young for her, though I think she tried not to notice that; she never compared me to Noël, never complained that I wasn't playing the plays quite the way that he had. In fact, we didn't do at all badly on the road, but once we got into New York those notices were killers and we were off within the month. 'This theatre is far too empty,' she said to me in the interval one night, 'I think I shall insist that the management remove three or four rows of stalls.' It was a curious experience, but I wouldn't have missed working with her for all the world.'

But she was tiring now, in retrospect perhaps tiring faster than a woman of fifty ought to have been, especially one who had never had a serious illness. She vowed that the tour of *Tonight at 8.30* would be her last, that from now on she would only play seasons on Broadway or in London or at the Cape. Somebody else could take over as 'Queen of the Road'.

That summer, her contribution to the Cape Playhouse season was Rattigan's *O Mistress Mine*, in which she played the Lynn Fontanne role, as she noted smugly in a letter to her old English secretary Evie Williams, 'just as well as Miss Fontanne did it on Broadway and with a great many more laughs!'. But by now she had even better news for Evie: in the post, unexpected and unheralded to the Cape, had come a script. It was a new play, a drama about a self-centred young artist who marries a young girl and then falls deeply in love with her mother—this, of course, was the role for Gertie. The author of the play was the novelist Daphne du Maurier, known already to both Aldriches because Gertie had worked with her father, Sir Gerald, and Richard had often been a guest at the du Maurier home in Cornwall when he was stationed there during the war.

Daphne's original plan had been for Gertie to take the play to Broadway that autumn of 1948, but Aldrich took the view that it was altogether too English for that market. Gertie, however, was determined not to lose the role, the best she had been offered in a long time and, though she agreed that the play might just not work out in America, she knew very well that she could make a success of it in London. Plans were therefore made with the H. M. Tennent management and in October Gertie sailed for Southampton on board the *Mauretania*, not best pleased to have discovered that in her absence her husband was to stage a play on Broadway starring none other than her old rival for the affections of Philip Astley, Madeleine Carroll.

Gertie was thus all the more determined that her return to London should be a triumphal and triumphant one. She needed a success in a new play at this point in her career, since for the best part of the last decade she had been doing nothing but revivals; she also wanted very much to re-establish herself in her home city, and to prove to English audiences that she had become a dramatic actress of considerable quality.

To some extent, *September Tide* eventually fulfilled all those requirements, though Gertie's first arrival back in London was a disillusioning experience. Her brief holiday there the year before had still not acclimatized her to all the changes that had overtaken the city and the people of London, both of which

Gertie still thought of in terms of the 1930s. As Graham Payn said: 'I think she found the whole thing very disillusioning; nobody hung around the stage door waiting to see her any more, and a lot of her old friends had disappeared, and somehow the whole stardom thing had already changed and she seemed already to belong to a different era, a theatre that had now vanished from the post-war world. It had after all been twelve years since she'd last played in London and a lot had happened in the meantime.'

Her letters home to Aldrich were at first less than buoyant: Fanny, still nervous about the constantly precarious state of Gertie's finances, had sent her over with no more than two hundred dollars, all of which vanished at once, either paying for the cables she sent to all and sundry from the *Mauretania* announcing her imminent arrival, or else in paying duty on the various presents she was bringing with her to old English friends and ex-servants from her pre-war life.

Though there were ritual articles of welcome in the press and a few photographs, London signally failed to hang out the flags for Gertie and she minded that very much indeed. It was not that anybody much cared (though Gertie of course leapt to the conclusion that they might) about her having spent almost the whole of the war in America, or married an American—if it had been that simple, the truth might have been easier to face—but the truth was quite simply that London had lost interest in her. She was back to do a play, fine; if she had a success, fine. There would of course be critics out in force to cover the first night. But that, in the old days, had only been a small part of Gertie's press coverage. What she missed now was all the old interest in what she was wearing, who she was seeing after rehearsal, where she was going in the evenings. In fact she wasn't going anywhere much, because there was no longer (in terms of nightclubs) anywhere much to go. But in some vague way it annoyed and worried her that nobody any longer much cared about the private life of Gertrude Lawrence. London had ceased to be star-struck by her, and she could never really quite come to terms with that realization.

But one of the great delights of *September Tide* was to be the friendship it formed between author and star. Daphne du Maurier recalled it thus:

Cinders, I called her, but why? Cinderella. Surely Gertrude was the last person in the world to make anyone want to call her by that name? Yet I did. Cinders . . . someone of importance had given a party to which she hadn't been invited. I mocked her. 'Poor old Cinders.' It was her name from then on. She retaliated by calling me

Dumb—Du M. I have been searching my shelves for a copy of the play. I can remember only that it was about a charming, unspoilt widow [Stella] of early middle age who discovers that she and the husband of the daughter she adores fall in love. Not a line of the play comes back to me now. I cannot remember how Cinders looked, what she wore, far less what she said. I close my eyes and it is not my play I see but *Private Lives* with Gertrude and Noël standing beside each other and she is singing 'Someday I'll Find You'. . . . That surely was 1930, eighteen years before she appeared in *September Tide*. A few years later she played the lead with my father Gerald in *Behold We Live*, and still I had not met her. I was either in France or in Cornwall and I never saw the play. Then comes the gap of years. I marry, I have three children, I write books, two other plays and then—heaven knows why—*September Tide*. It must have been Binkie Beaumont of H. M. Tennent, who knew she wanted to come to London and offered her the part of Stella. I went and met Gertrude, not Cinders yet, at the station. She was wearing a fur coat. I remembered that Gerald, my father, always gave his leading ladies presents and took them to lunch at the Savoy. I must do the same. I asked Gertrude to lunch at a small table at the Savoy Grill, where we could talk uninterrupted about the play. She took one look at the table, 'But nobody will see me here.' We hastily moved to a table where everyone could see her as they walked into the Grill. She was so right. Then I do recollect presents of champagne, a fur rug either for her flat or her car, I've no idea, but I had an account at Fortnum's, so to some extent I was doing a Gerald.

There was a try-out of the play at Oxford. I remember nothing about it except that Kenneth Tynan, then still an undergraduate, was there. I did not go to the first night in London. First nights of a play written by myself were naturally taboo.

She had taken a flat in London somewhere, and I remember going to see her there one afternoon; she put the kettle on for tea and then shook her finger at it. 'Now don't you go and boil over.' I stared.

'Do you always talk to your kettle?' I asked.

'Always,' she said, 'and it never boils over.'

TURN OF THE TIDE

'As I walk through the streets of London this winter of 1948 I see that we are no longer a nation of shopkeepers', wrote Gertie in an appallingly patronizing 'homecoming' piece for an American magazine, 'but a nation of really hard workers. Teenagers are doing wonderful things which surprise their elders. Britain is on the mend!' Privately, however, she was considerably less enthusiastic about being back in London; they were having to rehearse *September Tide* in the bombed-out remains of the Queen's Theatre, every other stage being fully occupied at the time, and a nasty contractual row had broken out with her old friend and agent Bill O'Bryen, who had looked after her at the time of the first bankruptcy hearings in London but had later been ousted from a share in her affairs by the Holtzmann takeover.

From New York, the news was that Aldrich had had a success with Madeleine Carroll on Broadway ('Your star owed me a good turn' was Gertie's acid comment) and before the West End opening of *September Tide* there was a long provincial tour through Blackpool, Leeds, Liverpool and Manchester in a winter of thick fogs and fuel cuts, neither of which did much for the box-office. Still, business was generally good and playing opposite her, in his first major West End role, was a thirty-year-old Michael Gough:

In rehearsal she was marvellous, very helpful, very generous, used to bring in bottles of champagne, but she was like a creature from a pre-war world that had evaporated. She was now very lonely. Her husband was in America, and all her old friends from before the war seemed to have disappeared into the woodwork, as if they didn't want to be reminded of a life she had shared with them.

She was full of little tricks on the stage; she used to put scent on the hem of her dress and then on her first entrance do a turn so that the dress would swing out and a marvellous smell would fill the auditorium. Other times, when her hair was a bit greasy, she used to put cotton-wool soaked in cleaning fluid on a comb and then streak it through her head so that her hair literally shone. But in other ways she was a very traditional, rather old-fashioned actress even for that time. If we had a break in rehearsal, she'd always talk about the play or others she'd been in; her whole life was the theatre. She didn't seem to have any other interests or topics of conversation. The world for her was the theatre; anything which happened outside it was simply irrelevant. That made for a rather narrow view, but she had a fascinating intensity; one night I remember going into her dressing-room and just listening while she and Noël reminisced about their pasts. It was like being a guest in the most wonderful theatrical boarding-house in the world.

She didn't really understand why everybody wasn't more interested in her return; she felt she'd been a hero in the war, going over to Normandy and all that, and she expected a hero's welcome which somehow just never happened. Those of her friends who were still around and free to take her out in the evenings found her very highly-strung and terribly demanding. She had a very 1930s idea of how the star should behave in the theatre, and more importantly of how people should behave towards her. I was having an affair with Anne Leon at the time, who was playing Gertie's daughter and whom I later married, and some nights Gertie would summon me to the dressing-room to take her out for dinner and then be furious to discover that I'd made a plan to go out with Anne. It wasn't that she was in love with me or anything like that, merely that as her leading man I was expected to be available, a sort of consort.

She was very bitchy about me and Anne, because I think she was lonely and felt that life was already passing her by; also she never seemed terribly well. Looking back, I think perhaps that final illness had already started.

As a company I think we disappointed her; she loved the play, enjoyed doing it every night, but was furious about Anne and me and somehow couldn't understand how life had changed backstage. Before the war, you see, a company really was a company – they lived together, in and out of the theatre. Or at least the stars lived in one world and the supporting players in another, but they were still within the same family unit, like parents and children. But now, in 1948, that just wasn't true any more; we all had our own private lives away from the theatre and away from her and she could never really come to terms with that.

Also working on this production, as a young assistant stage manager, was the agent Rosalind Chatto:

Gertie was a mixture of very nasty and very nice, and looking back I think perhaps we should have realized that she wasn't really very well by then. She used to get very cross because nobody waited outside the stage door for her as they had in the old days; also most of us in the company were under thirty and had been children when she'd had all her big London hits before the war, so we didn't really know a great deal about her. Another problem was that the author and the director [Irene Hentschel] were both women and she wasn't used to that. Usually the director and the author were the people who took her out for dinner afterwards; she liked to have gentlemen around and there just weren't any except Michael, who was already falling in love with Anne Leon. Gertie didn't care for that either, so all in all I don't think any of us saw Miss Lawrence at her best.

Dressed in long pale green chiffon, unlikely perhaps for a Cornish village drama but it was what she insisted on wearing, Gertie would play one scene while cooking an omelette, so my task off-stage was to get the omelette ready and then shove it through the fireplace to where she was standing. I only got the job because I could cook, though this was still the time of powdered eggs and rationing so she used to complain a lot until I started putting jam in the middle.

She spent a lot of the time being very, very cross; one day her dresser didn't turn up, so I had to help her with a quick change and I caught her in a zip and in a voice which reverberated round the theatre she said, 'Fucking bitch', and then a second later the curtain was up and the audience, who must all have heard her, were treated to the full graciousness. For the sake of reality she used to slip into a chic little apron for the cooking, but the rest of the time it was all green chiffon.

The audience always seemed to us immensely old, I suppose because most of them were her pre-war customers, and she used to get very angry with them too if she thought there weren't quite enough of them out front at a matinée. Once, when things were going badly on the tour, she said, 'I haven't come five thousand miles to work with a crowd of fucking amateurs,' which surprised us all a bit, as a second or two later there she was being terribly charming again. She was quite extraordinarily variable, and her moods would change in a matter of seconds. She used to make me tremble with fear, but then it was my first job and I don't think perhaps she knew how frightening her rages could be to people who weren't used to them.

One day I told her I was moving house and she announced we'd have an American 'shower' party, which she said meant everyone had to bring gifts. The company weren't best pleased, as you can imagine, but she also announced that it wouldn't be formal, so there were Anne and I in our little wool dresses and she arrived in the full black satin and said, 'Oh, aren't we dressing?' She actually said that. Her whole backstage life was made up of bizarre pre-war manoeuvres like that, and the terrible thing was that it all seemed somehow very irrelevant to London life in 1948.

For the actress Anne Leon, there are many of the same memories: 'Gertie didn't much care for me because I was starting to go out with Michael and she thought that was her privilege as the star. Once she hit me quite hard on the neck with a hairbrush, and I'm afraid we were all rather glad when she finally went back to America. But she could still be absolutely magical on stage, and looking back it was a great experience: once you'd worked with Gertrude Lawrence, you could work with anybody.'

September Tide opened in London at the Aldwych Theatre in mid-December to reviews that were rather better for Gertie than for the play: 'The return of Miss Lawrence,' wrote Eric Keown for *Punch*, 'is an occasion for rejoicing. We have missed her almost more than we care to say, for her utterly charming self and because at present in the English theatre there is no actress who can catch at our hearts as she can; but *September Tide* is an artificial piece of conventional sentiment which leaves the actress's talents unused.'

Others were more enthusiastic about the play, but the general feeling was that it had been a faintly muted return home for the star of *Private Lives*; Gertie had never been a mother before on the London stage, at least not of a daughter old enough to have a husband, and though in real life Pamela was soon to embark on her second marriage, the public was somehow faintly uneasy to be thus reminded of the passing years. If Gertie had grown that much older, she who had stood on that terrace in the South of France and talked to Noël about the impossibility of ageing, then surely they her audiences must also have grown that much older? It was not a reassuring thought.

Nevertheless, business at the Aldwych held up well through the winter and into the spring of 1949; also in that *September Tide* cast was a young actor called Bryan Forbes, who later recalled one particularly hilarious matinée:

I had an arrangement with Michael Gough whereby I partly shared the services of his dresser, an engaging and eccentric character named Herbert. Herbert's principal responsibility came during the second act, when Micky had to dive from the balcony of the house into the harbour to rescue the drifting boat. He dived, of course, into a pile of mattresses strategically placed off-stage and out of sight of the audience. He then had to plunge into a bath of lukewarm water to simulate the real thing for his reappearance. Herbert had to be standing by to assist. During one matinée, when the Aldwych was packed with middle-aged matrons all balancing tea-trays on their knees, one of the cleats securing Michael Relph's weighty set suddenly gave way. Ossie [the stage manager Osmond Wilson] dashed in search of stage-hands to repair the damage before the set caved in. Now, it so happened that this incident took place a few minutes before Micky was due to make his celebrated plunge into the harbour. Herbert was waiting in the wings and before he disappeared, Ossie handed him a support rope and told him to hang on to it until help arrived. Meanwhile, on-stage, Gertie and Micky continued with the scene, unaware of the drama being enacted in the wings. Micky leapt from the balcony and groped his way in semi-darkness to the bath of water. During his absence Gertie went to a cupboard in the supposedly deserted house and took some towels out in readiness for Micky's drenched return. It was a vital plot point and carefully established in the dialogue that she and her son-in-law were isolated and alone – the storm was raging and there was nobody for miles around. Unbeknown to Gertie, Herbert was standing holding the rope on the other side of the cupboard door. It was a hot afternoon and he was curiously dressed in pin-stripe trousers, collarless shirt and white tennis shoes. I should also add that he had a small Hitler moustache. The total effect was startling. Gertie opened the cupboard door as she had done for the last two hundred performances, and revealed Herbert. She was too dumbfounded to close the door again, and for a few seconds she and Herbert stood transfixed like characters in a Disney cartoon. Herbert, being of the old school of theatrical dressers, was also a stickler for etiquette. He couldn't help himself. He gave a little bow and said, 'Good afternoon, Miss Lawrence.' Up to this point the audience had been mystified but not unduly alarmed by this sudden plot twist. After all, since they hadn't seen the play before, it was conceivable that Miss du Maurier had intended that her central character be suddenly confronted with Hitler in tennis shoes inside a cupboard. But when Herbert paid his respects to Miss Lawrence, the game was up. Gertie managed to close the door and then started to collapse. She turned away upstage in a futile attempt to conceal her mounting hysteria, of course minus towels . . . . I know many a star who would have reacted in anger to such a situation and had the polite and unfortunate Herbert fired on the spot, but Gertie loved a joke.

On another celebrated occasion the audience at *September Tide* one evening included none other than the Queen Mother, then of course Queen Mary. Rumour had it that she was not Gertie's greatest fan, largely because she suspected, not without justification, that the actress had once had a brief affair with her eldest son, who was now Duke of Windsor. Gertie was thrilled at the idea of a royal visit, and had all the company assembled backstage afterwards. Michael Gough recalled: 'Queen Mary came down the line, shaking all our hands and saying how much she'd enjoyed it. Then she got to the end of the line, where Gertie was standing, and said it had been a lovely evening except that she had found it a little hard to hear the ends of sentences. "Do you hear," said Gertie, turning to the rest of us, "now you've all got to speak up."

"Not all them," said the Queen Mother to Gertie, "just you." ' '

Richard Aldrich had flown over to be with his wife at the first night of *September Tide*, after which there had been a poignant meeting in her dressing-room between him and (now Colonel) Philip Astley. But then Aldrich had to return to New York, leaving Gertie to stay alone in London for the rest of the run. In the interests of (minor) economies she had now moved out of the Savoy and into a flat in Park Street, Mayfair, from where she wrote indignant letters home to Richard about the expense, inconvenience and general difficulty of post-war London life.

She did, however, manage to start up a splendid friendship with Bernard Shaw, who took her in the Royal Box to that year's Palladium pantomime. She also became a frequent Sunday visitor to his home at Ayot St Lawrence and so devoted did Shaw become that he gave her one of his last plays, *Buoyant Billions*, in the hope that she might play it in America, though sadly she never did. She did though manage to get him to grant her husband the Broadway rights in *Caesar and Cleopatra*, which the Aldrich management were keen to present the following winter, and even drove Lilli Palmer down to Ayot St Lawrence so that Shaw might approve her being cast as Cleopatra to Cedric Hardwicke's Caesar. There were times now when Gertie had become the ideal Mrs Richard Aldrich.

She was beginning to build up some kind of a social life (Danny Kaye was then in London and he, she and the then Oliviers would sometimes make up a four for after-theatre dinner) but the run of *September Tide* was still not an easy time for her. On the one hand she felt she had lost touch with her native land, and sometimes thought of nothing but getting back to Aldrich and the Cape for the summer. On the other hand she regarded that as an admission of some sort of defeat; she was still immensely English, not only by birth but by temperament, and simply to let the play close and go back to an American life would be an admission that things had not worked out, that she was no longer at home where she felt she still had the most right to be at home.

Aldrich lay low, refusing to beg her to return to him and determined that when she did go back to America it would be of her own free will. *September*

Tide did not seem to lead to any other British offers, and though Noël was already talking about a play called *Island Fling* (which would eventually surface five years later as *South Sea Bubble* with Vivien Leigh in the role originally intended for Gertie) that was still very far from completion, let alone production.

Towards the summer she did some BBC radio work including 'In Town Tonight' and a special called 'The Gertrude Lawrence Success Story' for which Shaw allowed her to do again her celebrated thirty-minute version of *Pygmalion*. But there was really nothing else happening, and by July 1949 with the *September Tide* business starting to fall off, she decided to pack up and head back to America: her telegram to Aldrich read SPIT ON THE BRASS CLEAR THE DECKS GET THAT WOMAN OUT OF THE HOUSE AM LEAVING SHOW IN ONE MONTH AND COMING HOME LOVE MRS A.

Though intended and indeed understood as a joke, 'Get that woman out of the house' now had a faintly uneasy ring to it. In the nine years since their marriage, the roles of Mr and Mrs Richard Aldrich had undergone a curious kind of reversal. She had married an unknown theatrical manager, who then had to go away to war, so for at least the first six years of their married life it was always she who made both the running and the news. But now, since the end of the war, Aldrich had built up a thriving Broadway theatrical management, one which frequently involved him in entertaining glamorous actresses in the course of his duties. The press were not slow to notice this, and neither was Gertie; the point was not necessarily that he was unfaithful to her, nor even that he had frequent opportunities to be; the point was that Gertie could now be seen in public, if not in private, as an ageing actress with a handsome husband often photographed in the company of other women.

It did not actually matter that both Gertie and Richard and some of their closer friends knew the marriage was still strong, or at any rate as strong as it had ever been; what mattered was the subtle shift in Gertie's image from that of the glamorous, romantic, all-winning superstar to that of a middle-aged actress with potential marital difficulties. It had now been three years since she had opened on Broadway in *Pygmalion*, and in three years Broadway was apt to forget. The easy solution would have been for her to grab at the first script, musical or non-musical, that offered her a chance of Broadway stardom for the 1949-50 season and it is hugely to Gertie's credit that on this occasion she took a considerably more difficult and dangerous option instead.

First she did her ritual week at the Cape Playhouse in *September Tide* and then, rather against the judgement of the two who were closest to her, Richard Aldrich and Fanny Holtzmann, both of whom argued for Broadway, she headed out to Hollywood instead. The offer that had come from there was a curious one: to play the mother of Jane Wyman in the film version of Tennessee Williams's *The Glass Menagerie*, a role for which both Tallulah Bankhead and Bette Davis had unsuccessfully tested already.

Almost everything was against Gertie in this: Laurette Taylor had enjoyed a huge success in the stage original, one that Gertie was unlikely to be able to beat on film. Indeed she had not made a film since *Rembrandt* back in England fifteen years earlier, had never worked in Hollywood, and had never played a major role on screen that required anything more from her than minimal acting and very good looks.

Yet now, precisely because it was such a challenge, she was prepared to plunge into a role that many more classically trained and American actresses would have had second thoughts about. It required her to wear 20 lbs of padding in order to age up for the impoverished old Southern belle struggling to preserve a dream of grandeur for her disillusioned children. It also required her to take second billing to Miss Wyman (with Kirk Douglas and Arthur Kennedy also sharing the posters) and to cope with a deep-south accent. It required her, in short, to travel as far professionally as she had ever travelled away from her usual casting, and there were both friends and critics who thought that her courage here bordered on the reckless.

But then Gertie had never been an exactly fearful lady, and in one sense perhaps she knew she had not too much to lose; if the film worked, it would open up a whole new career for her as a character actress on screen, a route that Gladys Cooper and number of other one-time West End stars had by now chosen. If the film did not work, Broadway was still there and far enough away not to be affected by her California failure.

In the event it *was* a failure; Tennessee Williams himself thought her casting 'a dismal error' and the film itself the worst he had ever seen of any of his work. Other critics were more respectful, but they too had to admit that a once-great stage role had been turned, as Bosley Crowther put it for the *New York Times* 'by the screenplay and by Miss Lawrence into a farcically exaggerated shrew with the zeal of a burlesque comedienne to see her diffident daughter wed . . . Miss Lawrence peeks and listens behind the curtains of the tiny dining-room, giving a perfect imitation of a nervous Mama in domestic comedy. This is not what *The Glass Menagerie* is all about.'

British critics generally found Gertie 'over-theatrical' and objected on Tennessee Williams's behalf to a tacked-on 'happy ending' as well as to Kirk Douglas's idea of the gentleman caller. But now, in 1980, there are (still admittedly faint) signs that the film may be due for reappraisal. Doug McClelland, writing in a recent issue of the magazine *Filmograph*: 'Now that we have been exposed in subsequent stage and television productions of Tennessee Williams's semi-autobiographical play to such ludicrous Amanda Wingfields as Shirley Booth, Maureen Stapleton and Katharine Hepburn, Miss Lawrence's multi-faceted characterisation looks very good. So does the movie'; and it had other defenders even at the time, most notably Richard Griffith who wrote for the *Saturday Review* about Gertie that 'not since Garbo has there been anything like the naked eloquence of her face, with its amazing play of thought and emotion'. Not altogether bad for her very first Hollywood effort. Sadly it was also to be her last.

22

HOLLYWOOD MENAGERIE

Gertie had never had much luck on film, and *The Glass Menagerie* was to prove no exception to the rule; she did not much enjoy the shooting, did not much care for the Hollywood life (Hollywood was, after all, where her once great mentor, André Charlot, king of the West End and Broadway pre-war revues, was now being allowed to fade quietly away as an extra in B pictures) and she could not wait to get back East, where, in her view, real actors belonged. Sadly, in her haste to escape after the shooting was completed in January 1950, she missed one of the great film roles of all time. Joseph L. Mankiewicz was at this time just starting to cast his classic *All About Eve*; having fought off Darryl Zanuck's idea that Marlene Dietrich should play the role, which eventually went to Bette Davis, Mankiewicz first signed Claudette Colbert. When, however, she accidentally wrenched her back and had to withdraw, Mankiewicz's second choice fell on Gertie. He recalled later:

Submitting the actual screenplay to her suddenly became a highly complicated procedure. To this day, I don't quite know whether Gertie ever did read it; I'm quite sure that if she had, she would have crawled back to California to play it. Somehow, a protocol of approach to Miss Lawrence had come into being. All scripts were first submitted to, and approved by, the redoubtable Fanny Holtzmann. Miss Holtzmann read the screenplay and called me at home to say she found it very good. There were only two changes she would insist upon: (1) The drunk scenes would have to be eliminated. It would be preferable, in fact, if Miss Lawrence neither drank, nor smoked at all on the screen. (2) During the party sequence, the

183

pianist was not to play 'Liebestraum'. Instead, he would accompany Miss Lawrence as she sang a torch song about Bill. (Something I thought Helen Morgan had already done, rather successfully.) Since my own lawyer had always admonished me to respond to other lawyers with either 'yes' or 'no' and urged me to 'keep the witty ripostes for when you're shaving', I said nothing but 'no'. And that's how Gertrude Lawrence did not play Margo Channing.

Later Gertie would claim in a press interview that it was nothing to do with Fanny, nor yet (as had been reported elsewhere) a dispute with Mankiewicz over dollars. Instead, insisted Gertie, 'I did not wish to play the part of the actress as she was characterized in the original script. As a star of twenty-five years in the legitimate theatre, I felt the part would give an unfair impression to the film public of the character and the private lives of leading ladies in my profession.' And, in particular, of her? Meanwhile Aldrich was claiming that she had given up the film purely and simply to get back to his side, and yet again to 'patch up' a marriage of which the last year had been spent by him in New York and her first in London with *September Tide* and then in California with *Glass Menagerie*. Whatever the real reason, for more probably a combination of all these reasons, Gertie was, alas, never to be Margo Channing.

On a holiday with her husband in Florida early in 1950, Gertie had now apparently decided that her marriage was at last to become the most important thing in her life. Aware perhaps that she was nearly fifty-two and that she no longer had any real English affiliations and that Hollywood was a foreign country where things were done differently, she settled back into an East Coast American life as Mrs Aldrich. She was genuinely happy now at the Cape; her initial over-theatrical embrace of the Aldrich way of life had matured and settled into a real devotion to him and his summer theatre. There after all she was the resident queen, able to play gracious hostess to visiting stars from New York on the annual summer-stock circuit. There everybody knew who she was, and she could choose her roles. There too there was a community, of the kind she had once found and loved around the West End but which now existed nowhere else for her.

She was getting on well with her Aldrich step-children (one of whom was to be sent off later that year to Korea), and the marriage to Aldrich himself had at last settled down to the point where each had learnt to live with the other. He now had acquired the confidence of a successful career, she had begun to lose the insecurity which demanded he give her all of his time and attention. Ten years after her wedding, and with only two years left of her life, Gertie had at last learnt about marriage.

For the next year, she announced, she would be devoting herself to Richard and the Cape Playhouse; she was, however, entirely open to offers for 1951 and Fanny at once started on a search for a suitable new vehicle. Clearly it needed to be on stage rather than on screen, since the advance notices were already starting to come in for *Glass Menagerie*. Ideally, perhaps, it should be a stage reunion with Noël, but he had unaccountably still not finished his *Island Fling* comedy for Gertie and in the meantime had nothing else that might suit her. Fanny was now thinking big, perhaps aware that Gertie's career had begun to slide as she moved however gracefully into her fifties. This time it would be no good settling for another safe Shaw or Coward revival, no good just picking up a light comedy and hoping to run with it. Gertie needed something very big, something very starry, and above all something that she could make first and uniquely her own thing. It had, in other words, to be a première, and preferably a musical première.

The choice was a difficult one; it had been nine years since *Lady in the Dark*, and in that time a lot had happened to the Broadway musical. New producers, new composers, new dance directors had come along and none of them were thinking much about Gertrude Lawrence. Mary Martin and Ethel Merman were the big musical stars of the moment; Gertie was associated with pre-war smaller-scale revues and Coward comedies. She was not, in short, getting anything like first pick of the 1950 musicals.

Undaunted as ever, and at her best when faced by this sort of a challenge, Fanny decided that if musicals were not coming in by post then one would simply have to be created for Gertie and expressly commissioned for her. This fairly revolutionary idea (few actresses had ever actually commisssioned a musical) would, assuming it could be made to work, have certain distinct advantages: Gertie would not just be another hired hand, but in at the very wrapping of the package and therefore artistically and financially very much more strongly placed. It would be, whoever wrote it and whoever directed it, her musical.

By the spring of 1950 Fanny had all this worked out; what she still lacked was any idea at all as to what the show might be. Then, as if to prove that miracles did still happen, a book arrived on her desk. It was Margaret Landon's 1944 best-seller *Anna and the King of Siam*, and the William Morris office who represented the author had vague hopes that Gertie might fancy doing it as a play. As a film, of course, it had already been done a couple of years earlier with Irene Dunne playing Anna and Rex Harrison the King.

Fanny read it, gave to Gertie, and the two of them immediately reached the same conclusion: here was not a play, but a musical. The only trouble was that somebody still had to write it as such. Gertie suggested Cole Porter, who seemed less than enthusiastic. Fanny Holtzmann's biographer, Edward Berkman remembers: 'Fanny hurried down Madison Avenue, the names of composer-lyricist teams whirling through her mind. Crossing 63rd Street, she found herself abreast of Dorothy Hammerstein who was hastening in the same direction. Dorothy waved a gloved hand: "Can't talk now, Fanny. On my way to Sammy's Deli to get a sour pickle for Ockie". Ockie. but of course. What greater master of mellow sentiment and wry humour than Oscar Hammerstein II? And who could pour out melodies as tender as those of his partner, Richard Rodgers, with whom he had already written *Oklahoma!*, *Carousel* and *South Pacific?*'

Anna and the King of Siam was hastily despatched to Rodgers and Hammerstein for an opinion. Hammerstein was immediately keen to tackle this real-life saga of the British widow who, in the 1860s, went out to Siam to tutor King Mongkut's children and ended up tutoring him too; indeed so keen was he on the whole idea of the foreign governess who eventually wins the children and the heart of a crusty despot that ten years later he wrote the whole thing all over again and called it *The Sound of Music*.

Rodgers, however, was considerably less enthusiastic at first: 'We had never before written a musical specifically with one actor or actress in mind, and we were concerned that such an arrangement might not give us the freedom to write what we wanted the way we wanted. What also bothered us was that while we both admired Gertie tremendously, we felt that her vocal range was minimal and that she had never been able to overcome an unfortunate tendency to sing flat.'

But Fanny had moved fast and buttoned up the musical rights, which meant that if anybody wanted to set *Anna and the King of Siam* to music then they had to do it for Gertie. It was as simple as that, and Fanny had gambled on it eventually proving irresistible even on those conditions to Rodgers and Hammerstein, which indeed it did. They screened the film a couple of times, and as Rodgers later wrote:

That did it. It was obvious that the story of an English governess who travels to

Siam to become a teacher to the children of a semibarbaric monarch had the makings of a beautiful musical play. There was the contrast between Eastern and Western cultures; there was the intangibility of the attraction between teacher and king; there was the tragic sub-plot of the doomed love between the king's Burmese wife and the Burmese emissary; there was the warmth of the relationship between Anna and her royal pupils; there was the theme of democratic teachings triumphing over autocratic rule; and lastly, there were the added features of Oriental pomp and atmosphere. Here was a project Oscar and I could really believe in, and we notified Fanny that we were ready to go to work.

The King and I was now under way; the Holtzmann office announced the project as a vehicle for Gertie to open on Broadway early in 1951, which gave Rodgers and Hammerstein time to write and Gertie herself the unknown luxury of a year off with no need to worry about what was going to happen at the end of it. From several vaguely unsatisfactory postwar months in London and Hollywood her career had taken another of its sudden lurches upwards, to the point where she was able to announce that Rodgers and Hammerstein were writing her a musical. Ethel Merman and Mary Martin had never been so lucky.

That summer of 1950 Gertie stayed on the Cape, playing housewife and doing a couple of weeks in what was to prove her last part there, Beatrice in the comedy *Travellers' Joy*, which she did for a week at Dennis and a week over at Falmouth where Aldrich now had a second summer theatre. By now she was the undisputed ruler of the straw-hat circuit and even organized the setting up of the first Music Tent on the Cape at Hyannis. This idea of doing shows under canvas, which had recently been pioneered in Florida, was to become a permanent part of the Massachusetts summer theatre scene but it is doubtful if it would have got off to quite so well-publicized or rapid a start in 1950 had it not become a Gertrude Lawrence promotion. She even made sure, typically enough, that 'her' tent at Hyannis had the smartest powder rooms on the whole of the Cape.

She also spent a good deal of time that year redecorating The Berries, playing weekend hostess to the Aldrich New England clan and the various actors who worked the theatre, knitting mittens for Bernard Shaw in the forlorn hope he would give her the Broadway rights to *Doctor's Dilemma*, and organizing picnics for such special guests as Bea Lillie and Robert Flemyng. She also took part in a cabaret at one of her husband's Harvard College reunions and even learned to cook, so determined was she now to prove to the Aldrich family that their boy had not after all made too disastrous a marriage.

Back in New York that autumn, she made a few personal appearances to help *The Glass Menagerie* on its way, but her time was now increasingly being taken up with costume fittings and pre-rehearsal preparations for *The King and I*. With the start of the Korean War, Aldrich had been called back into Naval Intelligence and sent to Washington, so she was now alone again in New York and available for constant casting and other discussions on the new show.

The first idea for the King had been Rex Harrison, who'd already played the part on film; but (this was six years before *My Fair Lady*) he was unenthusiastic about his chances of survival in a musical and in any case already committed to an Edinburgh Festival and London run of T. S. Eliot's *The Cocktail Party*.

The Holtzmann office also made vague overtures to Noël, who of all people Gertie would most like to have played opposite; but he was not about to commit himself to a long run in somebody else's musical (he was also to turn down *My Fair Lady* in later years) and meanwhile Richard Rodgers was suggesting Alfred Drake, his *Oklahoma!* hero, who had just had another big success in *Kiss Me Kate*.

Drake however was only willing to sign for six months, and by now the production had already grown to the point where a run of years rather than months had to be economically envisaged. Aldrich himself had refused to take on the role of producer, sticking to his old belief in not confusing private with professional partnerships, and as a result *The King and I* was to become a Rodgers and Hammerstein presentation. The team they built for it during this autumn of 1950 was one of the greatest and most distinguished that Broadway had ever seen; though the King was still proving tricky to cast, the combination of Gertie and Rodgers and Hammerstein (and an already tried and tested vehicle which had made money as a book and a film) meant that the project attracted the very cream of Broadway's production talent. Thus a young choreographer called Jerome Robbins was handling the dances, Jo Mielziner was doing the settings and lighting, Irene Sharaff was doing the costumes, Robert Russell Bennett the orchestrations and the director was to be none other than Gertie's old playwright friend from *Behold We Live*, John van Druten, who had recently made a name for himself as a director of his own postwar successes *Bell, Book and Candle* and *I am a Camera*. Originally

Hammerstein had hoped that Josh Logan, who had worked with him on *South Pacific*, would handle the production of *The King and I* and co-author the book, but when that offer was declined Hammerstein decided he would handle the book himself and the production then became van Druten's.

But still they had no King and they, therefore, began auditioning, since there was no other star actor to whom they could think of offering it. Richard Rodgers: 'The first candidate who walked out from the wings was a bald, muscular fellow with a bony oriental face. He was dressed casually and carried a guitar. His name, we were told, was Yul Brynner, which meant nothing to us. He scowled in our direction, sat down on the stage and crossed his legs tailor-fashion, then plunked one whacking chord on his guitar and began to howl in a strange language that no one could understand. He looked savage, he sounded savage, and there was no denying that he projected a feeling of controlled ferocity. When he read for us, we again were impressed by his authority and conviction. Oscar and I looked at each other and nodded.'

Brynner's entire subsequent career can be charted in terms of his rise through the ranks of this musical: when it first opened on Broadway, Gertrude Lawrence was alone above the title and he well below it. For the film, a decade later, he was above the title, but sharing the billing there with Deborah Kerr; for the Broadway and London Palladium revival two decades later still, he was alone above the title, despite the fact that it remains fundamentally Anna's story and show.

But he was, even in 1950, not quite the unknown that Rodgers had taken him for; a former circus acrobat, Brynner had already worked with Mary Martin in a short-lived Broadway musical called *Lute Song* and was a pioneer New York television director then currently hosting his own CBS musical variety show each week, one he was reluctant to quit for the financially less secure offer of a below-the-title Broadway job. But Mary Martin urged Rodgers and Hammerstein to 'kidnap him if necessary—you'll never find a better King' and eventually Brynner was persuaded to quit his television career and start rehearsing.

The King and I was budgeted at $360,000 making it the most expensive Rodgers and Hammerstein musical to date, but there was no shortage of backers: Twentieth Century Fox, who owned the film, came in for $40,000 and other investors included Josh Logan and Mary Martin from *South Pacific*, the composers' families, Billy Rose and Leland Hayward. Gertie was on 10%

of the gross plus 5% of the profits, but neither Brynner nor any of Gertie's successors in the role in either New York or London did better than a straight salary. By the end of 1953, profits were running at over $700,000 and that was well before the release of the film or summer-stock rights. One New York lawyer who had originally put in $37,000 eventually took home another $44,000, meaning that the show in its first run was to return a profit of something like 117%.

The money wasn't made easily though; rehearsals got off to a bad start when Rodgers, thinking to be helpful, arranged for Gertie to attend a piano run-through of the entire score sung by Doretta Morrow, who had been cast as Tuptim, the king's Burmese wife. Gertie refused thereafter to speak to him for the first few weeks of rehearsal, perhaps because she had taken offence at Rodgers allowing Miss Morrow to sing 'her' songs, but more probably because it had panicked her into a realization of the demands of the score and the limitations of her own voice which were even greater than ever before. She had never tackled a show of the musical complexity of *King and I*, which, though rightly regarded as a classic of its kind, did not give her any of the chances for lyrical jokiness which she had always discovered in Coward and Cole Porter and the Gershwins. This was closer to being an operetta, and it frightened the hell out of her.

As a result she was throughout rehearsal edgy and very difficult indeed; she knew she couldn't be sacked, so deeply had she been built in to the show's construction, but she also began to think quite seriously that she had here taken on more than she could handle. As her director, van Druten found himself inexperienced at musicals, and the control therefore reverted quickly to Rodgers and Hammerstein, both of whom had to admit that for all her very considerable comic graces Gertie was not the kind of tough Mary Martin stage star they had grown accustomed to, but instead a very much more fragile and variable creature, given to moods and tantrums which identified her as a rather ghostly 1930s figure instead of a fully functioning part of the new postwar Broadway machine. She was, in short, trouble.

Her singing voice was shaky and very often flat, but Hammerstein was the first to acknowledge that she had a kind of 'magic light' on stage and Rodgers had been careful to write numbers for her in a limited vocal range ('I Whistle a Happy Tune', 'Hello Young Lovers', 'Shall We Dance?') while giving his more demanding songs ('Something Wonderful', 'We Kiss in a Shadow') to the professionally trained singers, Doretta Morrow and Dorothy Sarnoff.

Even so there were complaints about Gertie's flat singing all through rehearsals, and by the time they opened the pre-Broadway tour in New Haven on 27 February 1951 they were in considerable trouble. Expectations were high, bookings were high, but the show was running for almost four hours thanks to Jerome Robbins's immensely long (though innovative) ballet for the 'Uncle Tom's Cabin' sequence. Moreover Gertie had missed the dress rehearsal on account of laryngitis, and had already been replaced at that performance (as at so many others she was later to be) by her old friend and understudy from the Charlot revues Constance Carpenter, who thus became perhaps the first understudy in history to go on for a star even before the show had actually opened.

Still, they seemed to have a winner, though the *Variety* critic thought this was 'not nearly such a sure thing as the earlier Rodgers-Hammerstein creations' despite the fact that Yul Brynner's performance was 'stand-out thesping' and that 'Miss Lawrence, despite a recent illness that kept her away from rehearsals, slinks, acts, cavorts and in general exhibits exceedingly well her several facets for entertaining.'

The *Philadelphia Bulletin*, however, thought that 'Miss Lawrence's already thin voice is now starting to wear a great deal thinner' and this in the very first try-out week; moreover her loss of voice in the final rehearsals had already started to cause a split in the relationship between Gertie and Fanny on one side of the fence and Rodgers and Hammerstein on the other; Gertie wanted to delay the New Haven opening until she was feeling totally back on form. The producers wouldn't hear of it; despite her immense value to the show, the days were long gone when a single star could hold up an entire production simply by getting ill.

The health of Gertrude Lawrence was to be a constant source of worry and acrimony throughout the run of *The King and I*; but neither she, nor her husband, nor anyone involved with the show was to know that she was already dying of cancer, and her frequent indisposition was thus to have two highly contrasting interpretations. Those who loved her took the view that for a woman of fifty-two to have to carry, as Anna does carry, an entire $3\frac{1}{2}$-hour musical during the course of which she walked four miles around the stage at every performances and wore a total of seven massively heavy costumes each weighing 75 lbs and complete with steel hoops which bruised her legs every time she tried to curtsy to the King, was simply asking too much of an actress brought up in a gentler pre-war tradition of British leading ladies. Those who did not love her, and there were a great many of them too, took the not totally irreconcilable view that she was simply past it and masking her inability to sing and her jealousy of Brynner's success by a series of psychosomatic collapses.

In fact, Brynner's triumph was no problem at all: she had lived through all that with Danny Kaye and *Lady in the Dark* a decade before, and was genuinely delighted to have helped make them both into stars, just so long as they never lost sight of the fact that she had got there first. He was not a worry and nor were the collapses psychosomatic; she was beginning to be very sick indeed, though still blissfully unaware of the cause of her physical and vocal exhaustion. *The King and I*, after all, provided a perfect alibi; it was an extremely exhausting show.

It was also, on the pre-Broadway tour, a show in a constant state of change; from New Haven they had progressed to Boston where reviews were quite alarmingly unenthusiastic at first, and it was Gertie who came up with one at least of the show-saving solutions. Between bouts of laryngitis and ill health, and still plagued by a score set in a key too high for her, Gertie yet retained enough of her old-style star's instinct to realize that one of the show's first-half problems was that after 'I Whistle A Happy Tune', sung as the ship docks, she then didn't have another song for a very long time. She was after all still alone above the title, and audiences didn't expect to wait that long to realize why; what she needed was another song up front. Rodgers agreed, and in New Haven suddenly recalled a song he'd written for the young Naval lieutenant to sing to Liat in *South Pacific*. In the event, he'd then written them 'Younger Than Springtime' and abandoned this earlier effort which was still therefore unheard. It was called 'Getting To Know You', and he gave it to Gertie to sing to her Siamese charges when she first is seen with them.

By the time they'd got to Boston they'd also put in the complete 'Shall We Dance?' sequence which was to become the show's most lingering and evocative memory, and by the time they left there for Broadway, Elliott Norton was able to report, '*The King and I* left here with three new songs already inserted; understood Bing Crosby and others already recording, including Sinatra.' Indeed they were; by now the show had excellent word-of-mouth reports going for it, plus a final number which as Irene Sharaff, the costume designer, noted with justifiable pride 'starred Gertrude Lawrence, Yul Brynner and a pale pink satin ball-gown.' Even the fifteen Siamese children had stopped trying to flush their hats down the toilets, and all was set fair for a massive Broadway success, which was exactly what they got: 'an original and beautiful excursion into the rich splendors of the Far East,' thought Brooks Atkinson, while Richard Watts reckoned he'd seen 'a show of a thousand delights with the magic of Gertrude Lawrence and a remarkably believable performance by Yul Brynner.'

True there were those who argued that *Call Me Madam* and a revival of *Pal Joey*, the other main musicals of that 1951 season, were dramatically more exciting, but when it came to Tony award time *The King and I* swept the board: Gertie, Yul Brynner, Rodgers, Hammerstein, Jo Mielziner and Irene Sharaff all won in their respective categories.

Critics began going back to the show at three- or six-monthly intervals, to see how it, and specifically Gertie, were holding up; at first all was well. The rapturous first night, followed by rave reviews and a sense of being the musical queen of Broadway again for the first time in ten years, did wonders for Gertie's spirits. She had signed for two years, which would take her through to the end of 1952, and already she was then making plans to star at Drury Lane in what was to be the Coronation summer of 1953. Then, all being well, there would be the film; she was, therefore, to be Mrs Anna for at least the next four years, and all she had to do was survive them. No need to think about other properties or to worry about her career again: *The King and I* had seen to all of that.

Sadly, her health soon began to give way again; in rehearsal her weight had dropped to 110 lb, she was looking painfully drawn, and by the time the summer came, the heat backstage at the St James was almost more than she could bear. Ironically, this was happening at a time when (singing apart) she had seldom been closer to the top of her form; as her director John van Druten noted: 'Her comedy in the part was gentler, Victorian, almost evasive, and her touch on the sweeter and more personal notes was stronger and surer . . . her radiance was there, and her star quality indefinable but intensely vivid . . . she had a power to move not only the audience, but the very boards of the stage as she stepped on them.'

That was on the nights she was playing; this time her contract did not allow for her ritual summer holiday on the Cape, but Constance Carpenter was being kept on constant stand-by and was gradually beginning to take over at certain matinées: 'Gertie had never really had an understudy before, and I think (although she was always very sweet to me) that it unnerved her to see me around, because she knew that it meant the management were worried about her health. So was she: I think she knew that even allowing for the demands of the show she ought not to have been getting as exhausted as she was, but though she frequently went for check-ups nobody at that stage seemed to think there was anything very much wrong with her. At first she was furious to have me standing by, but gradually she got used to it and began sending me flowers and little notes when I took over.'

= 23 =

EXIT MRS ANNA

In the autumn, as the heat receded, Gertie seemed to get her strength back for a while; indeed apart from playing eight shows a week as Mrs Anna, she also agreed to teach a weekly, Thursday afternoon class in drama at the Columbia School of Dramatic Arts and this, so far from leading to further exhaustion, used paradoxically to give her a kind of energy with which to face the rest of the week on stage. Her fees here were used to found a scholarship in drama at Columbia, and she recruited such old allies as André Charlot and John Golden to provide her students with scripts and further advice. She had seldom been happier: for all the years that she had been told she was 'lightweight', a revue star without the intellectual equipment to make the leap into serious theatre, here at last was a kind of revenge. She was now a 'Professor of Drama' and loving every moment of it.

She also threw herself into organizing the charity appeal in the name of Helen Hayes' daughter, Mary MacArthur, who had died an early and tragic death only a few months after playing a season with her mother at the Cape Playhouse and staying there with Gertie. But by Christmas a combination of exhaustion and a recurrence of a bout of pleurisy had left Gertie so weak that she was herself finally sent into hospital for a full week of tests. The medical report at the end of that week, just nine months before her death, read that she 'had the physique of a woman in her twenties and although somewhat tired, this could be ascribed to her having worked through an excessively hot summer without a vacation.'

So there was nothing much to worry about. *The King and I* played into 1952, while the management started to make plans for moving the show to London in the following year. This was proving difficult, as the child labour laws there currently forbade the use on stage of very small children, except for brief periods, and Gertie let it be known backstage that she was 'totally opposed to the use of midgets' for the Siamese princelings.

February brought bronchitis, another week away from the show, and considerably worsening relations with Rodgers and Hammerstein; Gertie and Aldrich (who on frequent trips to New York from his Washington naval assignment was getting increasingly worried about his wife's health, whatever the doctors might have said) asked the R & H management if they would consider closing the show for Holy Week. This they regretted would be impossible; however, they would release her for six weeks from the end of June and put Celeste Holm in as a summer replacement.

Meanwhile, though, the composer and lyricist of *The King and I* were getting more than a little disturbed and irate at Gertie's worsening performances; a letter from them to her dated 20 May 1952 is marked in their files 'not mailed' but there can be no doubt that it only puts on paper what Gertie already knew they were thinking and saying about her work: 'Eight times a week you are losing the respect of 1,500 people. This is a serious thing to be happening to one of the great women of our theatre, and it would be dishonest and unfriendly of us to stand by any longer without making you aware of the tarnish you are putting on your past triumphs and your future prospects.'

Everyone except Gertie, it seemed, wanted Gertie out of that show. Audiences were now growing audibly restive at the standards of her singing, boos had even been heard at one or two performances, and both her friends and her enemies were agreed that for Gertie, and for *The King and I*, the best thing would be a parting of the ways. But Gertie was a stubborn fighter. *The King and I* was hers and she was not about to let go, whatever the cost to her health. Nothing had been finally signed about its London run, and if she let go now she might also be losing the chance of what she most wanted, a Coronation summer in a massive hit at Drury Lane; a royal return home.

So she played on, refusing to listen to even her beloved Noël, who that spring begged her for her own good to leave the show and have a prolonged rest, after which he promised her a less demanding light comedy of his own for the autumn, the one that was to become _South Sea Bubble_. But she was not willing to consider that either, and Noël went to Jamaica faintly worried about her unusual state of exhaustion, but having not the remotest idea that he would never see his darling Gertie again.

The summer came and, as Celeste Holm moved into the star dressing-room (turning the show, said one acid reviewer, into 'Anna Get Your King'), Gertie went back to the Cape for a prolonged and idyllic rest. True, they did find her one morning in an apparent faint, but that was put down to the humidity or possibly an unfavourable reaction to a course of injections she had been receiving for a poison-ivy rash on her arm. By Monday 11 August the holiday over, she was apparently fit and fine again, and back in the show, only faintly indignant to discover that the neon light announcing her name outside the theatre had fused, making her once again, she said, a 'lady in the dark'.

Through a sweltering August she played eight shows a week until one Saturday, after the matinée, she fainted on her way back to the dressing-room. Constance Carpenter again took over as Mrs Anna, and Gertie went into a New York hospital, where doctors now said she was suffering from hepatitis, a painful, but seldom fatal disease of the liver. Aldrich was called to the bedside, friends all over the world were alerted by Fanny, but again there seemed not to be too much to worry about. Gertie had after all been 'off' a good deal this past year, and perhaps at last, now the trouble had been diagnosed, she might start on a proper recovery. That at least was the thinking until 6 September. Her ex-son-in-law, Dr Bill Cahan, recalls:

Pamela and I had long since been divorced, and I therefore hadn't seen much of Gertie these last few years. I was now working across the street from New York Hospital but, although we had remained reasonably friendly, I didn't want to put in a sudden appearance at her bedside for fear of frightening her. The question of cancer did arise, and I had sent one or two of our experts over to have a look at her, but the general view was that this was definitely hepatitis, though we had decided that on the morning of Saturday 6 September there would be an emergency biopsy to see just what was wrong with her liver. I was then living a bachelor life on 69th Street and at six that morning the phone rang and it was Dick Aldrich saying would I come right over, as Gertrude was in a terrible state. I raced over and there she was in a big private room and she was in coma suddenly; I tried to work out what had happened, and apparently we managed to get her out of shock, because she opened her eyes and gave me a 'What the hell are *you* doing here?' kind of look, and then she died. The autopsy, which I attended, showed that she had a cancer which had been cryptic, very silent, and had completely taken over her liver. We never did find out where it had come from; some thought the gall bladder, others thought the pancreas. Either way, she died of cancer.

By mid-morning the death of Gertrude Lawrence was known all over New York, and by the end of that September Saturday it was known all over the world. Cole Lesley recalled: 'We had gone that afternoon to Folkestone Races, where we had great fun, backed several winners and drank rather a lot of cherry brandy. We also, naturally, had to back a horse called Bitter-Sweet, running in the first race at a course somewhere in the north of England. After the last race I ran to get an evening paper to find out if Bitter-Sweet had won, turned to the back page, and in the Stop Press was stupefied to read in large black letters GERTRUDE LAWRENCE DEAD. Noël's grief was dreadful to see, his face ashen during the drive home, and once at home he broke down completely.'

A day or two later, Noël wrote in *The Times*: 'We first worked together as child actors in the Playhouse Theatre, Liverpool; since then, whether we have been acting together or not, we have been integrally part of each other's lives . . . I wish so very deeply that I could have seen her just once more, acting in a play of mine, for no one I have ever known, however brilliant and however gifted, has contributed quite what she contributed to my work. Her quality was, to me, unique and her magic imperishable.'

Other tributes began to pour into the Aldrich home and the Holtzmann office from all round the world; that night, in the old 'show must go on' tradition, Constance Carpenter played for Gertie, as she had so often in recent weeks, but it was decided that on the following Tuesday, the day of the funeral, the theatre would close and, in a unique and so far unrepeated trans-Atlantic tribute, the lights would also be dimmed for two minutes all along Broadway and, that same evening, all along Shaftesbury Avenue and Hollywood Boulevard as well. This tribute was fixed, need one add, by Fanny, who reckoned it was no more than Gertie would have wished.

Morton Gottlieb described it thus: 'Like most people I was out of town the weekend Gertie died, but as soon as I heard the news I went straight to the Holtzmann office to see if I could help. All the phones were going, with calls coming in from all over the world, and it was decided that we'd manage the funeral just like a Broadway opening night. We sent out invitations to all the drama critics, we had special tickets reserved for her friends, like house seats, and as I was the only one who could instantly recognize all the Broadway people and all the people from Cape Cod as well I stood out front with the police, telling them who to let in. It was a lovely funeral. Dick Aldrich played ''Getting To Know You'' on the organ.'

In London Pamela heard the news of her mother's death via a phone call from Fanny, and caught the next plane to New York: 'It was grisly. We had this terrible meeting what can only be called backstage at the church, where there was a great boardroom table and there round it were Rodgers and Hammerstein, who had been so awful about her singing, and I thought this is a real mockery. There had been an autopsy and someone had patched her all up and made her face up a kind of putty colour and put her in the last-act ''Shall We Dance?'' dress from the show. It was pure Evelyn Waugh, the whole affair. Grotesque. Then we all trailed up to Massachusetts where she was buried with the Aldrich family, and there were photographers practically standing in the grave. I do wish my mother had died in England and was buried here instead. It's where she belongs.'

But America had by now claimed Gertrude Lawrence as its own: five thousand people jammed the pavement outside the Fifth Avenue Presbyterian Church at 55th Street, while there were another eighteen hundred inside – among them Richard and Pamela, of course, and Fanny and David Holtzmann, and the cast of *The King and I*, and Bea Lillie whom Gertie had understudied thirty-five years earlier. Dietrich was there, and Moss Hart, and an entire roll-call of the Broadway stage. Oscar Hammerstein gave the oration:

Gertrude had a magic light. It had nothing to do with technique, although her technical equipment was considerable. It had nothing to do with physical grace, although no trained dancer could move more gracefully than she. I think it had something to do with a great, warm love for the world and an eagerness to have the world love her. I think she wanted to do things for people to make them love her. And so she harnessed this burning desire and drove it through many theatres until she learned the shortest and most direct ways to the heart of an audience. Nothing was more important to her than this. She cheerfully dedicated her own life to a series of elaborate and glorious imitations of life – imitations that were just a little better, a little brighter, than life itself. This was her fun. This was her mission. This was why she gave herself to us. God bless her for it.

The tributes continued: on television that Sunday night Ed Sullivan put together a weird memorial programme consisting largely of Gracie Fields, Judith Anderson and Winston Churchill's daughter Sarah, none of whom had ever really known her; NBC came up with a rather better documentary tribute to her career, and on the day of the funeral, flags were lowered at Columbia University, where she had so recently been teaching, and by an army entertainments unit out in Korea. Her permanent memorial is a granite seat in Lakeview Cemetery, Upton, Massachusetts, where her body lies next to that of Richard Aldrich's mother and surrounded by other members of the Aldrich clan.

Her estate, left to her husband and daughter, was valued for probate at 'more than twenty thousand dollars'; quite how much more was never publicly established, though it was known that she had recently made £30,000 out of the filming of *Glass Menagerie* and that shortly before her death she had been getting more than £2,000 a week as her share of *The King and I*.

The Museum of the City of New York soon staged a retrospective exhibition in celebration of her career, and one City hospital named its cancer wing in her honour. Two years after his wife's death, Richard Aldrich published a memoir of their life together and Hollywood promptly announced that it was to be filmed with Greer Garson as 'the greatest love story ever told', a plan that came somewhat unstuck when, during the negotiations, Mr Aldrich married a young model whom he had first met during Gertie's lifetime.

When, in the end, they did make a film of Gertie's life it was the 1968 Julie Andrews musical *Star!* That, mercifully, exists now only on occasional late-night American television screenings in a cut version called rather more poignantly *Those Were The Happy Times*.

Yet Gertie lives on: not only as a shadowy figure in white dancing her way through the Royal Ballet production of *The Grand Tour* but also as that enchanting, heartbreaking voice echoing through the many reissues of her few recordings that are now a part of the stock of every London and New York nostalgia store.

Some years after Gertie's sudden death, Daphne du Maurier happened to meet Noël Coward at a party in London; the conversation turned to their mutual and now long-lost friend, and Daphne happened to say that Gertie had once told her how bitterly she regretted never having sung his 'I'll See You

Again' in *Bitter-Sweet*. A few minutes later, Noël was at the piano singing that very song; only now, its closing words had been altered:

> Though my life may go awry,
> And I never said goodbye,
> I shall love you till I die . . .

BIBLIOGRAPHY

The following is a list of those books which proved most useful to me while I was researching and writing this biography; some afforded anecdotes or direct quotations as indicated in the text, but many more were used as background material and for cross-checking references and dates and opinions. To all the authors, executors and publishers I am most grateful.

Agate, James *Ego* Hamish Hamilton, London, 1935 et seq
Aldrich, Richard Stoddard *Gertrude Lawrence as Mrs A* Odhams, London, 1954
Baral, Robert *Revue* Fleet, New York, 1970
Barker, Felix *The Oliviers* Hamish Hamilton, London, 1953
Barrow, Andrew *Gossip* Hamish Hamilton, London, 1978
Berkman, Edward *The Lady and the Law* Little Brown, Boston, 1976
Brown, John Mason *Seeing Things* Hamish Hamilton, London, 1950
Cazalet-Keir, Thelma *Homage to P. G. Wodehouse* Barrie & Jenkins, London, 1973
Cochran, Charles Blake *Secrets of a Showman* Heinemann, London, 1925; *Cock-a-Doodle-Do* Dent, London, 1941
Coward, Noël *Present Indicative* Heinemann, London, 1937; *Play Parades* Heinemann, London, 1934–55
Curtis, Anthony (ed.) *The Rise and Fall of the Matinée Idol* Weidenfeld, London, 1974
Dean, Basil *Seven Ages* Hutchinson, London, 1970; *Mind's Eye* Hutchinson, London, 1973

De Mille, Agnes *Speak to Me, Dance with Me* Atlantic Little Brown, Boston, 1973

Du Maurier, Daphne *Gerald, a Portrait* Gollancz, London, 1934

Eells, George *The Life That Late He Led* W. H. Allen, London, 1967

Engel, Lehman *This Bright Day* Macmillan, New York, 1974

Ewen, David *A Journey To Greatness* Holt, New York, 1956

Forbes, Bryan *Notes For a Life* Collins, London, 1974

Fordin, Hugh *Getting To Know Him* Random House, New York, 1977

Forsyth, James *Tyrone Guthrie* Hamish Hamilton, London, 1976

French, Harold *I Swore I Never Would* Secker, London, 1970; *I Thought I Never Could* Secker, London, 1973

Gershwin, Ira *Lyrics on Several Occasions* Elm Tree, London, 1977

Gielgud, John *Distinguished Company* Heinemann, London, 1972

Gifford, Denis *British Film Catalogue* David & Charles, Exeter, 1973

Gottfried, Martin *Broadway Musicals* Abrams, New York, 1979

Green, Stanley *World of Musical Comedy* Barnes, New York, 1968

Guthrie, Tyrone *A Life In The Theatre* Hamish Hamilton, London, 1960

Hardwicke, Cedric *A Victorian In Orbit* Methuen, London, 1961

Harris, Radie *Radie's World* W. H. Allen, London, 1975

Harrison, Rex *Rex* Macmillan, London, 1974

Heppner, Sam *Cockie* Frewin, London, 1969

Hoyt, Edwin P. *The Man Who Came to Dinner* Abelard Schuman, New York, 1973

Jablonski & Stewart *The Gershwin Years* Athenaeum, New York, 1973

Jason, David A. *The Theatre of P. G. Wodehouse* Batsford, London, 1979

Jenkins, Alan *The Twenties; The Thirties; The Forties* Heinemann, London, 1974 et seq

June, *The Glass Ladder* Heinemann, London, 1960

Kaufman and Hennessey *Letters of Alexander Woollcott* Cassell, London, 1946

Kimball and Simon *The Gershwins* Athenaeum, New York, 1973

Korda, Michael *Charmed Lives* Random House, 1979

Kulik, Karol *Alexander Korda* W. H. Allen, London, 1975

Laufe, Abe *Broadway's Greatest Musicals* Funk & Wagnalls, New York, 1977

Laver, James *Museum Piece* Deutsch, London, 1963

Lawrence, Gertrude *A Star Danced* Doubleday, New York, 1945

Leavitt, Richard *The World of Tennessee Williams* W. H. Allen, London, 1978

Lesley, Cole *Remembered Laughter, The Life of Noël Coward* Jonathan Cape, London, 1976

Lillie, Beatrice *Every Other Inch a Lady* W. H. Allen, London, 1973

Mankiewicz, Joseph L. *More About All About Eve* Random House, New York, 1972

Mander, Raymond and Mitchenson, Joe, with J. C. Trewin *The Gay Twenties* Macdonald, 1958; *The Turbulent Thirties* Macdonald 1960

Mander, Raymond and Mitchenson, Joe *Theatrical Companion to Noël Coward* Rockliff, London, 1957; *Musical Comedy* Peter Davies, London, 1969; *Revue* Peter Davies, London, 1971

Marshall, Michael *Top Hat and Tails* Elm Tree, London, 1978

Massey Raymond *A Hundred Different Lives* Robson, London, 1979

Matthews, Jessie *Over My Shoulder* W. H. Allen, London, 1974

Nichols, Beverley *The Sweet and Twenties* Weidenfeld, London, 1958

Nolan, Frederick *The Sound of Their Music* Dent, London, 1978

Rodgers, Richard *Musical Stages* W. H. Allen, London, 1976

Rust, Brian *London Musical Shows on Record* Gramophone, London, 1977

Schwartz, Charles *Gershwin* Abelard Schuman, New York 1973

Smith, Cecil *Musical Comedy in America* Theater Arts Books, New York, 1950

Thornton, Michael *Jessie Matthews* Hart-Davis MacGibbon, London, 1974

Wodehouse, P. G. *Performing Flea* Herbert Jenkins, London, 1954; *Over Seventy* Herbert Jenkins, London, 1957

APPENDIX: THEATRE, FILMS AND RECORDS

Theatre

(Gertrude Lawrence born 4 July 1898)

1908: (debut) Child dancer in *Babes in the Wood* (Brixton Theatre, London)

1911: Chorister in *The Miracle* (Olympia, London)

1912: Variety tours and principal dancer, *Fifinella* (Liverpool Repertory Theatre)

1913: Angel in *Hannele* (Liverpool Repertory Theatre); toured in chorus *All Aboard*

1914: Toured in chorus *Miss Lamb of Canterbury*

1915: Toured in chorus *Miss Plaster of Paris*

1916: Blanche-Marie in *The Little Michus* (tour); in chorus of *Money For Nothing* (tour); understudy and chorus in *Some* (Vaudeville, London and tour)

1917: Understudy and chorus in *Cheep!* (Vaudeville, London and tour)

1918: Understudy for Bea Lillie and featured roles in *Tabs* (Vaudeville, London)

1919: *Buzz-Buzz* (Vaudeville, London)

1920: Cabaret, Murray's Club, London, and *Midnight Frolics* (tour); also understudied Phyllis Dare in *Aladdin* (London Hippodrome)

1921: Variety tour of Britain with Walter Williams; *A to Z* (Prince of Wales, London)

1922: Denise in *Dédé* (Garrick, London); *Midnight Follies* (Hotel Metropole, London)

1923: *Rats* (Vaudeville); *London Calling!* (Duke of York's)

1924: *André Charlot's London Revue of 1924* (Times Square, New York, and tour)

1925: *Charlot's Revue* (Prince of Wales's, London); *Charlot's Revue of 1926* (Selwyn Theatre, New York, and tour)

1926: Kay in *Oh, Kay!* (Imperial, New York)

1927: Kay in *Oh, Kay!* (His Majesty's, London)

1928: Jane Crosby in *Icebound* (Sunday Play Society, London); Ann Wainwright in *Treasure Girl* (Alvin, New York)

1929: Marie in *Candle-Light* (Southampton, England, then Empire, New York)

1930: *The International Revue* (Majestic, New York); Amanda in *Private Lives* (Phoenix, London)

1931: Amanda in *Private Lives* (Times Square, New York); Diana in *Take Two From One*, (Haymarket, London); Harriet in *Can The Leopard . . .?* (Haymarket, London)

1932: Sarah Cazenove in *Behold We Live* (St James's, London)

1933: Jill in *This Inconstancy* (Wyndham's, London); Evangeline in *Nymph Errant* (Adelphi, London)

1934: Deirdre in *The Winding Journey* (British tour); Josephine in *Moonlight is Silver* (Queen's London)

1935: Sophy in *Hervey House* (His Majesty's, London); nine roles in *Tonight at 8.30* (British tour)

1936: *Tonight at 8.30* (Phoenix, London; National, New York)

1937: Susan Trexel in *Susan and God* (Plymouth, New York)

1938: *Susan and God* (us tour)

1939: Lydia Kenyon in *Skylark* (us tour and Morosco, New York)

1940: *Skylark* (us tour); Amanda in *Private Lives* (Cape Playhouse, Cape Cod, us)

1941: Liza Elliott in *Lady in the Dark* (Alvin, New York); Sarah in *Behold We Live* (Cape Playhouse)

1942: *Lady in the Dark* (tour) and Julia in *Fallen Angels* (Cape Playhouse)

1943: *Lady in the Dark* (Broadway revival)

1944: ENSA wartime tour of England, France and Belgium; Bernice in *Errand For Bernice* (us tour)

1945: USO wartime tour of the Pacific; Elvira in *Blithe Spirit* (Hawaii); Eliza in *Pygmalion* (Ethel Barrymore, New York)

1946 *Pygmalion* (US tour and Cape Playhouse); Crystal in *The Man in Possession* (Cape Playhouse)

1947: Six roles in *Tonight at 8.30* (US tour); Lady Maria in *Lady Maria* (Cape Playhouse)

1948: *Tonight at 8.30* (National, New York); Olivia in *O Mistress Mine* (Cape Playhouse); Stella in *September Tide* (Aldwych, London)

1949: *September Tide* (Cape Playhouse)

1950: Beatrice in *Travellers' Joy* (Cape Playhouse)

1951: Anna in *The King and I* (St James, New York)
(Gertrude Lawrence died 6 September 1952)

Films

(dates refer to the first British or American release)

1929: (debut) *The Battle of Paris* with Charlie Ruggles, Arthur Treacher; Paramount, New York; dir. Robert Florey; songs by Cole Porter.

1932: *Aren't We All?* with Hugh Wakefield, Owen Nares, Marie Löhr; Paramount British; dir. Harry Lachman; from the play by Frederick Lonsdale.
Lord Camber's Ladies with Gerald du Maurier, Benita Hume, Nigel Bruce; BIP Wardour films, London; dir. Benn Levy; prod. by Alfred Hitchcock.
No Funny Business with Laurence Olivier, Jill Esmond, Gibb McLaughlin; United Artists, London; dir. John Stafford and Victor Hanbury.

1935: *Mimi* with Douglas Fairbanks Jr, Diana Napier, Austin Trevor; BIP Wardour films, London; dir. Paul Stein from *La Vie Bohême*.

1936: *Rembrandt* with Charles Laughton, Elsa Lanchester, John Clements, Walter Hudd; London Films; prod. and dir. Alexander Korda
Men Are Not Gods with Rex Harrison, Sebastian Shaw, Miriam Hopkins; London Films; dir. Walter Reisch; prod. Alexander Korda.

1950: *The Glass Menagerie* with Jane Wyman, Kirk Douglas, Arthur Kennedy; Warners, Hollywood; dir. Irving Rapper from the play by Tennessee Williams.

Radio, Television and Recordings

In 1943, Gertrude Lawrence took to the American air waves with her own weekly series of radio shows, some in a 'guest night' format and others adapting current Hollywood successes into half-hour dramas. She also frequently appeared as a guest on other shows, and in Britain both before and after the war made occasional appearances on BBC interview and variety broadcasts. In America she did a pioneering telecast of *Susan and God* in August 1938 and later a production of Shaw's *Great Catherine* for NBC (1947); later she made promotional appearances on various chat shows during the rehearsals of *The King and I*.

Of her many recordings, those that are still available include the following LPS:

The King and I	Brunswick LAT 8026
A Bright Particular Star	MCA MUP 336
George Gershwin in London	EMI SH 185
Cole Porter in London	EMI SHB 26
The Star Herself	EMI MFP 1245
Noël Coward: The Master	EMI SHB 50
Noël and Gertie	HMV CLP 1050
Noël Coward: The Great Shows	EMI SH 179/180

A complete listing of her original 78 rpm recordings was compiled for *The Gramophone* by Brian Rust in 1977:

Acc. by the Vaudeville Theatre Orchestra.   London, c. 15 January 1919
(All four titles are from *BUZZ, BUZZ*)

76349-1	I've Been Waiting For Someone Like You (w/Walter Williams)	Col L-1296
76350-1	Winnie The Window-Cleaner (w/chorus)	—
76351-1	I've Lost My Heart In Maoriland (w/ch)	Col L-1293
76352-1	Miss Sunshine And Mr. Rain (w/Margaret Bannerman)	Rejected

Orch. acc. cond. by George W. Byng.		Hayes, Middlesex, 31 March 1922.
B6-1172-1-2	When I'm Dressed in Blue ("A To Z")	HMV rejected
B6-1173-1-2	Come On And Kiss Your Angel Child, Sweetie Dear ("A To Z")	—

Acc. by alto sax., violin, piano and banjo		Hayes, Middlesex, 6 May 1925.
Cc-6097-2	Broadway Medley—Part 1 (Intro. Sweet And Low/ Lazy/So This Is Venice/ My Honey Lou/Doo Wacka Doo/Big Boy) (w/Beatrice Lillie)	HMV C-1206
Cc-6098-1	Broadway Medley—Part 2 (Intro. Chloe/Cover Me Up With The Sunshine of Virginia/I Wonder What's Become of Sally?/I'm So Unlucky/My Best Girl) (w/Beatrice Lillie)	

Piano acc. by R. H. Bowers		New York, 17 November 1925.
141271-2	A Cup Of Coffee, A Sandwich And You (w/Jack Buchanan)	Col 512-D
141272-2	Poor Little Rich Girl	Col 513-D
141273	Russian Blues	Col 514-D
141274-2	Carrie	Col 512-D

NOTE:- All the above four titles are from THE CHARLOT REVUE, 1926.

Piano acc. by Tom Waring.		Camden, N. J., 29 October 1926.
BVE-36653-3	Do-Do-Do ("Oh, Kay!")	Vic 20332, HMV B-2563
BVE-36654-3	Someone To Watch Over Me ("Oh Kay!")	—

Piano acc. by Milton Rettenberg. Camden, N. J., 15 November 1926.

BVE-36653-5-6-7	Do-Do-Do ("Oh Kay!")	Vic rejected
BVE-36654-4	Someone To Watch Over Me (w/Nat Shilkret—(2nd Piano) also) ("Oh Kay!")	—

Acc. by His Majesty's Theatre Orchestra, cond. by Arthur Wood. (All three titles are from OH, KAY!) His Majesty's Theatre, London, 4 Oct 1927

WA-6325-1-2	Do-Do-Do (w/Harold French)	Col rejected
WA-6326-1-2	Someone To Watch Over Me	—
WA-6327-1-2	Maybe (w/Harold French)	—

His Majesty's Theatre, London, 17 Oct 1927

WA-6327-3	Maybe (w/Harold French)	Col rejected

His Majesty's Theatre, London, 25 Oct 1927

WA-6325-4	Do-Do-Do (w/Harold French)	Col 4617
WA-6326-4	Someone to Watch Over Me	Col 4618
WA-6327-5	Maybe (w/Harold French)	—

Dialogue with Noël Coward, with orch. cond. by Ray Noble. Small Queen's Hall, London, 15 September 1930

Cc-20202-2	Private Lives: Scene from Act 2	HMV C-2043, Vic 36034
Cc-20203-2	Private Lives: Love Scene from Act 1 (Intro. Someday I'll Find You)	—

Piano acc. by Ord Hamilton. London, 2 October 1931

GB-3352-1-2	At Your Command	Dec rejected

		London, 5 October 1931.
GB-3370-1-2	You're My Decline and Fall	Dec rejected
		London, 13 October 1931.
GB-3352-3-4	At Your Command	Dec rejected
GB-3370-3-4-5	You're My Decline and Fall	—
		London, 20 October 1931.
GB-3352-7	At Your Command	Dec F-2577
GB-3370-6	You're My Decline And Fall	—
GB-3464-2	Now You Are Here	Dec F-2755
GB-3465-	Impossible You	Ace of Clubs ACL-1171 (LP)
Orch. acc.		London, 3 November 1931.
GB-3520-1	Limehouse Blues ("A To Z")	Dec F-3578
GB-3521-	Parisian Pierrot ("London Calling")	Ace of Clubs ACL-1171 (LP)
		London, 21 December 1931.
GB-3464-5	Now You Are Here	Dec F-3578
GB-3744-1-2-3	Stealing For You	Rejected
GB-3745-2	You're Blasé ("Bow Bells")	Dec F-2755
		London, 11 March 1932.
GB-4079-1	My Sweet (Film "Aren't We All?")	Dec F-3140, M-400
GB-4080-1	Someday I'll Find You ("Private Lives")	—
Piano acc. by Claude Ivy, with 'cello.		London, 13 May 1932.
GB-4483-1	Tired	Dec F-3141, M-412
GB-4484-1-3	Shadows On The Window	—

213

London, 27 September 1932.

GB-4944-3	Nothing But A Lie	Dec F-3192
GB-4945-2	Why Waste Your Tears?	—

Orch. acc., with piano by Claude Ivy.　　　　London, 11 October 1932.

GB-5004-3	Let's Say Goodbye	Dec F-3214
GB-5005-2	Mad About The Boy	—

NOTE:- Both the above titles are from WORDS AND MUSIC.

London, 24 November 1932.

Piano acc. by Claude Ivy.

GA-5247-	Songs She Made Famous— Part 1 (Intro. I Said Goodbye/You Were Meant For Me)	Dec K-689
GA-5248-	Songs She Made Famous— Part 2 (Intro. A Cup Of Coffee, A Sandwich And You/Someone To Watch Over Me)	—

Orch. acc. cond. by Ray Noble.　　　　London, 11 October 1933.

OB-5381-1-2	How Could We Be Wrong?	HMV B-8030
OB-5382-2	It's Bad For Me	—

London, 18 October 1933.

OB-5137-2	The Physician	HMV B-8029
OB-5138-2	Experiment	—
OB-5139-1-2	Nymph Errant	HMV B-8031

NOTE:- All the above five titles are from NYMPH ERRANT.

London, 7 February 1934.

OB-5880-2	An Hour Ago This Minute	HMV B-8137
OB-5881-2	What Now?	—

Dialogue and singing with Douglas Fairbanks,   London, 20 November 1934.
Jnr., with orch. cond. by Carroll Gibbons.

| 2EA-693-2 | Moonlight Is Silver: Scene and Song | HMV C-2710 |
| 2EA-694-2 | Moonlight Is Silver: As above, Part 2 | — |

Dialogue and singing with Noël Coward,   London, 15 January 1936.
acc. by the Phoenix Theatre Orchestra,
cond. by Clifford Greenwood

2EA-2666-1	Then/Play, Orchestra, Play ("Shadow Play")	HMV C-2816, Vic 36191
2EA-2667-2	You Were There ("Shadow Play")	—
2EA-2668-1	Has Anybody Seen Our Ship? ("Red Peppers")	HMV C-2815, Vic 36193
2EA-2669-1	Men About Town ("Red Peppers")	—

London, 16 January 1936.

| 2EA-2670-2 | Here's A Toast (w/supporting cast) | HMV C-2817, Vic 36192 |
| 2EA-2671-2 | Hearts And Flowers (The Musical Box) (w/supporting cast) | — |

NOTE:- Both above titles are from FAMILY ALBUM.

Orch. acc. by Carroll Gibbons.   London, 4 March 1936.

| 2EA-2708-1 | Gertrude Lawrence Medley (Medley of Song Successes) —Part 1 (Intro. Limehouse Blues/You Were Meant For Me/Do-Do-Do) | HMV C-2833, C-4198 |
| 2EA-2709-2 | Gertrude Lawrence Medley (Medley of Song Successes) —Part 2 (Intro. Someone To Watch Over Me/A Cup Of Coffee, A Sandwich And You/Wild Thyme/ Experiment) | — |

Orch. acc. cond. by Leonard Joy.		New York, 23 February 1941.
BS-060679-1	This Is New	Vic 27331
BS-060680-1	One Life To Live	—
BS-060681-1	The Princess Of Pure Delight	Vic 27332
BS-060682-1-2	My Ship	Vic 27330
BS-060683-1	Jenny	—
BS-060684-1	Glamor Music (Gertrude Lawrence sings HUXLEY; the other two songs on the side are by a male quartet)	Vic 27332

Orch. acc. cond. by Harry Sosnik.		New York, April 1944.
71997-A	A Guy Named Joe	Dec 23446
72039-A	Poor John	Dec 23446

Acc. by small instrumental group.		New York, c. 18 December 1950.
80280-A	Limehouse Blues ("A To Z")	Dec , Br 05001

Orch. acc. cond. by Jay Blackton.		New York, c. 3 January 1951.
80308-A	Someday I'll Find You ("Private Lives")	Dec , Br 05001

Acc. by "The King and I" Orchestra, cond. by Frederick Dvonch.		New York, April 1951.
80856-	I Whistle A Happy Tune	Dec , Br 05167
80858-	Hello, Young Lovers	Dec , Br 05169
80861-	Getting To Know You	Dec , Br 05171
80863-	Shall I Tell You What I Think Of You?	Dec , Br 05169
80866-	Shall We Dance? (w/Yul Brynner)	Dec , Br 05166

# INDEX